ACTIVE SOCIAL POLICIES IN THE EU

Inclusion through participation?

Edited by Rik van Berkel and Iver

The POLICY
PP
PRESS

First published in Great Britain in September 2002 by

The Policy Press
34 Tyndall's Park Road
Bristol BS8 1PY
UK

Tel +44 (0)117 954 6800
Fax +44 (0)117 973 7308
e-mail tpp@bristol.ac.uk
www.policypress.org.uk

British Library Cataloguing in Publication Data

A catalogue record for this book is available from the British Library

ISBN 1 86134 280 2 paperback

A hardcover version of this book is also available

Rik van Berkel is Researcher and Lecturer in Labour and Welfare State Studies, Faculty of Social Sciences, Utrecht University, the Netherlands, **Iver Hornemann Møller** is Professor in Comparative Welfare Research, Centre for Social Integration and Differentiation, Denmark.

Cover design by Qube Design Associates, Bristol.

Printed and bound in Great Britain by Bell & Bain Ltd, Glasgow.

Contents

List of figures and tables

Figures

Tables

Acknowledgements

This book is the result of Inclusion through Participation (INPART), a research project that brought together an international group of researchers in 1998 and 1999. Funds for the research project were made available through the EU's Fourth Framework Programme, Targeted Socio-Economic Research (TSER, contract number SOE2-CT97-3043). The researchers had already been working together on the Social Exclusion and the Development of European Citizenship (SEDEC) project, an international social-scientific network. However, INPART, an internationally comparative research project, proved to be a challenging, interesting and instructive experience, if occasionally time and energy consuming, and complex! INPART was a process of continuous learning, especially for the young researchers who did the bulk of the research work. It was also a new experience, a cooperation in debate and problem solving that made great demands on the creativity, flexibility, inventiveness and patience of the participants. Cooperation increased because the participating teams came from different welfare state, theoretical and methodological traditions. And since doing research always means managing and coping with scarce resources, we had to resort to pragmatic solutions more often than we would like to admit. Therefore, we are the first to acknowledge that our project has its weaknesses, such as balancing the use of various research methodologies, optimising the comparability of empirical data, or elaborating the theoretical and conceptual framework (something which we did to a large extent while writing this book, rather than during the research process).

Producing valid, reliable and useful knowledge through research is no easy task, and that goes especially for the relatively new branch of internationally comparative research. Nevertheless, we think that our project has produced interesting results, and hope that this book will contribute to the debates on activating welfare states in the EU, which is its main objective.

Not all of the INPART researchers contributed to this book. We would like to thank them here, since their contribution to the research work and, by extension, to this book, has been considerable: Jacques Vilrokx (senior researcher with the Belgian team), Joanne Cook (responsible for the case study into part-time work in the UK), Jan Windebank (who cooperated in the case study into informal work in the UK), Ana Matos (who did most of the data collection and data analysis for the Portuguese case studies), Fernando Ruivo (senior member of the Portuguese team), and Cyril Tholen (main researcher with the Dutch team). Furthermore, we are grateful to our respondents for their insights into participation in types of work, as well as to the people that helped us in getting access to our field of research. Also, we would like to thank Fadila Boughanémi of the Directorate General Research of the EU (the scientific officer of the DG in charge of the INPART project). We would like to thank The Policy Press, especially Karen Bowler (editor) and Dawn Rushen (editorial manager). Finally, we would like to thank our anonymous referees for their comments, which have significantly improved this book.

May 2002

Notes on contributors

Jan de Schampheleire is a psychologist and sociologist, whose research focuses on industrial relations and the sociology of labour. He is a correspondent of the journal EIRONline (European Foundation for the Improvement of Living and Working Conditions) (www.eiro.eurofound.ie). His publications include 'Collective bargaining in Belgian metalworking under EMU: between ideals and constraints' (with J.Vilrokx and J. Oste in T. Schulten and R. Bispinck [eds] *Collective bargaining under the Euro: Experiences from the European metal industry*, ETUI, 2001), 'The activation approach in Dutch and Belgian social policies' (with R. van Berkel, *Journal of European Area Studies*, 2001), and 'Subsidised work in Belgium and the Netherlands' (*Transfer*, 2000/1).

Marisol García lectures at the University of Barcelona. She is a member of the editorial board of the *International Journal of Urban and Regional Research* (Oxford: Blackwell). She is also president of the Research Committee on Urban and Regional Research within the International Sociological Association. She has been Visiting Fellow at St. Antony's College (Oxford), Research Fellow at the Royal Institute of International Affairs (London), and Visiting Researcher at the European University Institute (Florence), and at the University of Amsterdam. Her publications include 'Cities and citizenship' (*International Journal of Urban and Regional Research*, 1996) and 'Ciudadanía: justicia social, identidad y participación' (with S. Lukes; Siglo Veintiuno de España Editores, 1999).

Aitor Gómez González is a doctoral sociology student at the University of Barcelona, having graduated from that university with a degree in Anthropology. He is a member of the Research Centre on Citizenship and Civil Society of the University of Barcelona, where his research focuses on citizenship, the labour market and activation policies. His recent publications include 'The Southern European model' (with A. Andreotti, S. García, P. Hespanha, Y. Kazepov and E. Mingione, *Journal of European Area Studies*, 2001), 'Activerend sociaal beleid en arbeidsmarktregulering in Spanje' (with M. García; *Tijdschrift voor Arbeid en Participatie*, 2000) and 'Erfaringer med kapitaliseringen af arbejdsløshedsunderstøttelsen I Spanien' (*Arbejdsliv*, 2000).

Iver Hornemann Møller is research director of the Centre for Social Integration and Differentiation in Copenhagen, and Professor at the University of Coimbra (Portugal). He has published numerous books and articles on the labour market and social policy issues, including 'Social integration and labour market marginalisation in Scandinavia' (in M. Roche and R. van Berkel [eds] *European citizenship and social exclusion*, Avebury, 1997) and *A textbook on social policy* (with J. Elm Larsen; Munksgaards Forlag, 1997). He co-edited *Inclusion and exclusion: Unemployment and non-standard employment in Europe* (Ashgate, 1999).

Recently he has published 'On activation in Denmark and Portugal' (with P. Hespanha; *Transfer*, 2000) and *On the labour market: Continuity and change* (with J. Lind; TemaNord, 2000).

Henning Hansen holds a Master's degree in Economics. He currently works as a consultant at the Danish Centre for Alternative Social Analysis (CASA), while researching living conditions, labour market policy, and social policy. He was editor of *Living conditions in Denmark – Compendium of statistics, 1984 and 1988*, and has contributed several publications on Danish social policies, including *Arbejdsmarkedsindsatsen – hvad er det der virker* (CASA, 1995), *Er der noget galt med Bistandsloven?* (CASA, 1996) and *Arbejde, aktivering og arbejdsløshed* (Samfundslitteratur, 2001).

Pedro Hespanha is Professor of Sociology at the School of Economics, University of Coimbra (Portugal), and a founding member of the Centre for Social Studies (CES). He has been developing studies on welfare pluralism, social non-governmental organisations (NGOs), the globalisation trend, and rural poverty. He has published widely on these themes. He is currently coordinating an observatory on social change at the University of Aveiro.

Jens Lind lectures at the Department of Social Studies and Organisation, University of Åalborg (Denmark). His research focuses on the labour market and labour-market policies, industrial relations, unemployment, the welfare state, and comparative studies in these areas. Recent publications in English include 'Recent issues on the social pact in Denmark' (in P. Pochet and G. Fajertag [eds] *Social pacts in Europe: New dynamics*, ETUI and OSE, 2000) and 'Denmark: private service growth – towards a new trajectory for employment and regulation?' (in J.E. Dølvik [ed] *At your service? Comparative perspectives on employment and labour relations in the European private sector services* (PIE-Peter Lang, 2001). He is co-editor of *Inclusion and exclusion: Perspectives on unemployment and non-standard employment* (Ashgate, 1999) and *Worlds of employment: Working life and employment relations on both sides of the world* (LEO, University of Åalborg, 2000).

Carlos Machado is a political scientist and has a Master's degree in European Science, Society and Technology (ESST) from the University of East London and the Vrije Universiteit Brussel (Belgium). In 1998 he joined the VUB as a collaborator in two European TSER projects (SEDEC and INPART) within the Research Centre for Socio-economic Changes and Labour Relations (TESA). He has co-authored with other members of TESA several articles and publications in the area of social inclusion policies, most recently 'Tackling inequality and exclusion: towards a dimension of active citizenship participation' (with J. Vilrokx; in A. Woodward and M. Kohli [eds] *Inclusions and exclusions in European societies*, Routledge, 2001).

Maurice Roche is Reader in Sociology at the University of Sheffield. His research is concerned with the sociology of citizenship and of social and cultural policy. His publications include *Mega-events and modernity* (Routledge, 2000), *Rethinking citizenship: Ideology, welfare and change in modern society* (Polity Press, 1996), *Renewing the European social model* (co-edited with C. Annesley; Berghahn Books, 2003: forthcoming) and *European citizenship and social exclusion* (co-edited with R. van Berkel; Ashgate, 1997). Since 1994 he has coordinated the SEDEC European social research network, which has received EC funding for work on European social inclusion policies.

Ben Valkenburg lectures at the Faculty of Social Sciences of Utrecht University (The Netherlands). He has been involved in various research projects of Dutch activation policies, including research into the Dutch 'Melkert-1' scheme, and the labour-market reintegration of disabled people. He is currently involved in several research projects in which an individual, client-centred approach in active social policies is being developed and implemented, both at the delivery and management levels. He is co-editor of the European journal *Transfer*. His publications include 'Atypical employment in the Netherlands' (with L. Beukema; in J. Lind and I. Hornemann Møller [eds] *Inclusion and exclusion: Unemployment and non-standard employment in Europe* (Ashgate, 1999), 'Individualization and solidarity: the challenge of modernization' (in P. Leisink, J. van Leemput and J. Vilrok [eds] *The challenge to trade unions in Europe: Innovation or adaptation*, Edward Elgar, 1996) and 'Work and inclusion' (with J. Lind and R. van Berkel; *Transfer*, 2000/1).

Rik van Berkel is a researcher at the Department of General Social Sciences in the Faculty of Social Sciences of Utrecht University (the Netherlands), and coordinator of the TSER research project Inclusion through Participation (INPART). His main research areas are social policies, labour-market policies and unemployment. His publications include *European citizenship and social exclusion* (with M. Roche; Ashgate, 1997), *Beyond marginality? Social movements of social security claimants in the EU* (with H. Coenen and R. Vlek; Ashgate, 1998) and 'Workfare in the Netherlands: young unemployed people and the Jobseekers' Employment Act' (with H. Spies; in I. Lødemel and H. Trickey [eds] *An offer you can't refuse*, The Policy Press, 2001).

Colin C. Williams is Reader in Economic Geography at the University of Leicester. His recent publications include *Community self-help* (Palgrave, 2002), *Bridges into work* (The Policy Press, 2001), *Revitalising deprived urban neighbourhoods: An assisted self-help approach* (Ashgate, 2001), *A helping hand: Harnessing self-help to combat social exclusion* (York Publishing Services, 1999) and *Informal employment in the advanced economies* (Routledge, 1998).

ONE

Introduction

Rik van Berkel and Iver Hornemann Møller

Setting the scene

This book reports and reflects on the results of Inclusion through Participation (INPART), a research project that took place during 1998 and 1999, and funded in the context of the European Commission's Targeted Socio-Economic Research programme. INPART's aim was to shed light on the inclusionary and exclusionary potentials of various types of work. In other words, to find out to what degree participation in various types of paid or unpaid work contributes to inclusion or exclusion. This objective was formulated against the background of the growing concern in social policy debates and social policy practices with the issue of 'activation'. Put simply, activation implies a shift in the inclusion discourse from 'inclusion through decent income provisions' towards 'inclusion through participation in work'. This transition from 'passive' social policies (income provision), to an emphasis on 'active' social policies (the promotion or enforcement of participation; see Chapter Three of this volume) is taking place in all member states of the EU, and is exacerbated by various policy initiatives of the EU, mainly the European Employment Strategy and the open coordination method on Social Inclusion.

INPART involved research teams from six EU countries: Belgium, Denmark, the Netherlands, Portugal, Spain, and the UK. Although we do not want to claim that this group of EU countries can be considered a representative sample, it does represent the various welfare-state regimes of the EU. Belgium is a corporatist welfare state; Denmark is an exponent of the social democratic welfare state. The UK is a liberal welfare state, while the Netherlands is a 'mixed' or 'hybrid' welfare state regime, combining corporatist and social democratic characteristics (Esping-Andersen, 1999). Portugal and Spain are Southern European, sub-protective or 'familistic' welfare states (Gallie and Paugam, 2000; Andreotti et al, 2001). Of course, welfare regime typologies have been developed on the basis of an analysis of 'passive' rather than 'active' social policy characteristics. It is not yet clear whether or not specific 'passive' regimes correspond with specific 'active' regimes, or how and to what degree the introduction of activation influences income protection schemes.

Nevertheless, the countries involved in INPART reveal significant differences with respect to the 'activation' characteristics of their social policies as well. For example, Denmark has a long tradition of some types of active labour-market policies. Traditionally, active labour-market policies were considered to reflect the commitment to full employment of social democratic welfare states (see Therborn, 1986). During the last decades, the obligatory character of participation in activation programmes has increased significantly. By now, Denmark has a highly differentiated set of activation schemes, covering increasing parts of the unemployed population. The latter also applies to the Netherlands, but here the transition towards a more activating welfare state implied a clear move away from corporatist elements in its social policies. During the late 1970s and the early 1980s, the Netherlands responded to increasing unemployment by reducing labour supply, a typical corporatist or conservative regime strategy (Esping-Andersen, 1999). Older workers left the labour market massively, either due to early retirement schemes or by what has become the most notorious Dutch exit option: disability benefits. During the 1980s, this strategy was subjected to strong criticism, and gradually made way for a strategy aiming at an increase of labour-market participation rates, to be supported by activation policies.

Other countries, such as Spain, Portugal and the UK, have started the introduction of activation programmes even more recently. In the UK, this seems to reflect different policy priorities of the successive conservative and New Labour governments of the 1990s. In Spain and Portugal, the relative weakness of the state is often mentioned as an important factor in explaining the fact that activation schemes have been introduced only recently. The weakness of the state in these countries also influences the nature of the activation schemes that are being introduced as well as the actors that are involved in making the transition towards a more active welfare state (cf Saraceno, 2002). For example, the Spanish activation programme that we investigated (the Capitalisation of Unemployment Benefits; see Chapter Seven of this volume) is characterised by the absence of a central role of the state, and in the case of Portugal, third sector organisations, such as non-governmental organisations (NGOs) play a significant role in activation and the implementation of active social policies.

Therefore, the role of the state in making social policies more active differs according to each country involved in the project. For example, in Denmark, the Netherlands and the UK, the state plays a dominant role in active social policies, even though, as Saraceno (2002) points out and as Lødemel and Trickey (2001) illustrate with respect to workfare programmes, there can be considerable differences in the degree to which central, regional and local state authorities and institutions are involved in the design and delivery of social policies. Portugal and Belgium are examples of countries where other actors and institutions, such as NGOs and third sector or system organisations (discussed later in this chapter), are important. Against these backgrounds of different 'pathways' towards more activating welfare states and of different activation 'arenas', the impact on the various countries of the European Employment Strategy and other EU initiatives to promote activation, differs as well. For Portugal, for example, the impact of these EU initiatives has been significant, whereas their impact on countries such as Denmark and the Netherlands seems to be marginal.

This book aims to contribute to the debate on the activating welfare state in a number of ways:

- by presenting empirical results about the contribution to inclusion of participation in types of work;
- by theoretical reflection on central concepts and assumptions in the 'activation' debate;
- by analysing the conditions under which activating welfare states may contribute to inclusion.

Of course, we cannot deal with each relevant issue and topic in great detail in this book. Therefore, three central themes constitute the theoretical pivots:

1. The concepts of inclusion and exclusion underlying social policy debates, and interventions to combat (unwanted) exclusion and promote (wanted) inclusion;
2. The heterogeneity of work and its implications for social policies promoting participation in work as an important instrument of inclusion;
3. The variety of activation approaches that lies behind the strong political and public consensus on the activation objective.

Naturally, these themes are closely related. As a matter of fact, one of the main concerns of the research project was to classify the ways in which activation policies and programmes define and interconnect inclusion, work and activation. In the mainstream of active social policies, regular paid work is considered both the most desirable *form* of inclusion, and the most important *instrument* for inclusion in a wider sense – for example, into social networks, political participation, economic independence, and so on. Due to this conviction, and the benefits labour-market participation is thought to produce both for the individuals involved and for society in general, activation is believed to be a legitimate policy objective, even when it involves certain degrees of compulsion. Against this background, this book wants to critically assess the assumptions underlying mainstream activation policy thinking, and the consequences of these assumptions for the objectives and means of activation. In addition, it hopes to contribute to the development of alternative activation approaches.

Inclusion and exclusion: the development of a discourse

The themes of inclusion, exclusion and – closely related – marginalisation, which are often debated in connection with the concepts of differentiation and integration, are back on the agenda. In both policy and politics, for example in the EU and the social sciences, the categories of differentiation/integration and inclusion/exclusion have been widely used in the 1990s. This book attempts to link the themes of integration/differentiation and inclusion/exclusion across policy debate and scientific discourse. Prior to describing INPART, the research project on which this book is based, and presenting an overview of the different chapters, it would be worthwhile positioning this widespread interest within the social sciences (a review partly based on Gough and Olofsson, 1999).

The emergence of differentiation/integration theories can be located in the latter half of the 19th century, in the works of Karl Marx, Herbert Spencer, and especially Emile Durkheim. Key themes in the work of Marx are the divisions of labour on the societal level (town–country, production–circulation), and within the labour process. The same applies to his treatment of class struggle and social contradictions in general, as well as to his theory of tension between the forces of production and the relations of production. Spencer saw societal evolution in a rather abstract and general way as being shaped by increasing differentiation and the emergence of new forms of integration. Durkheim transformed Spencer's suggestions and categories into concepts and articulated a special theory of social development.

Durkheim, in particular, analysed the forms and effects of differentiation. He also developed a theory of integration. His focus was the transformation of a traditional social order grounded on status hierarchies, to a society with an increasing division of labour, provoking class conflicts and lacking a natural, or easy-to-find, principle of integration. His fundamental and, in a sense, very modern question was: how is integration, and a well-functioning society, possible in a differentiated and individualised social order? Spencer's answer – a generalisation of the view of economists – was that the problem would be solved by society's own 'invisible' forces without political interference. In contrast, Durkheim envisaged a new 'organic solidarity' grounded in the moral experiences deriving from the contemporary work roles, and supported by a development of law and state institutions.

Unlike integration, the notion of 'exclusion' has played a far from central role in social science. Only Max Weber – one of its 'founding fathers' – worked intensively with the concept. He noted that the creation of 'social closure' advances efforts by the powerful to exclude less powerful people from the full benefits of joint enterprise.

From the 1940s to the 1960s, differentiation/integration theory was further developed by Talcott Parsons. Clear emphasis was placed on the forms or mechanisms of integration. The basic form of integration was seen as a system of norms, taking shape in a civil and political culture within the framework of stable institutions and a modern state. Parsons' theory, developed in the shadow of the Cold War, may be seen as an argument for the integration of society based on a consensus about fundamental civil, political and social rights and an acceptance of pluralism in more specific values and norms. This linked directly to Durkheim, who argued that consensus in highly differentiated societies must rest on the only thing we still have in common – our humanity. Hence his belief that modern societies require for their cohesion a respect for human rights.

Post-'May 1968' social theory became fragmented in many directions: different kinds of conflict theory, different schools of neo-Marxism, Foucault's theories of the construction of the modern subject, renewals of German critical theory, an upsurge of micro-social scientific theories, and, from the beginning of the 1980s, postmodernism. As a major paradigm, differentiation/integration theory was largely absent. Types of differentiation and types of integration were studied, of course, often taking the shape of Marxian class studies or Weberian stratification theories. (Frank Parkin, for example, saw Weber's concept of social closure as an alternative to class analyses.) Strategies of exclusion are seen as the predominant mode of closure in stratified systems. In addition, studies of poverty, subcultural changes and new social movements, and studies and theories of the role of the state and mass media were undertaken as forms of systemic integration. However, these themes were dealt with under diverging theoretical schemes, and were not subordinated to some kind of unified differentiation/integration paradigm.

Nowadays, contemporary social scientists have once again begun to devote serious intellectual efforts to the general themes of differentiation/integration. However, preoccupation with this theme and the related notions of inclusion, exclusion and marginalisation has re-emerged within a new historical and social context. The theoretical cast is also different. In addition, what has re-emerged is a more divergent and complex issue: where the conceptual emblems of the 1950s were industrialism, modernisation, democratisation, spreading equality and affluence, the conceptual emblems of the late 1980s and 1990s were instead risks of globalisation, the re-emergence of nationalism and ethnicity, technological and organisational complexity and flexibility, and modes of duality. New social differentiation and increasing social divisions, poverty, long-term unemployment and exclusion from several systems by the same persons, were identified as key social problems of integration/inclusion and social stratification. The fragile, even unstable, balance between economic competitiveness, societal differentiation and social stability was again at the centre of the debate. Therefore, in the 1990s a new set of societal problems and diagnoses for political reflection and intervention had taken hold in European social theory and political practice. This book is part of this new development.

We argue that the new political debate and the scientific discourse on inclusion/exclusion and differentiation/integration are addressing a new societal situation. Both at a political level and a theoretical level, conceptualisation of these themes takes place on a much broader scale than before. On the political level, the range of relevant actors has increased. A significant aspect of the present understanding is that it systematically identifies a multilayered range of actors: local, national, and supranational political/administrative actors, as well as companies, organisations and voluntary organisations. As a theory, it addresses complex systemic and social differentiation and different understandings and types of integration, inclusion, exclusion and marginality at both the national and the international level.

Inclusion through Participation (INPART): the research project

This book reports and analyses results of an international comparative research project that was carried out in the context of the EU research programme Targeted Socio-Economic Research. The objectives of the project were:

- To analyse and compare views on inclusion and exclusion from two connected, but at the same time distinct, perspectives: inclusion and exclusion as embodied in social policies, and inclusion and exclusion as experienced by different groups of people (that is, in the context of our research project, participants in different forms of work).
- To gain insight into determinants of success and failure of inclusion policies, taking into account the kind of participation (work) being stimulated by these policies and the systems or domains of inclusion these policies aim at, as well as the characteristics of the persons these policies are aimed at.
- To gain insight into, and to test the validity of, several of the assumptions underlying mainstream active social policies: first, that unemployment equals exclusion; secondly, that participation in paid work equals inclusion; and thirdly, that non-paid forms of work by itself cannot achieve inclusion.
- To develop recommendations concerning active social policies (for example, with respect to the conditions under which various types of work might contribute to inclusion), and the degree to which tailor-made rather than universal or target-group oriented approaches to problems of exclusion are desirable and feasible.

The main part of the research was devoted to a study of the inclusionary and exclusionary potentials of various types of work. Given the policy background of INPART, that is, the transition towards activating welfare states, we paid considerable attention to forms of work promoted by active social policies. Nevertheless, we did not limit ourselves to types of work covered by these policies. It is quite clear that, whereas active social policies stimulate, and even create, certain forms of work, they also neglect or even counteract others. From this point of view, we can see active social policies themselves as one of the factors constituting the inclusionary and exclusionary potentials of forms of work. As we explained earlier in this chapter, the project did not want to uncritically reproduce the emphasis of most active social policies on (regular) paid work as the royal road towards inclusion. Therefore, we also paid attention to forms of work that hardly receive attention in the active social policy mainstream. During the various steps of INPART, the diversity and heterogeneity of 'work' were taken into account by distinguishing between:

- participation on the regular or 'primary' labour market;
- participation on a 'secondary' labour market of state-subsidised, 'additional' jobs, specifically created for unemployed people;

- unpaid and paid informal work;
- participation in training and education activities.

By adopting this broad approach to work, we hoped to generate two kinds of policy recommendation. First, recommendations with respect to adjusting existing active social policies so as to enhance their effectiveness in terms of inclusion. Secondly, recommendations with respect to the creation of new active social policies that recognise the inclusionary potential of forms of work currently not covered by social policies.

In studying the inclusionary potential of forms of work, we not only wanted to take into account the differentiation of work, but also the differentiation of people's situations, experiences, expectations, ambitions, and so on. In other words, we adopted as a starting point whether or not a given form of work contributes to inclusion (or exclusion) not only depends on characteristics of that specific type of work but also on characteristics of the persons involved. Consequently, the match between forms of work and the people participating in them is a recurring theme of this book.

The work of INPART was divided into four subsequent steps. The first aimed at making a comparative analysis of active social policies in the countries involved in the project, taking into account policy developments at the EU level. Furthermore, an analysis was made of the national and transnational policy discourses accompanying the transformation of welfare states and the introduction of active social policies. As part of this, the views on exclusion and inclusion that more or less explicitly underlie policy debates and practices were studied.

The second step involved an analysis of the research literature on experiences of inclusion and exclusion of social groups related to participation in various forms of work. This included a review of evaluation research into the effects of active social policies in terms of inclusion and exclusion.

During the third step, national case studies were carried out with the objective of gathering empirical data to gain insight into experiences of inclusion and exclusion related to participation in various forms of work. In the case studies, the perspective of the participants in forms of work and participation was given much attention. Table 1.1 gives a graphical presentation of the case studies, grouped according to the four main types of work we distinguished earlier in this chapter. (The case studies and the types of work that they refer to, especially those that deal with activation programmes, are elaborated in Chapter Five of this volume.) Case studies marked with an asterisk deal with activation programmes.

In terms of the methodologies used in the case studies, we started from a methodologically pluralist point of view. We did this not only to respect the various methodological backgrounds and traditions of the participants in the project, but also because we think that a combination of qualitative and quantitative methodologies creates the opportunity to gain both in-depth insight into people's experiences with participation in types of work and their situations

Table 1.1: INPART case studies

	'Primary' labour market	'Secondary' labour market	Unpaid/ informal work	Training and education
Belgium		*Local social economy activities within Third System Organisations		*Education and work-training in Third System Organisations
Denmark	Regular paid work	*Subsidised work	Voluntary work	*Educational projects
The Netherlands		*Subsidised work: Melkert I	*Unpaid work: Social Activation	
Portugal		*Occupational Programmes		*Measure 2, INTE-GRAR sub-programme
Spain		*Capitalisation of unemployment benefits		
UK	Part-time work		Unpaid (and informal paid) work	

in terms of inclusion and exclusion, and to validate these insights by investigating a larger group of people. Due to practical resource limitations, it turned out to be impossible to realise this combination of methodologies at the level of all separate case studies[1]. Most, though not all, of INPART's research teams decided to use in-depth interviews for their case studies, which explains why the data reported in this book are predominantly of a qualitative nature, though partly also of a quantitative character. Both kinds of data are presented, of course, but the combination of qualitative and quantitative data precludes the graphic presentation of data in tables familiar to readers of reports based on quantitative research.

Finally, the fourth step aimed at integrating and synthesising the data collected during research. Its objective was to assess the strengths and weaknesses of forms of work and of active social policies in terms of their inclusionary and exclusionary potential, and to develop policy recommendations.

The structure of the book

This book is comprised of three main parts. When we commenced writing this book after the completion of INPART, we started with the elaboration of the theoretical and conceptual framework in more depth than we were able to maintain during the course of the research. The results of this are presented in Chapters Two and Three. These chapters make explicit our conceptualisation of inclusion/exclusion and work, and elaborate the concept of 'activation' which is at the core of the research project. On the basis of this, intensive analyses and re-analyses of the project results have been made. These are presented in the second part of the book, Chapters Four to Seven. The third part of the book, Chapters Eight and Nine, reflect on the project and its results. Chapter Eight does this from a methodological perspective, by evaluating our experiences with comparative research and with combining qualitative and quantitative research methods. Chapter Nine formulates policy recommendations on the basis of the results of the research project.

Chapter Two presents the central concepts applied in the book: inclusion, exclusion and marginalisation on the one hand, and the concept of work on the other. The concepts of inclusion, exclusion and marginalisation are related to the more comprehensive themes of differentiation and integration. A central distinction is between integration in the macro-sociological sense, and integration understood as individuals' inclusion into societal systems. It is in this second distinction that the problematic of inclusion/exclusion seems to be applied most effectively. A further exploration of the meanings and contexts of inclusion and exclusion, however, reveals the necessity of making explicit what one means by inclusion, exclusion and marginalisation when using the concepts. In our view, individuals can, willingly or unwillingly, be in situations of inclusion, exclusion and marginalisation with respect to a multidimensionality of domains, practices, institutions or systems. This is seen as referring to processes rather than any particular state of affairs. In order to understand people's experiences of inclusion and exclusion, and to determine the objectives of social policy interventions as well as to assess their outcomes, insight into the temporal aspects of the concepts is significant.

The debates and discourses on the concept of work have their own backgrounds. Nevertheless, the concept of work is closely connected to those of inclusion, exclusion and marginalisation. This is so, not only because we are specifically interested in the inclusionary and exclusionary potentials of various forms of work, but also because inclusion policies put great emphasis on the meaning of work in creating social cohesion in societies and providing individuals with a social identity and a sense of 'belonging'. Chapter Two tries to explain how social policies are fixated on jobs as the 'royal roads' to 'full' participation, and argues that there are various reasons for recognising and re-evaluating work beyond employment.

Chapter Three explores the development of active social policies, and elaborates the concept of activation. The chapter analyses the shift from passive to active social policies in the EU in general, and at the EU policy making level in particular, as a paradigm shift in which the main objective of social policies is being transformed from protection to participation. The chapter argues that activation is not a uniform concept and distinguishes four ideal activation approaches in order to elaborate the variety of views on, and practices of, activation:

1. The autonomy optimists' approach;
2. The welfare independence optimists' approach;
3. The paternalism optimists' approach;
4. The activation optimists' approach.

Furthermore, it offers a first analysis of how the development of active social policies can be interpreted in the context of attempts of welfare states to adapt to a changing social reality. Chapter Three concludes with a discussion of why activation did emerge, and explores activation expenditures and institutional developments taking place against the background of the process of making welfare states and social policies more activating.

Having outlined the conceptual framework of the book in these two chapters, the results of the project are then presented. Before describing the results and findings of the case studies, Chapter Four provides an overview of the research literature on the inclusionary and exclusionary potentials of various forms of work. The chapter elaborates on the more general discussion of the concept of work in Chapter Two. It examines research on how work participation affects people's inclusion. In this context, the (albeit quite small number of) studies that address the effects of active social policies in terms of inclusion and exclusion is reviewed as well. Following the distinction of types of work presented earlier, Chapter Four looks at participation in 'standard' work, part-time work and flexi-work, employment programmes and training, unpaid work, and informal paid work. The latter has not received much attention in our case studies, but is nevertheless dealt with since it is an important form of participation in South European countries. The purpose of this review is, firstly, to explore issues that should be central to research into the inclusionary and exclusionary potentials of forms of work and social policies promoting them. Secondly, it puts the findings of our case studies in a broader perspective.

Chapter Five is the first of three chapters that report on the findings of our case studies. As Table 1.1 shows, several case studies were related to active social policy schemes, in the sense that they involved specific programmes aimed at (mostly long-term) unemployed people. Initially, the chapter pays attention to the development of active social policies in the EU countries, and to EU level policy initiatives that strengthen and stimulate this development. It also focuses on two types of activation programmes that received specific attention in our case studies: subsidised employment for the unemployed, and education and training programmes. Secondly, the chapter presents a short description of the design of the case studies and of the types of work they investigated. Specific attention is paid to the case studies into activation programmes, since these involve participation, employment and training schemes which may be unfamiliar to many readers. There follows an analysis of inclusion opportunities as well as exclusion risks for each form of work. Since the variety *within* the types of work is as relevant as the variety *between* them, the analysis involves both types of comparison. The data show that there are no clear and stable borderlines between concrete types of work on the one hand, and specific forms of (wanted) inclusion or (unwanted) exclusion on the other. Chapter Five concludes by stating that policy *matters* when it comes to the contribution of different types of work to inclusion. This is not only true in the sense that policies can, and actually do, influence the inclusion opportunities and exclusion risks of types of work, but also in the sense that activation processes can play an important role in matching these opportunities with the wishes, ambitions and needs of the target groups of activation.

Inclusion and exclusion, as we said earlier, are multidimensional concepts. People can be included in, or excluded from, a wide variety of systems or 'domains' of society (income, work, different types of networks, culture, politics, sports, other leisure-time activities, and so on). Chapter Six analyses the results of the case studies from this multidimensional perspective and some of the hypotheses that can be derived from it. Among others, it analyses the occurrence of virtuous and vicious circles in relation to various domains of participation, as well as the frequently claimed dominance of labour-market inclusion. The data show that there are no tendencies to significant accumulation of good or bad situations: the same person's inclusion into or exclusion from many systems. An important exception was found with respect to the extended family in the Portuguese case studies. Furthermore, no evidence was found to support the research in the interwar period, which strongly suggested that unemployment leads to the collapse of people's social networks. As far as the 'paid work as the royal road to inclusion' issue is concerned, income seems to be of greater importance than work for the inclusion of people into other systems. The data suggests that there are few 'automatic' inclusion, or exclusion positions in one system based on positions in other systems. Consequently, it seems that many people act strategically. In other words, they formulate strategies according to their preferences: some voluntarily exclude themselves, others try to include themselves into various systems or to compensate for unwanted exclusion and again others formulate strategies for bridging their inclusion into two or more systems at the same time.

Although the overall focus of this book is on cross-national analysis, Chapter Seven pays specific attention to one of the case studies, one quite distinct from the schemes we find in other countries: the so-called Capitalisation of Unemployment Benefits programme, which is the most important employment scheme in Spain (although, as the chapter states, the importance of the scheme is not located in its quantitative impact). This programme allows the unemployed who are entitled to unemployment benefits to capitalise the total value of these benefits and invest it in a new or already-established social company. Although it involves elements that we find in schemes in the other countries under investigation, the programme stands out because of a number of specific characteristics. After a general introduction to the programme, Chapter Seven discusses these specific characteristics and the way the scheme differs from the mainstream of employment programmes in the EU countries. Then, the experiences of participants in the scheme in terms of its contribution to inclusion and exclusion are analysed. An important aspect of these experiences, which is absent in most activation programmes, is the fact that by capitalising unemployment benefits in a social economy, workers become co-owners of the company where they work. In other words, the scheme promotes 'entrepreneurial activation'. This increases autonomy and responsibility at work, which elicits different reactions and is experienced in different ways by the participants. Another characteristic of the scheme is the limited role of the state in implementing and delivering the programme, which is analysed, as was mentioned earlier, as a specific characteristic of Southern European welfare states.

Chapters Eight and Nine reflect from two different perspectives on the results of, and experiences during, the project. Chapter Eight does this from a research perspective. It argues that the increasing emphasis in social scientific research on international comparisons, of which INPART is an example, is taking place against the background of a 'reflexive turn' in the social sciences. The empirical analytical model of social scientific research, which is based on theory testing, large-scale research, and the collection of quantitative data and aims at generalising explanations of social behaviour in terms of causality, meets increasing criticism from a reflexive strand in social sciences. The reflexive strand starts from central notions such as viewing actors under investigation as competent actors, relating common sense and scientific knowledge in terms of reciprocal adequacy, and the contextuality of knowledge. The chapter briefly summarises the orthodox consensus and the reflexive turn. Then, it discusses and analyses the implications the reflexive turn has for social research. It continues by elaborating how INPART dealt with these implications, for example, in terms of the contextuality of knowledge and in terms of the competence of actors (that is, in our case studies, participants in different types of work). It concludes by highlighting some of the challenges confronting internationally comparative research in the context of the reflexive turn in social sciences.

Chapter Nine reflects on the research results from an active social policy perspective. Since the development of social policies increasingly takes place in a context of EU policy making, the chapter elaborates this broader socio-political context. It then picks up the theme of reflexivity, introduced in Chapter Eight, and elaborates on it in the context of debates on the future of active social policies. On the basis of INPART's results, the chapter identifies several core issues of activation: heterogeneity and policy differentiation, objectives of activation, matching resources of work and people's needs, the relation between participation and income, and the recognition of non-labour-market inclusion strategies. It argues that, in general, two approaches to these issues can be distinguished, which – following the terminology of Chapter Eight – are called the 'orthodox consensus' of activation and 'reflexive' activation. Whereas the first is characterised by paternalist, labourist and top-down orientations, the latter not only emphasises the competence and autonomy of policy clients, but is strongly bottom-up oriented and uses broader concepts of inclusion and participation. Chapter Nine then returns to the issue that 'policy matters' where the inclusionary and exclusionary potentials of types of work are concerned, and formulates some conditions to strengthen the contribution of activation programmes to (wanted) inclusion. Finally, it argues in favour of treating activation as a process that involves activation not only of policy clients but also of the institutions involved in designing, implementing and delivering social policies. Some issues involved in the process of 'institutional activation' are discussed.

Note

[1] The Danish team acquired additional funding from the Danish Ministry of Labour. These extra resources enabled the team to realise a combination of qualitative and quantitative research methods.

References

Andreotti, A., García, S., Gómez, A., Hespanha, P., Kazepov, Y. and Mingione, E. (2001) 'Does a South European model exist? Some evidence of its presence', *Journal of European Area Studies*, vol 9, no 1, pp 43-63.

Esping-Andersen, G. (1999) *Social foundations of post-industrial economics*, Oxford: Oxford University Press.

Gallie, D. and Paugam, S. (eds) (2000) *Welfare regimes and the experience of unemployment in Europe*, Oxford: Oxford University Press.

Gough, I. and Olofsson, G. (1999) 'Introduction', in I. Gough and G. Olofsson (eds) *Capitalism and social cohesion. Essays on exclusion and integration*, London: Macmillan.

Lødemel, I. and Trickey, H. (eds) (2001) *'An offer you can't refuse': Workfare in international perspective*, Bristol: The Policy Press.

Saraceno, C. (ed) (2002) *Social assistance dynamics in Europe: National and local poverty regimes*, Bristol: The Policy Press.

Therborn, G. (1986) *Why some people are more unemployed than others: The strange paradox of growth and unemployment*, London: Verso.

TWO

The concept of inclusion/exclusion and the concept of work

Rik van Berkel, Iver Hornemann Møller and Colin C. Williams

Introduction

The introduction of active social policies throughout the EU can be seen as a reconsideration of the importance of work. In the context of such policies, the emphasis on participating in work is embedded to varying degrees in discourses stressing work as an 'entitlement' and work as an 'obligation'. It is similarly the case with discourses on the 'empowering' and 'disciplining' elements of work. Policy makers consider work to provide people with the material and non-material resources to be, as it is called, 'fully included in social life'. At the same time, participation in work is an obligation in the sense that when included in work, people fulfil their societal responsibilities by contributing to social production and preventing dependency on social security.

In emphasising participation in work, social policies do not usually refer to work in the general sense of "the carrying out of tasks, involving expenditure of mental and physical effort, which have as their objectives the production of goods and services that cater to human needs" (Giddens, 1989, p 481). As a rule, 'work', as conceived in social policies, refers to paid work or formal jobs. Often in Southern Europe, work on the informal market is not officially recognised as including people in the labour market or society. The size and importance of this market, however, make it a most central precondition for the official social policies and labour-market inclusion programmes. Contrary to the Southern European labour markets, work that is not taking place in the context of the regular and/or regularised labour market in Northern Europe is usually not considered of relevance with respect to the objectives social policies set themselves. Informal and non-regular work, including forms of unpaid work, are not recognised for their inclusion potentials, nor as one of the ways in which people might contribute to society; that is, as a way to fulfil their social responsibilities. In some cases, it is even considered a barrier to inclusion, as this is – explicitly or implicitly – defined by social policies. This happens, for example, when social security claimants are denied the opportunity to engage in voluntary work, because this is supposed to decrease their labour-market availability. It also happens when single parents on benefits are refused the right to raise their children and instead are expected to make use of childcare facilities to secure their labour-market availability.

In consequence, this chapter first centres on two groups of highly related issues:

- The problematic around the theme of exclusion, marginalisation and inclusion;
- The theme of integration and differentiation.

In addition, and as a result of the very high priority EU policy makers give to the inclusion specifically in paid work, the concept of work is dealt with at the end of this chapter.

Exclusion is one of the central concepts of INPART. It is our contention, however, that to get a more profound understanding of the contents and breadth of the theme of exclusion (plus marginalisation and inclusion), the concept of integration should be dealt with first. This is because it is both meaningful and productive to analyse the concept of exclusion in relation to insights and understandings of related concepts. Of all such concepts, integration is the broadest, and that is why we have chosen to start here. As is demonstrated later in this chapter, integration is a multidimensional concept which, throughout the last two centuries and up to the present, has been applied in a multitude of ways in varying societal contexts. In a way, integration is an umbrella concept.

Sometimes, inclusion is also seen to be synonymous with integration. There is a growing tendency, however, at least in scientific discourses, to use the concept of inclusion in a much narrower way than integration. In this new vein, inclusion has a tendency to be applied as the opposite of exclusion. Furthermore, the two concepts, inclusion and exclusion, are either conceived as dichotomies (for example, Luhmann, 1997) or, as with INPART, as two opposite poles with an area of marginalisation in between. So, in this way, exclusion, marginalisation and inclusion constitute a single theme. What then distinguishes this from the concept of integration is that the former is applied (tendencially) at the micro or meso level of analysis only.

This book adheres to this tendency and, as a consequence, conceives integration as a multidimensional concept that is most fruitfully applied to macro phenomena and in macro contexts. Exclusion, and its two related concepts of inclusion and marginalisation however, constitute themes that should be related to individuals and groups of persons only. Therefore, before presenting our understanding of exclusion (plus inclusion and marginalisation), we shall say a few words about the meanings of integration.

Different notions of integration

Integration is a key theme in sociology, maybe *the* key theme. Even a cursory glance at the literature reveals that the concept has many different meanings and is used in many different contexts: from the classic texts of Marx, via Tonnies, Spencer, Durkheim and Parsons to the 'modern classic' writings of Lockwood, Habermas, Giddens, Luhmann and Mouzelis.

In some approaches to integration, the micro–macro dimension plays a central role, or is an important – although sometimes rather implicit – principle of analysis (Habermas, Luhmann). Other approaches turn on the actor–structure dimension as a most relevant distinction (Lockwood, Mouzelis), while yet others focus on the duality objective versus subjective (Weber) or face-to-face relations versus indirect relations (Giddens)[1].

David Lockwood's article, 'Social integration and system integration' (1964), in many ways sets the scene for the debate on integration and disintegration that was to occur over the following decades. When Lockwood and those who followed him (such as, Habermas, Rex and Mouzelis) talk about system integration and social integration, they clearly do not use the term integration to denote the involvement or attachment of individuals or groups of individuals to functionally differentiated systems, cultural life worlds or collective movements. Rather, they are concerned with structures and actors at the macro level. System integration, according to Lockwood, is then conceived as involving more or less compatible relationships between different parts or subsystems in the society at large, while social integration is seen as involving more or less orderly (as opposed to conflicting) relations between collective actors of a social system.

In Mouzelis' (1995) elaboration on Lockwood's work, social integration focuses on collective actors. Here, institutions are at the periphery while actors are at the centre in the sense that rules are seen in connection with the complex methodologies the actors employ for the purpose of applying (or managing not to apply) these rules when playing specific games. From a system integration viewpoint, however, the main concern is no longer how such rules are actually applied by actors in specific interactions, but their relevance or irrelevance to a social system's functioning and its basic conditions of existence.

Habermas (1981) has taken up Lockwood's concepts and linked them to his own famous concepts of system world and life world. The result is a conception of social integration that differs from that of Lockwood. Habermas sees social integration as a matter of the unhindered working of the communicative reproduction of the life world or, more precisely, the reproduction of the life world's ability to secure cultural meanings, solidaristic social norms and personal identities. In his latest works, Habermas' view of integration becomes more blurred between micro and macro. It now denotes at one and the same time the specific kind of communication that takes place in a certain part of society, and the basis on which individuals or groups participate in a given part: social integration works on the basis of identity. In a coalition of social integration, people identify in crucial ways with each other and with the community of which they see themselves as a part. Mutual understanding is possible because one can assume that the other communication partners share the same implicit notions and conceptions as oneself. Habermas' notion of political integration works on the basis of a principle for communication that is both stronger and weaker than identity. The partners do not have to identify with each other, but they must accept each other's right to mean what they mean. In the sense of not demanding identification, political integration is less demanding than social integration; but in requiring rational argumentation it is more demanding than social integration.

For system integration, the requirements to the participants are much weaker than social and political integration. What is needed is the acceptance of some symbolically generalised media such as money, power, love or truth. The working of these media makes a very simplified mode of communication possible. It requires neither identification nor argumentation but just a mutual acceptance of use of the media. One can make business with total strangers and read scientific articles by persons that one need not like or even know.

In contrast to Lockwood and his tradition, Giddens pays explicit attention to the micro level, to face-to-face interaction, and to the question of micro versus macro levels of analysis. Social integration means reciprocity between actors in contexts of co-presence. In the course of their daily activities individuals encounter each other in situated contexts of interaction – interaction with others who are co-present. System integration means reciprocity between actors or collectives across extended time-space. Giddens emphasises the point that social and system integration is closely bound: the routines of day-to-day life are fundamental to even the most elaborated forms of societal organisation. The merit of Giddens' definition of social and system integration is that dimensions of time and space are explicitly taken into account. In consequence, the discussion about integration opens up a question sidestepped by Lockwood and his tradition: how does it occur that actions can be coordinated or integrated over large spans of time and space where actors are not in direct interaction with each other?

In contrast to most others, Luhmann addresses inclusion and exclusion to the issue of whether or not individuals have a role in one of the subsystems. He reserves the concept of integration to denote loose or strong connections between individuals' inclusion and exclusion within the different subsystems.

From Lockwood, Mouzelis, Habermas, Giddens and Luhmann, one could easily go on to catalogue many other and different meanings of integration. The literature referred to above should, however, be sufficient to illustrate the point that many different understandings of integration coexist. As a result, the notion of integration is applied in many different ways in contemporary political discussions and in a good deal of empirical work. This ranges from the integration of immigrants and psychiatric patients into the rest of the society, through integration of the unemployed into the labour market, to integration of new nation states into the EU, or of 'predator' states into the westernised ways of thinking.

The many different conceptions of integration, and its many different connotations, should not be seen as a fault. Indeed, the goal should not be a single unitary conception of integration in society. Rather, the different conceptions and connotations reflect a real complexity in society. More precisely, they reflect the fact that a diversity of observations about 'integration in society' can often be made at one and the same time, without any of them standing out as irrefutably more salient than the others. Confusion over concepts and connotations here arises when society can be observed from quite different yet nonetheless all relevant viewpoints.

The different conceptualisations are then only in occasional conflict with each other. The numerous different observations of 'integration into parts of society' *are complementary* – they are not competing. Quite simply, *society needs many different conceptions of integration at the same time.* Confusion may reflect situations where society is observed in ways that may seem mutually contradictory yet can be taken also as complementary. For example, the way the economic and the political subsystems are integrated or not integrated cannot and should not be analysed by the same concepts used to analyse integration of physically disabled people or the integration of new member nations into the European Community.

The lessons from this section, therefore, are first, that the social sciences need a variety of integration concepts and, second, that integration is an *umbrella concept* that embraces a host of meanings.

Different notions of differentiation

A central distinction regarding integration, then, is that between the macro sociological sense, and integration understood as individuals' and groups' inclusion into societal systems and subsystems. It is in the latter connection that the problematic of inclusion/exclusion and marginalisation seems to be most effectively applicable.

INPART is about inclusion policies. It is, however, evident that without any exclusion there would not be any inclusion (policies): inclusion, so to speak, presupposes the existence of exclusion. Without exclusion there would be no need to talk about inclusion since everyone would *ipso facto* be included. Instead of a section examining inclusion alone, we have here devoted space, as a consequence, to examining different notions of exclusion.

One often finds not only politicians but also commentators and even social scientists talking about 'exclusion' or 'exclusion from society'. This is not very informative or enlightening unless the speakers then at least specify:

(a) exclusion from (inclusion into) which part of society;
(b) exclusion in what connotation (for example, exclusion of North Korea from the international community; exclusion of foreign students from the university);
(c) in what sense/meaning/understanding of the word (for example, exclusion/ inclusion as a dichotomy or as a continuum).

From the first requirement, one needs to draw on the concept of differentiation. For it should now be clear – at least for those who have agreed with the argument so far – that differentiation comes *before* exclusion; it is meaningless to talk about exclusion before one has made clear the types of societal differentiation into which exclusion is to be examined. This is logic: without differentiation in the society or a social system there is no need to talk about exclusion. In a 'whole' society without difference, everyone is included. Consequently, before it is meaningful to choose from the various connotations and the different understandings of exclusion/inclusion, it needs to be made clear how society's differentiation is conceived and which of the prevailing features of differentiation are most relevant for the types of problems being analysed.

According to most sociological theories, inclusion/integration and differentiation do not oppose each other. Spencer, Marx, Durkheim, Parsons, Habermas and Luhmann, each in his own way, worked with models of growing societal differentiation followed by new types of integration and its opposite, disintegration. Spencer saw societal development happening by way of an evolutionary trend towards increasing differentiation followed by changing types of integration. In industrial society, he therefore envisaged that a specific agency for integration, such as the state, was no longer necessary because integration would come about of its own accord, by means of something like Adam Smith's 'invisible hand'.

Marx did not use the terms 'differentiation' and 'integration', but was the first to distinguish social (dis)integration (of actors) from system (dis)integration (of institutions). And as long as economic reductionism is avoided, the Marxist paradigm still offers a most theoretically successful linkage between institutional analyses and analyses in terms of actors' strategic behaviour. The propensity to class antagonism (social disintegration) generally is a function of production relationships (including intra-class identification and communication). The dynamics of class antagonism, however, clearly arise from progressively growing contradictions in the economic system (system disintegration). The conflict that is decisive for change, then, is the system conflict stemming from contradictions between property institutions and forces of production. So, the work of Marx goes towards an interpretation of development in terms of incompatibilities between institutionalised complexes, as well as in terms of how actors do or do not perceive such incompatibilities. He analysed capitalist societies both in terms of growing institutional contradictions and in terms of agents' struggles; and he then posed the ever relevant questions: under what conditions does system disintegration lead to social disintegration? What are the complex ways in which system contradictions become or do not become associated with the development of class consciousness, class organisation and class action?

Durkheim's famous model centred on a change from mechanical to organic solidarity. He saw the integrating mechanism in modern societies as a new kind of social morality holding together people who are differentiated according to their diverse roles in the occupational structure. He also coined the term *anomie*, however, to describe a situation where organic solidarity had not developed, the results being, among others, industrial conflict and anomic suicides.

With Talcott Parsons the concept of system becomes crucial. Even though evolution means a continuous growth of differentiation into systems and further differentiations into subsystems, the process of development is kept together or 'integrated' through the ability of the cultural system to secure the necessary normative integration. Jürgen Habermas' and Niklas Luhmann's theories represent a significant increase of internal complexity in conceptions of differentiation and inclusion/integration. We shall return to some parts of Luhmann's theories later in this chapter.

There is, as one can see, no general agreement about which are the most outstanding types of differentiation in modern society. In general, however, differentiation is used as both a broader and weaker concept than exclusion/inclusion and integration. On the one hand, it may denote simply a classification of certain items (for example, countries, ethnicities). On the other hand, differentiation is sometimes deployed to characterise the evolution of whole societies or their structural make-up. This is the case whether the predominant characteristic of modern societal differentiation is class division or functional differentiation, a debate that goes back to the contrast between Karl Marx and Emile Durkheim and today centres around the positions of Pierre Bourdieu and Niklas Luhmann. The disagreement over whether hierarchical differentiation (Bourdieu) or functional differentiation (Luhmann) is the predominant feature of present societal differentiation may well not be open to definitive resolution. For empirical observations tend to show that modern society is differentiated into both functional systems and hierarchical groups and classes (Andersen, 1999; Larsen, 2000).

Consequently, and as a heuristic device, INPART has tried to combine Luhmann's principle of functional differentiation with Bourdieu's theory of capital and distinction. We take the latter then as complementary to Luhmann's theory of differentiation while addressed to the hierarchical structures of society. This combination, which underlines the co-presence of two very different forms of differentiation in contemporary society, will be presented later in this chapter. First however, it is time to take a look at the different notions of exclusion.

Different notions of exclusion/inclusion

Unlike integration, the notion of exclusion has rarely played a central role in sociology. Only one of the 'founding fathers', Max Weber, worked intensively with the concept. As he noted almost a century ago, the creation of 'social closure' advances efforts by the powerful to exclude less powerful people from the full benefits of joint enterprises, while at the same time, facilitating efforts by underdogs to organise for the seizure of benefits denied (Weber, 1968, pp 43-6). A relationship is likely to be closed, Weber (1968, p 43) remarked:

> ... in the following type of situation: a social relationship may provide the parties to it with opportunities for the satisfaction of spiritual or material interests. If the participants expect that the admission of others will lead to an improvement of their situation, an improvement in degree, in kind, in security or the value of satisfaction, their interest will be in keeping the relationship open. If, on the other hand, their expectations are of improving their position by monopolistic tactics, their interests is in a closed relationship.

He then points out, "such group action may provoke a corresponding reaction on the part of those against whom it is directed" (Weber, 1968). In other words, collective efforts to resist a pattern of dominance governed by exclusion principles can properly be regarded as the other half of the social closure equation.

Parkin (1974) sees, although in an embryonic form, Weber's concept of social closure as an alternative to class analysis. Modes of closure can be thought of as different means of mobilising power for the purpose of engaging in distributive struggle. Strategies of exclusion may be regarded as the predominant mode of closure in all stratification systems. The common element in the strategies is the attempt by a given social group to maintain or enhance its privileges by the process of subordination (that is, the creation of another group or stratum of ineligibles beneath it). Where the latter in their turn also succeed in closing off access to remaining rewards, so multiplying the number of substrata, the stratification order approaches that condition of political diffusion that represents the furthest point of contrast to the Marxist model of class polarisation. The traditional caste system provides one of the clearest illustrations of this type of closure pattern. Whereas, Parkin (1974) continues, exclusion is a form of closure that stabilises the stratification order, usurpation is one that contains a potential challenge to the prevailing system of distribution. Whole collectivist rules of closure would produce a communal situation, characterised by a total negative status, of which the apartheid system is the clearest example. The opposite extreme is represented by closure practices based wholly on individual criteria, thereby giving rise to a condition of segmental statuses – a classless society. In modern capitalist societies, says Parkin, the two main exclusionary devices by which the bourgeoisie constructs and maintains itself as a class are, first, those surrounding the property institutions and, second (and partly inspired by Bourdieu), academic or professional qualifications and credentials.

In the 1960s, and quite early in the development of his massive holistic theory of domination, Bourdieu, and his collaborator Passeron, developed their theory of symbolic violence, which crucially involves the notion of exclusion. In the theory, and in contrast to Weber's and Parkin's work, one recognises the lack of awareness on the part of the excluders as to what they are actually doing. The theory's two key propositions (Bourdieu and Passeron, 1977, pp 40-1) are:

- In any given social formation, the pedagogic work through which the dominant pedagogic agency is carried on always has the function of keeping order. In other words, by reproducing the structure of the power relations between the groups or classes, inasmuch as by inculcation or exclusion, it tends to impose recognition of the legitimacy of the dominant culture on the members of the dominated classes or groups. Furthermore, this makes them internalise, to a variable extent, disciplines and censorships which best serve the material and symbolic interests of the dominant groups or classes when they take the form of self-discipline and self-censorship.

• In any given social formation, because of the pedagogic work through which the dominant pedagogic agency tends to impose recognition of the legitimacy of the dominant culture on the members of the dominated groups or classes, it tends at the same time to impose on them, by inculcation and exclusion, recognition of the illegitimacy of their own culture.

More recently, Mancur Olson (1982) traced social exclusion to the collective action of exclusive groups and lobbies, and Charles Tilly (1998) identified 'opportunity hoarding' as a mechanism promoting durable inequality. It is very common, however, that the concept of exclusion is conceived much more narrowly. However, even in the broader understandings of Weber, Parkin, Bourdieu and Passeron, Olson and Tilly, exclusion is usually applied 'only' in relations to individuals, groups of persons or fractions of classes. It is not viewed in relation to different economic, political, cultural and other parts or institutions of society; or in relations between different nation states; or seldom in relations between classes.

Towards the end of the 1980s, it became generally assumed within the European Community that 'poverty' – in the Townsendian tradition of extreme class inequalities and lack of resources (Townsend, 1979) – was no longer the right word, and was replaced by 'social exclusion'. This term was intended to denote not just lack of material wealth, but also a condition of deprivation in respect of such dimensions as in particular wealth, social rights, attachment to the labour market and strength of informal networks in mutual interaction. An extensive debate about the distinctions between these two concepts and their contexts followed. Some commentators (for example, Abrahamsen, 1998) claimed that distinctions could be found according to:

• *Situation* (lack of resources versus lack of rights);
• *Causes* (needs versus discrimination);
• *Perspective* (static versus dynamic);
• *Societal type of differentiation* (hierarchical into classes versus horizontal into insiders and outsiders);
• *Remedies* (social transfer payments versus activation measures);
• *The disciplinary approach* (economics versus sociology).

Others (for example, Sen, 1998) argued that the idea of social exclusion was "not a novel concept and does not make a conceptual breakthrough.... The concept of social exclusion reinforces – rather than competes with – the understanding of poverty as capability deprivation by giving more focus to the relational routes through which deprivation may come about" (Sen, 1998, pp 4-5). Others in turn adopted more political interpretations. They argued that poverty was no longer an acceptable concept for well-developed welfare states; and as a by-product of this line of debate the point was underscored that "to enunciate 'problems', establish causalities, classify populations and prescribe solutions are inseparable moments of the same discourse ... to name groups is to draw social boundaries" (Silver, 1996, p 135).

Each concept (poverty, exclusion) has its own internal logic and dynamic, determining which aspects of a phenomenon are highlighted. Different concepts privilege different points of possible insight, just as different concepts lead up to different discourses; so that some topics are kept out while others are brought into central focus. As Levitas (1996) notes, the exclusion–inclusion discourse can obscure the fact that the positions into which people are included through paid work are fundamentally unequal (as to class, gender and ethnicity).

Recently, Room (1999) has tried to specify the conceptual relationship between poverty and social exclusion:

(a) While poverty tends to focus on financial hardship, exclusion deals with multidimensional disadvantages;
(b) Poverty is predominantly a static concept, whereas the focus of exclusion is dynamic;
(c) Poverty understandings focus on the resources of the individual or household, whereas exclusion also deals with those of the local community;
(d) Poverty approaches tend to concentrate on distributional dimensions while exclusion approaches deal with relational dimensions of stratification and disadvantage;
(e) When leaving the poverty understanding and moving into exclusion one moves from focus on a continuum of inequality to a focus on catastrophic rupture.

Room (1999) rightly points to the fact that the 'traditional' poverty studies did partly include the 'new'. For example, the multidimensional approach was salient in several of Townsend's studies and also in Mack and Lansley's survey of 'Breadline Britain' (Mack and Lansley, 1985). Townsend also claimed that there was a 'kink' in the income hierarchy below which the consequences of income deprivation were disproportionately great and therefore had catastrophic effects. What matters then to Room are the co-presence of all five elements and their high degree of irreversibility. He concludes that:

> [I]n short, then, to use the notion of social exclusion carries the implication that we are speaking of people who are suffering such a degree of multidimensional disadvantage, of such duration, and reinforced by such material and cultural degradation of the neighbourhoods in which they live,

that their relational links with the wider society are ruptured to a degree which is to some considerable degree irreversible. (Room, 1999, p 171)

Room's works have to some extent been trendsetting in various EU contexts. It is therefore important to draw attention to the fact that the understanding of exclusion applied in INPART, and to which we now shall turn in the next two sections, have both similarities and differences in comparison with Room's. First of all, the way INPART contextualises and conceptualises exclusion is rather different from Room's which implies, among other things, that we do not necessarily conceive exclusion as associated with 'ruptures' and 'irreversibility'. Rather, we understand exclusion as a process which, over shorter or longer periods of time, may or may not be followed by positions of inclusion, of marginalisation and also of further exclusion.

When comparing the concept of integration with the concept of exclusion (and inclusion), it should now be clear that integration has many more and much broader understandings than exclusion. It is also applied in many more different contexts. Contrary to integration, exclusion is not an umbrella concept, and with very few exceptions exclusion is always used in connection with individuals or groups of individuals who for one reason or another are out of one or more of the (sub)systems in focus.

Functional and hierarchical differentiation

Three forms of societal differentiation are prevalent in present society. *Segmentary differentiation* – the first of Luhmann's three forms of evolutionarily developed differentiation – implies differentiation into a number of similar units. The units may be families, ethnic groups, clans, tribes, and so on, where the unit has some character of a partly self-contained community or *Gemeinschaft* to it, based upon the principles of co-presence and co-locality of its members.

The next type of differentiation – the second in Luhmann's evolutionary series and arising from further differentiation of certain roles, for example, chieftains and sacred roles, in the segmentary society – is *hierarchical differentiation*, based on the principles of over/under. The development of hierarchical differentiation depends on conditions (for example, written language) that make possible forms of social organisation, including work organisation, that transcend the principles of co-presence and co-locality. Today, almost everybody belongs to and lives in a social group – at least the majority of people are raised within a family. And also most people are members of one or more organisations, often work organisations, where again they are part of a social unit. However, the social groups and organisations are often ordered hierarchically according to power, privilege and prestige. As social science has long observed and as Bourdieu reminds us, income, life courses, health, cultural taste, consumer taste, and so on are not alike for different people.

The third type of differentiation – the third step in Luhmann's evolutionary development of types of differentiation – is *functional differentiation*; that is, into functionally specific subsystems such as economy, polity, the juridical subsystem, religion, family and cultural subsystems. According to Luhmann, there is no final list of subsystems because new subsystems can develop such as, in recent years, the mass-sport subsystem, the ecological subsystem and the IT subsystem.

Observations of contemporary societies make it difficult, however, to agree with Luhmann on the overall importance and predominance of functional differentiation. Although most commentators can agree on an evolution from predominance of segmentary differentiation to predominance of more modern types of differentiation, empirical evidence from contemporary societies show all three principles to be involved at the same time but with great variations from one society to another. Family formations and ethnic groupings are clear examples of segmentary differentiation that remain present in many societies today. At the same time, unequal possessions of, or access to, various forms of capital (economic, social, cultural and symbolic), as pointed out by Bourdieu, are clear indications of the importance of hierarchical differentiation.

We can agree with Luhmann that communications and actions in the functionally differentiated subsystems are coordinated by various symbolically effective media (for example, money in the economic subsystem, power in the political subsystem, law and rules in the juridical subsystem, faith in the religious subsystem, and love in the subsystem of affinity) and that these codes are not translatable into each other. Each subsystem communicates within itself by means of its specific media. We can *also* agree with Bourdieu, however, that within many (but not all) functionally differentiated subsystems, there are struggles between the agents for the improvement of their respective positions and that in society as a whole there are processes of distinction based on the agents' unequal possessions of, or access to, economic, social and cultural capital.

So, while segmentary, hierarchical and functional differentiation on the one hand are leading principles of differentiation that have developed in some form of evolutionary succession, on the other hand, when looking at present societies, one finds empirical evidence for the coexistence of all three principles at the same time. In most societies, segmentary differentiation, although still relevant, plays a less important role today than previously. However, it is hard to find conclusive empirical evidence for Luhmann's general postulate that functional differentiation is now the primary or leading type of differentiation.

Central to Luhmann's understandings of systems of the functionally differentiated society is the absence of an overall societal force that keeps the subsystems together. The subsystems are 'structurally linked' to each other, but there is no 'Durkheimian common ethic', Adam Smith's 'invisible hand' or set of Parsonian 'cultural values' to secure the coherence of the society.

What in particular makes the notions of segmentary, hierarchical and functionally differentiated society so 'attractive' for analyses of exclusion and inclusion, however, is its almost perfect correspondence with the phenomenon that people do not any more belong to only one or two subsystems, the family and the work subsystem. Instead, most people today are included within many different subsystems (leisure-time subsystems, cultural subsystems, educational subsystems, and so on) not only over the course of their lifetime but also at any given point of time; a fact which makes this understanding of 'exclusion' and 'inclusion' dynamic. To this matter we shall return below when dealing with the micro and meso level issue of individuals' and groups' exclusion from and inclusion into society.

In sum, the outcome of this discussion of different conceptions of differentiation reveals an important finding. It shows that whether the emphasis is on functional differentiation, hierarchies, classes or any other type of overall differentiation in society, the concepts of exclusion/inclusion and integration, whether theoretical or applied, should always be analysed in relation to specified segments, hierarchies and functionally differentiated systems.

Exclusion, marginalisation and inclusion of individuals and groups in relation to different subsystems

There is no end to the number of (sub)systems in functionally differentiated society. New subsystems emerge, and inside the same subsystem, such as the educational subsystem, one can make an almost infinite amount of differentiations into (sub)subsystems: primary school, secondary school, a large number of types of vocational training schemes, different types of university education, and so on.

Luhmann's conception of being included means to have a role in a system from which one can communicate; without such a role one is excluded. The notion can be applied irrespective of who is to blame, whether the individual that is excluded or the excluding system or no one at all because the exclusion is voluntary and therefore wanted by the excluded individual. The merit of 'inclusion' and 'exclusion' is that they are well-suited to analyse the involvement or non-involvement, attachment or non-attachment of individuals or groups vis-à-vis different (sub)systems of society.

At any point in every individual's life trajectory, he/she will be included in some (sub)systems, and excluded from others. Furthermore, everybody will experience that the pattern of inclusions and exclusions will change during their life course: nearly all children, for example, will be included within a nuclear family but at the other end of the life cycle more than half of elderly North Europeans live in single-person households. Middle-aged people are often included in the labour market, while this is seldom the case for children and older people. This means that the concepts of inclusion and exclusion are *dynamic* concepts, in the sense that most individuals during their life trajectory will move into and out of quite a few (sub)systems. None, however, will be included in all (sub)systems or, conversely, excluded from them all at the same time (see below).

Figure 2.1 illustrates our understanding of the connection between inclusion, exclusion and marginalisation from a system-theoretical point of view. The term inclusion/exclusion presupposes a separation between system and environment, but, in contrast to Room's emphasis on 'irreversibility' and

Figure 2.1: Inclusion, exclusion, marginalisation

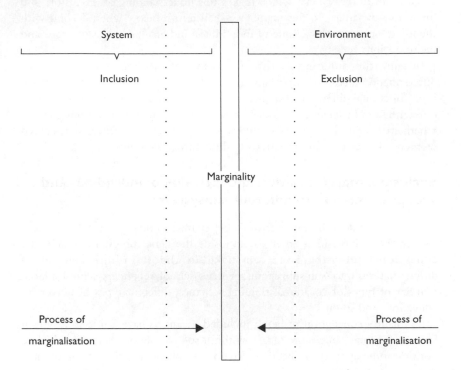

'ruptures', a door is added that makes movements possible into and out of the system. This corresponds with many empirical observations and consequently a zone is defined on both sides of the borderline where one can speak about marginality. Since we deal with processes over time, marginalisation may be conceived as a process whereby people voluntarily move or are pushed or pulled away into marginality and further into exclusion. Marginalisation is, however, also possible in the other direction; but in this case it is often conceived as a positive movement out of exclusion, into marginality and eventually maybe across the borderline into inclusion. There are, however, also processes which involve movements of people directly from inclusion into exclusion without a stage of marginality, for example when older workers retire or are fired overnight with very little chance of ever finding a new job.

It is of central importance that inclusion, marginality and exclusion should be analysed *in relation to a specific social system* (a segment, class or function system) since the means of inclusion – the code for communication applied within each system – differs from one system to another. Communication and so inclusion by way of money in the economic system is obviously quite different from communication by way of love in the system of affinity and affection.

An analytical advantage of conceiving inclusion–marginality–exclusion as a continuum – instead of, as Luhmann and Room suggest, treating inclusion and exclusion as a dichotomy – is that in many situations of 'real life', individuals are *more or less* included, *more or less* marginalised and *more or less* excluded. A sharp distinction between the three zones is not feasible. It is possible for each of the large number of (sub)systems to identify strong/weak positions within all three zones where individuals possess larger/smaller amounts of resources which allow them greater/lesser freedom of choice whether or not to maintain their present position. Consequently, it is more in accordance with empirical observations to conceive inclusion, marginality and exclusion as *relative concepts*: you can be more or less included, more or less excluded and more or less marginalised.

Exactly where on the continuum of inclusion–marginality–exclusion an individual is situated depends, to a major extent, on his/her overall possession of, and capacity to, *mobilise* not only economic resources but also *social, cultural* and *symbolic resources*. This typology corresponds with Bourdieu's productive distinction between different types of capital: *economic capital* in its various forms; *social capital*, which consists of resources based on connections and group membership (that is, networks of social relations – kin and otherwise – to further one's goals); *cultural capital* gained by acquisition of socially valued knowledge, artistic taste, literary skills and such like; and *symbolic capital*, which entails the idea of honour and social prestige (that is, the additional form the different types of capital take once they are perceived and recognised as legitimate).

Let us illustrate the relativity of positions within each of the three zones by some examples of inclusion/exclusion, specifically in relation to the subsystem of the paid labour market and the nuclear family subsystem. People possessing both an extensive network of social relations and such knowledge, skills and competencies as are strongly demanded in the paid labour market will, if they wish, nearly always be included and strongly placed within the paid labour market. Meanwhile, persons with a weak network and little demanded qualifications will, if at all included within the paid labour market, have relatively weak positions. In many countries, a significant segment of the labour force finds only casual employment during most of their life, and are consequently positioned at the margin of the market. There are also students and others with many more resources who, for shorter spells, find themselves in a marginalised position. As for excluded persons, most possess some (residual) but highly varying capacity to work. Among the excluded, those who have the highest residual work capacity in market terms are relatively best placed, and it is these who in some countries have been the particular target groups for policies towards 'activation'.

In Northern Europe today, many individuals live in single-person households. Some of these individuals possess few resources and, one would expect, are often then involuntarily excluded from the nuclear family subsystem. Others, however, possess many resources but have chosen – at least for some time to come – to exclude themselves from the nuclear family; or they try more intermediate forms of cohabitation and consequently could be seen as marginalised vis-à-vis the nuclear family subsystem.

In our view, therefore, exclusion, marginality and inclusion are seen as relative concepts that are related to each other. They can be applied specifically to each of modernity's almost unlimited number of segmented, hierarchically and functionally differentiated subsystems where the position of each individual within each subsystem is based on his/her possession of different types of capital. This, for us, is superior to seeing exclusion, marginality and inclusion as autonomous and relatively isolated phenomena.

As we demonstrated earlier in this chapter, exclusion is often conceived, defined and applied in relation to both marginalisation and inclusion. Also the very best studies deal with marginalisation in relation to inclusion or to exclusion or to both. Park (1928), for example, a pupil of Merton and the first to apply the concept of marginalisation, described the many Jewish immigrants to the US he studied as living at the margin. They were neither totally included into the new North American society nor had they maintained all their Jewish roots from their society of origin. When studying the millions of people living at the margins of Latin American societies, Germani (1980) defined marginalised persons as those possessing both the desire and capacity to fulfil societal norms, for example regarding work or education, while lacking the objective opportunities (for jobs or schools). In a more recent study Johannessen (1997) conceives labour-market marginalisation as a process of movement from the kernel of the market via more and more precarious labour-market positions towards the end where the individual is finally excluded.

Exclusion is not necessarily a *bad thing*, although it is this way of understanding which often implicitly dominates both the literature and the day-to-day use of the word. To restate our logic that differentiation comes before exclusion, the notion of labelling the concept 'good' or 'bad' ultimately depends on individuals' moral evaluations of the kind of differentiation studied (the parts, the subsystems, and so on). It is not good to be included into something bad, and if the subsystem studied is regarded as repulsive it is better to stay excluded. For example, many liberalists want to stay out of the trade-union movement and the federations of employers; some homeless people and drug-addicts may not want to be included in every aspect of the 'normal' society; and many people's moral evaluations make them decide to stay excluded from the religious subsystem, the political subsystem, the sport subsystem, the nuclear family subsystem, and so on. Not surprisingly, the individuals' perceptions of the 'good' and 'bad' dimensions of exclusions are, as shown in the second part of this book (Chapters Four to Seven), a most central part of the empirical side of INPART.

Another moral aspect arises with the questions: *who is to blame for the lack of wanted inclusion? Who has the responsibility?* The concepts of exclusion and inclusion as developed and understood by Luhmann coined no initial implications concerning who is to blame, the individual that is excluded or the excluding system. From the early 1970s onwards, however, a growing number of EU citizens became unemployed or marginalised in relation to the labour market. The issue of responsibility came to the fore; and there is not much doubt that since the end of that decade, focus on who was to blame shifted in most European countries from emphasis on society to emphasis on the unemployed themselves (Lind, 1995). This shift has been exacerbated with the emergence of activation policies across Europe, in connection with which not only liberals and conservatives but also labour politicians have increasingly talked about excluded persons' responsibilities for their own lives, and blamed them for their alleged unwillingness to be activated.

That being said, the question of who is to blame for involuntary exclusion is a central normative issue. There is then another, related and equally central issue: how aware are those who have set this agenda (to shift more responsibility on to the unemployed) of the strong likelihood that their own moralising will in turn serve to exclude the excluded further still?

If one considers the many ways society can be differentiated, the many ways of differentiating the subsystems and of combining the divisions and subdivisions with varying degrees of exclusion, marginalisation and inclusion, the result is an overwhelming number of conceivable combinations. Therefore, at the outset one has to accept that the almost infinite number of combinations may well lead to many competing and even contradictory analyses of exclusion, inclusion and marginalisation in modern societies.

It then makes sense, of course, to pare down the frame of reference. One way to limit the complexity is to identify those subsystems that are the *most important* for people. It is hard to imagine, for example, that adults in most societies could be totally excluded from the economic system over longer periods of time and so have no access at all to buying on the market. After all, unemployed and homeless people must find ways to prevent themselves from starving to death. Consequently, inclusion into the subsystem of paid work or other formal or informal income creating activities is generally recognised to have a high priority. The significance of this type of inclusion stands out at least in Western societies where paid work generates not only income but is often also conceived as 'the royal road to societal inclusion' via new networks, more status, more self-confidence and more recognition of doing something useful for society.

There is some ambivalence about the centrality of the nuclear family subsystem. It remains relatively important in Southern Europe but has been declining there, while it has seen some revitalisation in Northern Europe over the past decade or so. There are in any case many people who prefer, for shorter or longer periods of time, to live their life outside a nuclear family framework. As for the educational system on the other hand, there is a great deal of evidence of the growing salience of education for the proper functioning of individuals. It is often argued that education is an increasingly important precondition for a strong position in the paid labour market, in the income system, in the cultural system, in the leisure-time system and in the social network system.

One (sub)system, therefore, can be more important than others, either because

– as with the income system – it is (almost) impossible to survive without some degree of inclusion; or because inclusion in/exclusion from one specific system may lead to inclusion in/exclusion from other systems as well. Mortensen (2000) argues, for example, that there is much research evidence to show how the systems of paid labour, nuclear family formation and education come together to cumulative negative effect in processes of marginalisation and exclusion.

More generally, how far one can predict a person's positions within other (sub)systems from his/her position within one specific (sub)system becomes a very central question. Or, formulated in another way: *to what extent can we measure vicious circles (accumulation of bad life) and virtuous circles (accumulation of good life)?* St Matthew says: "Whoever has will be given more.... Whoever does not have, even what he has will be taken from him" (St Matthew's Gospel, 13:12). According to Luhmann, however, exclusion and marginality are characterised by vicious circles while inclusion is not characterised by virtuous circles: inclusion into one (sub)system is seldom linked to inclusion into other systems, while exclusion from one (sub)system probably involves exclusion from other systems. The argumentation is that when one is included into a (sub)system there is only a weak if any correlation between positions in the various (sub)systems. Each (sub)system has its own specific way of communication, its own codes, and its own mode of inclusion. Whether you are married or not has little to do with your political activity, your role in the economic system or in the religious system for instance. On the other hand, Luhmann claims, if you are excluded from one (sub)system there is a tendency to be excluded also from other (sub)systems.

It is the position of INPART that at the end of the day it is an empirical question how far Luhmann's 'half Matthew-principle' mirrors contemporary society. Chapter Six deals with the empirical results regarding this issue. Our emphasis on the empirical approach underlines, however, that we are, a priori, not reiterating the dominating norm and discourse about the overall importance of either paid work or income.

Last but not least, a few remarks about INPART's approach to *the objective-subjective dimension*. An objective approach rests on the assumption that it is reasonable to ascribe specific qualities or values to identities from the outside. There are two varieties of objectivistic approaches. The first emphasises rationality (for example, the categorisation of work to be discussed later); the other stresses empirical reference (for example, the typology of activation made in Chapter Three of this volume). A subjective approach claims that it is not proper to view societies or large parts of social life from an objectivistic point of view, because social phenomena must be seen from the inside, according to the meanings that actors and cultures have themselves. On the subjective side we can distinguish between a hermeneutic version focusing on meanings (phenomenology), and a pragmatic version focusing on actions (pragmatic interactionism). INPART did not take an either/or point of view: on the one hand, notions of exclusion, of different types of capital, of work, of activation and of other concepts have been theorised, adapted and developed both on the micro, meso and macro level. Such approaches are overwhelmingly objective. On the other hand, people's perceptions are not only taken into account but also brought into focus. This is done by way of their understanding and views on activation, work, income, family network, culture and other concepts related both to the micro, meso and macro level. These subjective approaches dominate the empirical parts of the study.

The concept of work

The meaning of work

Until now, we have outlined the diversity and complexity of the two themes of exclusion, inclusion, marginalisation on the one hand, and integration/differentiation on the other hand. In this section, another dimension is added that brings further complexity to the discussion. Much social policy is grounded in the assumption that employment is the 'royal road' to combating exclusion and promoting inclusion. Social policies seem to be based on a rather narrow definition of work, presuming that unemployment equals exclusion and employment equals inclusion. Our contention in this section is to highlight that it is necessary to rethink 'work' in the context of inclusion, exclusion and marginalisation. In doing so we shall analyse the previous attempts to redefine work as more than employment.

Apart from the 'narrow' concept of work underlying most social policies, these policies also operate a rather undifferentiated view on jobs. Generally, social policies start from the assumption that jobs contribute to citizenship, in the double meaning of being included and exercising one's responsibilities, irrespective of the goods and services being produced, the working conditions of the job, the quality of work, and so on. Of course, these issues may be subjected to policies in other fields (wage regulations, working time regulations, leave regulations, and so on), but social policies do not distinguish between 'bad' jobs and 'good' jobs when it comes to assessing the contribution of jobs to realising citizenship (although the EU summit in Lisbon in 2000 did speak about 'good' jobs in relation to combating exclusion). The only exceptions to this general picture are social security regulations with respect to work obligations. Some social security systems qualify work obligations, for example in terms of qualifications (people are obliged to look for 'suitable' jobs) or in terms of number of working hours (some categories of social security claimants have a part-time work obligation). However, most social security systems have strengthened rather than weakened work obligations during the last decades, thereby reducing claimants' opportunities to choose a job that meets their needs and demands.

How can social policies' fixation on jobs as the 'royal road' towards 'full' participation or citizenship be explained? One of the reasons for this is that jobs are supposed to give people access to wellbeing. Ironically, it has been social scientific research into the life worlds and experiences of unemployed people that has contributed considerably to establishing the exclusivity of jobs in linking work and citizenship. The work of Marie Jahoda and her colleagues, especially their research in the Austrian village of Marienthal in the 1930s, has been pioneering in gaining insight into the social-psychological wellbeing of the unemployed and, by implication, into the meanings of work (Jahoda et al, 1975; Jahoda, 1982). The characteristics, functions or meanings of work can be outlined as follows (Giddens, 1982, pp 506-7; italics in the original).

1. *Money*. A wage or salary is the main resource most people depend on to meet their needs. Without such an income, anxieties about coping with day-to-day life tend to multiply.

2. *Activity level*. Employment often provides a basis for the acquisition and exercise of skills and capacities. Even where work is routine, it offers a structured environment in which a person's energies may be absorbed. Without employment, the opportunity to exercise such skills and capacities may be reduced.

3. *Variety*. Employment provides access to contexts that contrast with domestic surroundings. In the working environment, even when the tasks are relatively dull, individuals may enjoy doing something different from home chores. Unemployment reduces this source of contrast with the domestic milieu.

4. *Temporal structure*. For people in regular employment, the day is usually organised around the rhythm of work. While this may sometimes be oppressive, it provides a sense of direction in daily activities. Those who are out of work frequently find boredom a major problem and develop a sense of apathy about time.

5. *Social contacts*. The work environment often provides friendships, and opportunities to participate in shared activities with others. Separated from the work setting, a person's circle of possible friends and acquaintances is likely to dwindle.

6. *Personal identity*. Employment is usually valued for the sense of stable social identity it offers. For men in particular, self-esteem is often bound up with the economic contribution they make to the maintenance of the household.

This list of meanings of employment is still often quoted when it comes to underlining the importance of jobs. However, several developments in society make it necessary to qualify this way of looking at the meanings of employment. First of all, employment has changed. The current 'post-Fordist' labour market shows an increased variety of jobs compared to 'Fordist' times (Lind and Møller, 1999; Standing, 1999), making it increasingly difficult to assume that each and every job provides the meanings and functions in the list above. For example, the 'temporal structure' provided by flexible jobs is quite different from the temporal structure of the 'traditional' full-time job. This does not exclude the possibility, of course, that unemployed people may prefer 'bad' jobs to situations of unemployment. However, it may help to explain why some unemployed people think they are better-off without a job than in a (particular) job, or why many unemployed people do not want to accept any job offered to them.

Second, the social circumstances in which the unemployed live and that influence their resources, experiences, options and choices, have changed. The development of welfare systems is of course very important in this respect. Although these systems have not put an end to poverty or removed processes of stigmatisation of unemployed people, they have increased resources unemployed people dispose of in absolute terms, which will influence the attractiveness and importance of jobs and labour market participation.

Third, people have changed. Educational levels have increased, people's needs have differentiated, and so have views on what constitutes a 'good life' and on the contribution employment can make to that. Once again, this does not imply that employment is no longer of importance to the unemployed. Nevertheless, research also shows that part of the unemployed has been successful in developing alternative participation strategies, partly out of free choice, partly out of necessity (Burman, 1988; van Berkel and Brand, 1996). Therefore, there are so-called 'good copers' among the unemployed (Fryer and Ullah, 1987), who, by being involved in other subsystems than the labour market, manage to prevent or decrease experiences of exclusion.

Against this background, one of the main arguments in this book will be that social policies that are really concerned with addressing issues of exclusion, marginalisation and inclusion, should avoid dichotomies such as 'employment versus unemployment', 'work versus non-work' and 'passive versus active citizens'. Rather, they should reflect critically on policy assumptions such as 'unemployment equals societal exclusion' and 'employment equals societal inclusion'.

Rethinking work

Rethinking work is an essential element of these reflections. Despite the fairly recent interest of some social policy analysts in rethinking the meaning of work, this has been on the agenda in the social sciences for over three decades. Since the 1970s a vast social science literature has explored the magnitude and character of work beyond employment and called for the recognition and revaluing of such work (Williams and Windebank, 1998; Gregory and Windebank, 2000). This demand to recognise and revalue work beyond employment has come in general from two camps.

First, there are those who view such a reconceptualisation as necessary due to the inequalities inherent in such work and/or their resulting consequences for disparities in paid employment. Primarily, this has been argued by feminist scholars who focus upon the unequal gender divisions of labour and/or the subjugation of women due to patriarchal and/or capitalist modes of production and reproduction (for example, Vaiou, 1997; WGSG, 1997). However, it has also been the rationale for those who analyse the oppressive dark side of social capital (for example, Shulman and Anderson, 1999), the polarisation between 'work busy' and 'work deprived' households (for example, Pahl, 1984), and the exploitative character of low-paid, informal employment (for example, Castells and Portes, 1989).

A second camp views this reconceptualisation to be necessary for more positive reasons. On the one hand, there are those who view this as a prerequisite for rethinking the future of work and developing more socially equitable futures (for example, Gorz, 1999). On the other hand (and often overlooked), it is asserted by those environmentalists who O'Riordan (1996) refers to as 'communalist ecocentrists'. Arguing that modern societies should alter their economic practices to be more eco-friendly, revaluing 'local work' is seen by them as a key part of the 'new localist' agenda required in order for sustainable development to be achieved (Robertson, 1998).

Although various reasons therefore exist for recognising and revaluing work beyond employment, a thorny issue that all analysts have had to confront is *how to define work once it is taken to mean more than employment*. Despite universal agreement that work cannot be distinguished from leisure by listing tasks (for example, cooking, ironing, and writing) and that the social relations within which activity is conducted need to be investigated, at this point, the two camps diverge. The former group, concerned to show how such work subjugates women and/or marginalised groups, emphasise the negative social relations (for example, its unremunerated, low-paid, oppressive and/or routine character) in their definitions. The latter group, meanwhile, points to the rewarding, autonomous and creative social relations involved. Defining work, therefore, is a *deeply political* project. It is embedded in the values, objectives and concerns of the writer and his/her situatedness. Recognising this inherent problem, the working definition here adopted is that work in contemporary advanced economies is *any task that one may wish to pay someone else to do*. This situates the definition of whether a task is work or leisure largely in the hands of the actor rather than the analyst.

Given the vast scope and heterogeneity of human activity covered by such a definition, most studies adopt a typology that divides work into four slightly more coherent categories (although there is still great diversity within each type of work):

• *Self-provisioning:* the unpaid work undertaken by household members for themselves and each other. This ranges from domestic labour through unpaid caring activities conducted for and by household members to do-it-yourself home improvements (DIY);

- *Community work:* work provided on an unpaid basis by the extended family, social or neighbourhood networks and more formal voluntary and community groups;
- *Paid informal exchange:* where legal goods and services are exchanged for money and gifts, which are unregistered by, or hidden from, the state for tax, social security or labour law purposes;
- *Formal employment:* paid work that is recorded in the official statistics.

Although this differentiation of work is useful for exploring the changing nature of work in contemporary society as well as forms of exclusion and inclusion, we recognise that there is still great diversity within each type of work. Therefore, it is often useful to divide each of these forms of work into a number of subcategories (Table 2.1).

Self-provisioning, or what Polanyi (1944) called 'householding', includes a diverse range of activities ranging from routine tasks such as housework to more creative activities such as DIY. These are often conducted under very different social relations and the motives underpinning participation often lie in stark contrast to each other. In consequence, and in response to much literature that has called for a distinction to be drawn for analytical purposes between routine domestic work and DIY (for example, Walby, 1998; Gregory and Windebank, 2000), such activities need to be divided into these two subcategories wherever appropriate.

Community work, similarly, can be subdivided for analytical purposes into three types: kinship work, friendship/neighbourly work, and voluntary work. Although there is a tendency in some analyses to further subdivide voluntary work into numerous sub-categories (for example, Burns and Taylor, 1998; Home Office, 1999), this is not here asserted to be necessary in order to understand everyday life in most of the EU. Micro level reciprocal exchange between kin, neighbours and friends in contrast is much more heavily relied upon and given the variations in the attitudes towards, and motives underpinning participation in such work (see Williams and Windebank, 1999; Williams et al, 2001), is

Table 2.1: Typology of forms of work

Type of work	Sub-categories
Self-provisioning	Domestic work
	DIY activity
Community work	Kinship work
	Friendship/neighbourly work
	Voluntary work
Paid informal exchange	Autonomous paid exchange
	The informal market
Formal employment	'Primary' labour market
	'Secondary' labour market

divided into unpaid kinship exchange and unpaid exchange between friends/neighbours.

Paid informal exchange, can be both market and non-market work. The market work is conducted by parts of the populations as an economic survival strategy. In particular, this is the case in Southern European countries where this form of work amounts to between one fourth and one third of the GNP and the labour force participation in the informal market plays a decisive social and system integrative role (Lockwood, 1964). From a social integration point of view, the informal work market functions as a normal resort for poor people when unemployed and/or very low paid. In this respect, the informal market works as a social policy buffer that reduces people's propensity to draw on community, family and public resources. And in this way the informal market contributes to society's social coherence. From a system integrative perspective, the informal work market lubricates the economy by expanding and contracting, varying with the business cycle and changes in the more public regulated formal economy.

This view on the informal market differs from the most common one in Central and Northern Europe where paid informal exchange is normally associated with profit-motivated monetary exchange and seen as an exploitative form of work. This is 'organised' paid informal work, and occurs where an employee conducts paid informal work for a formal or informal business and is conducted under social relations akin to formal employment for profit-motivated rationales.

Here we shall distinguish between two forms of informal paid exchange (Williams and Windebank, 2001). On the one hand, there is informal market work, described earlier. On the other hand, there is the 'autonomous' paid informal work, where people engage in paid exchange mostly for friends, relatives and neighbours. This variant of exchange is very much a form of non-market production and exchange. It is also a form of cooperative self-help rather than exploitative employment. The autonomous paid work is increasingly recognised as an important subsystem of work – an importance that is enhanced by its strong links to several of the social network's subsystems.

Based on this reconceptualisation of work, various attempts have been made to measure the amount of work beyond employment that is taking place and the degree to which work has been penetrated by employment. The emerging practice has been to quantify the volume and value of the inputs using time-budget studies. These analyse whether people perceive their activity as work or leisure and then measure the time that people spend engaged in various forms of work. Although this technique has a tendency to overestimate both the time spent in employment and its value relative to unpaid work (Luxton, 1997; Gregory and Windebank, 2000), the outputs provide a fascinating and illuminating insight into the nature and direction of work in contemporary advanced economies.

These studies (see among others, Gershuny and Jones, 1987; Murgatroyd and Neuburger, 1997) show that in the UK, France and the US, over half of all working time is spent engaged in unpaid work. Moreover, although the absolute amount of time spent in both employment and unpaid work is declining, the time spent in unpaid work is declining at a relatively slower rate. The result is that a greater proportion of the total working time is being spent in unpaid work. Therefore, work beyond employment, so long considered the residual and diminishing 'other', is not only larger than employment, measured in terms of the volume (and often value) of time inputs, but over the past thirty years, such work has taken up an ever greater proportion of total working time.

It is not only the sheer volume of such work that is important; so too is the distribution of such work. Up until now, the presupposition has sometimes been that households excluded from or having a marginal position in one subsystem of work (for example, formal employment) can compensate for this exclusion by their fuller inclusion in other subsystems (self-provisioning, community work, paid informal work). Throughout the advanced economies, however, the vast majority of studies have displayed that this is not the case. Households that have people in employment also conduct more self-provisioning, more unpaid community exchange and more paid informal work than jobless households.

As a consequence, it can no longer be simply assumed that those marginalised or excluded from formal employment compensate for their exclusion by being included into more informal subsystems of work. For example, it is often assumed that rural populations engage in higher amounts of unpaid community exchange than urban populations. A recent study in rural England explores this issue (Williams et al, 2001). It reveals that although unpaid community exchange is slightly higher amongst rural populations, it tends to be relatively affluent households in jobs who both give and receive the vast majority of this unpaid community exchange. Jobless rural households find themselves not only excluded from employment but also from social support networks that might ameliorate their situation. How this can be tackled is an important issue for social policy. Despite the interventions in the formal sphere, there has up until now been a relative laissez-faire approach adopted towards inclusion of social groups into informal subsystems of work. In part, this may be because it has been assumed that those social groups marginalised or excluded from employment are already compensating for their marginalisation and exclusion from this realm in these informal spheres. However, given that the vast majority of studies show that this is not the case, there is need for parallel interventions in these informal spheres. It is necessary to consider how these groups, excluded not only from employment but also informal spheres of participation, can be more included. To pursue active formal labour-market policies is to deal with one side of the equation only. Similar inclusion policies are also required to include these groups into other subsystems of work.

To conclude, we provide a short note on the 'typology' of work used in our research. This 'typology' should not be seen as an alternative to existing typologies. Rather, ours is a more pragmatic distinction, developed to serve the purposes of INPART. That is, the distinction reflects the diversity of types of work/participation as these are being stimulated by social policies, while at the same time paying explicit attention to 'paid informal exchange' and 'community work' – until now largely being neglected in activation programmes:

- *Participation in work in the 'primary' labour market.* In other words, paid work as formal employment;
- *Participation in work in the 'secondary' labour market.* This refers to paid work as formal employment as well, but focuses attention to 'additional', often state-subsidised job schemes targeted at categories of unemployed people;
- *Voluntary and informal work.* This refers to two types of work distinguished above: 'paid informal exchange' and 'community work';
- *Education and training.* Although this type of work is not included in the typology presented earlier, since education and training are important activation policy instruments and can be seen as a type of participation in themselves (even though, in the context of social policies, they are usually treated as a preparation for employment), we decided to make them a separate category.

Note

[1] For an earlier attempt to classify different types of integration concepts into a chart, see Mortensen, 1995. Later analyses, also by Mortensen, have suggested, however, that the concept of integration encompasses so many dimensions that a 'total mapping' is meaningless.

References

Abrahamson, P. (1998) *Postmodern governing of social exclusion: Social integration or risk management?*, Copenhagen: Sociologisk Institut, University of Copenhagen.

Andersen, J. (1999) 'Post-industrial solidarity or meritocracy?', *Acta Sociologica*, vol 42, no 4.

Bourdieu, P. and Passeron, J.-C. (1977) *Reproduction in education, society and culture*, London: Sage Publications.

Bourdieu, P. (1995) *Distinktionen*, Copenhagen: Det lille Forlag.

Bourdieu, P. (1997) *Af praktiske grunde*, Copenhagen: Hans Reitzels Forlag.

Bourdieu, P. (1998) *Acts of resistance: Against the new myths of our time*, Oxford: Polity Press.

Burman, P. (1988) *Killing time, losing ground. Experiences of unemployment*, Toronto, Canada: Thompson Educational Publishing.

Burns, D. and Taylor, M. (1998) *Mutual aid and self-help: Coping strategies for excluded communities*, Bristol/York: The Policy Press/Joseph Rowntree Foundation.

Castells, M. and Portes, A. (1989) 'World underneath: the origins, dynamics and effects of the informal economy', in A. Portes, M. Castells and L.A. Benton (eds) *The informal economy: Studies in advanced and less developing countries*, Baltimore, MD: Johns Hopkins University Press.

CEC (Commission of the European Communities) (2000) *Proposal for a Council decision on guidelines for Member States' employment policies for year 2001*, Brussels: CEC.

Fryer, D. and Ullah, P. (eds) (1987) *Unemployed people: Social and psychological perspectives*, Milton Keynes/Philadelphia, PA: Open University Press.

Germani, G. (1980) *Marginality*, Brunswick, NJ: Transaction Books.

Gershuny, J. and Jones, S. (1987) 'The changing work/leisure balance in Britain 1961-84', *Sociological Review Monograph*, no 33, pp 9-50.

Giddens, A. (1989) *Sociology*, Cambridge: Polity Press.

Gorz, A. (1999) *Reclaiming work: Beyond the wage-based society*, Cambridge: Polity Press.

Gregory, A. and Windebank, J. (2000) *Women and work in France and Britain: Theory, practice and policy*, Basingstoke: Macmillan.

Habermas, J. (1981) *Theorie des kommunikativen Handelns I, II*, Frankfurt: Suhrkamp.

Hansen, H. (2000) *Inclusion and exclusion in social policy and everyday experiences*, Copenhagen: Samfundslitteratur.

Hespanha, P. and Matos, A. (1999) *Inclusion policies for employment. An evaluation based on user experience*, INPART work package 3: The case studies, Coimbra: CES, University of Coimbra.

Home Office (1999) *Community self-help*, Report of Policy Action Team 9, London: Home Office.

Jahoda, M. (1982) *Employment and unemployment. A social-psychological analysis*, Cambridge: Cambridge University Press.

Jahoda, M., Lazersfeld, P. and Zeisel, H. (1975) *Die Arbeitslosen von Marienthal. Ein soziographischer Versuch über die Wirkungen langandauernder Arbeitslosigkeit*, Frankfurt: Campus.

Johannessen, A. (1997) 'Marginalitet som socialpolitisk utfordring', Paper presented at the 9th Nordic Social Policy Research Seminar, Copenhagen, 13-15 June.

Jordan, B. (1998) *A theory of poverty and social exclusion*, Cambridge: Polity Press.

Larsen, J.E. (2000) 'Klassebiografi og individuel biografi', in J.E. Larsen, J. Lind and I.H. Møller (eds) *Kontinuitet i forandring – kontinuiteter og forandringer i samfundets differentierings- og integrationsformer*, Copenhagen: Samfundslitteratur, pp 31-98.

Levitas, R. (1996) 'The concept of social exclusion and the new Durkheimian hegemony', *Critical Social Policy*, vol 16, no 1, pp 5-20.

Lind, J. (1995) 'Unemployment policy and social integration', in N. Mortensen (ed) *Social integration and marginalisation*, Copenhagen: Samfundslitteratur, pp 183-205.

Lind, J. and Hornemann Møller, I. (eds) (1999) *Inclusion and exclusion: Unemployment and non-standard employment in Europe*, Aldershot: Ashgate.

Lockwood, D. (1964) 'Social integration and system integration', in G.K. Zollschan and W. Hirsch (eds) *Explorations in social change*, London: Routledge.

Luhmann, N. (1982) *Differentiation of society*, New York, NY: University of Columbia Press.

Luhmann, N. (1990) *The political theory of the welfare state*, Berlin/New York, NY: De Gruyter.

Luhmann, N. (1997) *Die Gesellschaft der Gesellschaft I, II*, Frankfurt: Suhrkamp.

Luxton, M. (1997) 'The UN, women and household labour: measuring and valuing unpaid work', *Women's Studies International Forum*, vol 20, pp 431-9.

Mack, J. and Lansley, S. (1985) *Poor Britain*, London: George Allen & Unwin.

Møller, I.H. (1995) 'Some empirical and theoretical perspectives on labour-market marginalisation', in N. Mortensen (ed) *Social integration and marginalisation*, Copenhagen: Samfundslitteratur, pp 114-46.

Møller, I.H. (1997) 'Social integration and labour market marginalisation. The Scandinavian experience', in M. Roche and R. van Berkel (eds) *European citizenship and social exclusion*, Aldershot: Ashgate, pp 83-103.

Møller, I.H. (1998) 'On the spoor of conceptual clarification', Paper prepared for INPART.

Møller, I.H. (2000) *Understanding integration and differentiation – inclusion, marginalisation and exclusion*, Coimbra: University of Coimbra, Oficina do Centro de Estudos Sociais.

Mortensen, N. (1995) 'Mapping system integration and social integration', in N. Mortensen (ed) *Social integration and marginalisation*, Copenhagen: Samfundslitteratur, pp 18-48.

Mortensen, N. (2000) 'Differentieringer og integrationer – eksklusioner og inklusioner', in J.E. Larsen, J. Lind and I.H. Møller (eds) *Kontinuitet i forandring – kontinuiteter og forandringer i samfundets differentierings- og integrationsformer*, Copenhagen: Samfundslitteratur, pp 99-139.

Mouzelis, N. (1995) *Strategies of integration and socio-cultural differentiation*, CID-Studies No 11, Copenhagen: CID.

Murgatroyd, L. and Neuburger, H. (1997) 'A household satellite account for the UK', *Economic Trends*, no 527, pp 63-71.

Olofsson, G. (1995) 'Embeddedness and integration. An essay on Karl Polanyi's *The great transformation*', in N. Mortensen (ed) *Social integration and marginalisation*, Copenhagen: Samfundslitteratur, pp 72-113.

Olson, M. (1982) *The rise and decline of nations: Economic growth, stagflation and social rigidities*, New Haven, CT: Yale University Press.

O'Riordan, T. (1996) 'Environmentalism on the move', in I. Douglas, R. Huggett and M. Robinson (eds) *Companion encyclopaedia of geography*, London: Routledge.

Pahl, R.E. (1984) *Divisions of labour*, Oxford: Basil Blackwell.

Park, R.E. (1928) 'Human migration and the marginal man', *American Journal of Sociology*, no 33, pp 881-93.

Parkin, F. (1974) 'Strategies of social closure in class formation', in F. Parkin (ed) *Social analysis of class structure*, London: Tavistock Publications, pp 1-18.

Polanyi, K. (1944) *The great transformation*, Boston, MA: Beacon Press.

Robertson, J. (1998) *Beyond the dependency culture: People, power and responsibility*, London: Adamantine.

Room, G.J. (1999) 'Social exclusion, solidarity and the challenge of globalisation', *International social welfare*, no 8, pp 166-74.

Sen, A. (1998) 'Social exclusion: A critical assessment of the concept and its relevance', Paper presented to the Asian Development Bank.

Shulman, M.D. and Anderson, C. (1999) 'The dark side of the force: a case study of restructuring and social capital', *Rural Sociology*, vol 64, pp 351-72.

Silver, H. (1996) 'Culture, politics and national discourses of the new urban poverty', in E. Mingione (ed) *Urban poverty and the underclass*, Oxford: Blackwell, pp 105-38.

Standing, G. (1999) *Global labour flexibility. Seeking distributive justice*, Basingstoke: Macmillan.

Tilly, C. (1998) *Durable inequality*, Berkeley/Los Angeles, CA: University of California Press.

Townsend, P. (1979) *Poverty in the United Kingdom*, Harmondsworth: Penguin.

Vaiou, D. (1997) 'Informal cities? Women's work and informal activities on the margins of the European Union', in R. Lee and J. Wills (eds) *Geographies of economies*, London: Arnold, pp 321-30.

van Berkel, R. and Brand, A. (1996) 'Actors and factors in finding a job or remaining unemployed. Longitudinal research into the position of the long-term unemployed in the Rotterdam labour market', in C. Verhaar, P. de Klaver, M. de Goede, J. van Ophem and A. de Vries (eds) *On the challenges of unemployment in a regional Europe*, Aldershot: Avebury, pp 145-67.

Walby, S. (1997) *Gender transformations*, London: Routledge.

Weber, M. (1968) *Economy and society: An outline of interpretive sociology*, translated from *Wirtschaft und Gesellschaft* by G. Roth and C. Wittich, New York, NY: Bedminster Press.

Williams, C.C., White, R. and Aldridge, T. (2001) *Community self-help in rural England: Its role in tackling poverty and exclusion*, London: The Countryside Agency.

Williams, C.C. and Windebank, J. (1998) *Informal employment in the advanced economies: Implications for work and welfare*, London: Routledge.

Williams, C.C. and Windebank, J. (1999) 'The formalisation of work thesis: a critical evaluation', *Futures*, vol 31, pp 547-58.

Williams, C.C. and Windebank, J. (2001) 'Beyond profit-motivated exchange: some lessons from the study of paid informal work', *European urban and regional studies*, vol 8, pp 43-56.

WGSG (Women and Geography Study Group) (1997) *Feminist geographies: Explorations in diversity and difference*, Harlow: Longman.

THREE

The concept of activation

Rik van Berkel and Iver Hornemann Møller

Introduction

For more than two decades, the governments of the EU have presented welfare state reforms as reactions to rising levels of unemployment and other types of labour-market marginalisation, and in terms of their need to curb expenditures on social security. The growing use of public funds to support people of working age over the past 50 years evidently plays a major role in these reforms. However, welfare state reforms have gradually come to be placed in the context of broader developments in society. Rather than being seen as temporary measures to deal with economically hard times, more structural, fundamental and lasting needs for welfare state reforms came to the fore. Of course, the analysis of modernity and the challenges faced by welfare states are themselves contested. Nevertheless, the following issues are frequently mentioned as examples of major developments to which welfare states have to be adjusted.

- *Economic globalisation:* affects relations of competition around the world and, among other things, increases the pressure on national governments to create an attractive economic climate and adjust social policies accordingly.
- *Demographic changes:* encompass, for instance, the relative growth of the elderly population, changes in the composition of households, changes in the composition of the labour force and migration.
- *Labour-market changes:* the most cited manifestations are unemployment, long-term unemployment, underemployment, quantitative and qualitative changes in the demand for, and supply of, labour and labour-market flexibility.
- *Processes of differentiation and individualisation:* taking place in relation to these points. Society and the biographies of its citizens are becoming less standardised and more complex and unpredictable, partly due to the decreasing importance of institutions such as the family and the lifetime job. These processes also may affect patterns of inequality.
- *Reduced government spending:* the EU and specifically the Maastricht Treaty have forced national governments to keep government borrowing within strict limits.

These developments have been interpreted as elements of a transformation of modernity. For example, Beck (2000) talks about the transformation of 'primary modernity' into 'secondary modernity' or the 'risk society'. Others, such as Gorz (1999), prefer to use the concepts of 'Fordism' and 'post-Fordism'. These transformation processes force national governments into action. The direction of action, however, is subject to political debate, reflected in the 'challenge profiles' that national governments design with respect to their welfare state, as well as in the variety of reform programmes national governments have initiated. The following issues are examples of recurrent themes in debates on the nature of welfare state challenges.

First, there is the future of full employment. Is full employment an adequate objective of social policies in an era of 'new modernity', or should it be considered unfeasible (either against the background of labour-market modernisation, or because of presumed limitations to government regulation, or even against the background of the ecological risks of economic growth)?

Secondly, the issue of employment as a cornerstone of social policies is debated from yet another perspective. Are labour-market participation and access to paid work becoming more important in realising people's independence, autonomy and emancipation? Or do these objectives require an opposite strategy: granting people more autonomy in deciding over the forms of participation they want to be involved in, including forms of work other than paid jobs?

Thirdly, there is the debate on rights, obligations and responsibilities of the people benefiting from social security arrangements. What are the rights, obligations and responsibilities of social security claimants (if any), and who is to determine their content?

Fourthly, new 'modes of regulation' are being considered and introduced into welfare states and social policies. These question traditional balances between the state, the market, civil society and the citizen and his or her family or household members.

Fifthly, changes are taking place with respect to the universal or selective character of welfare state arrangements. Whereas some argue that social justice is enhanced by targeting social policies exclusively at those most at risk of social exclusion and poverty, others advocate a strengthening of the universality of welfare state arrangements.

This book deals with a solution that politicians, policy makers and scientists have come up with in trying to cope with welfare state challenges: the introduction into social policies of the so-called 'activation approach', which is taking place throughout the EU (and not only there). As has been mentioned before (and will be again in Chapters Five and Nine), there is a clear EU policy dimension to this process of strengthening the activation approach in social policies. Nevertheless, despite the 'unifying' impact this has on the social policies of the member states, the process of making welfare states more activating is one of both uniformity and diversity. This diversity not only relates to the ways in which countries of the EU conceptualise, legitimise and implement the activation approach, reflecting different ideological positions, welfare state traditions and political priorities, for example, concerning the issues of social inequality, exclusion and redistribution, the rights and obligations of citizens, and so on. Diversity is also clearly visible when we look at more concrete characteristics of active social policies, such as the government funds available for and spent on this type of policy, their target groups and coverage, the degree of compulsion used in activation programmes, the content and duration of programmes, the institutional context of their implementation and delivery, and so on. In other words, under the general heading of activation we can find a wide variety of programmes and practices, which (as will be discussed later in this chapter) can reflect quite different approaches to the issues concerning the future of welfare states we distinguished earlier.

This chapter deals with the concept of activation in an attempt to make explicit our approach to active social policies in this book. In doing so, we hope to avoid the lack of clarity and ambiguities often present in debates on active social policies, which partly explain differences in the appreciation of these policies. In section two we develop a typology of activation approaches that can be helpful in analysing the characteristics and the diversity of activation policies and programmes. In section three the relationship between the activation approach and existing typologies of welfare regimes is discussed. Then, in section four, we examine some theoretical points of view that can be helpful in explaining the rise of activation. At the same time, we conclude that they are insufficient in making sense of national preferences and priorities in shaping activation. Section five deals with some issues related to the introduction of activation. First we consider the growing rhetorical support for active social policies in the countries of the EU. We then confront this with some data on national expenditures on activation programmes. Finally, we will go into some institutional developments recursively related to the introduction of activation.

Conceptualising activation

The 'passive' unemployed

By using the concepts of 'activation' and of 'active' and 'passive' policies we do not intend to simply reproduce many politicians' view of unemployed people as passive and *in need* of activation or participation. As Chapter Two elaborated, most social policies are based on a narrow conceptualisation of inclusion and exclusion. Citizens are considered 'active' when they are in regular paid work and independent of social benefits or social assistance and, in the context of active social policies, when they are enrolled in programmes directed at realising labour-market participation and benefit independence. Social security claimants of working age who are not enrolled in activation programmes are considered 'passive', regardless of their involvement in activities and forms of paid or unpaid work outside the formal labour market. The lack of recognition in social policies of meaningful forms of participation outside the formal labour market has been pointed out by various authors (among others, Pahl, 1984; Jordan et al, 1992; Roche and van Berkel, 1997). The same goes for the inadequacy of treating the possession of a job, being included and being active as synonymous, or being unemployed, excluded and passive, for that matter. These are central topics of this book as well.

The perspective of recognition also highlights another potential meaning of the concepts of active and passive, that is the involvement of policy users or policy clients in policy making and policy delivery. As Lister writes:

> Here 'active' refers to the construction of welfare state users as active and creative participants in the process of welfare policy making and delivery, again reflecting an understanding of citizenship as a practice as well as a status bestowing rights. (2000, p 10)

In this context, Lister refers to forms of collective user involvement through social movements (see also, Swift et al, 1994; van Berkel et al, 1998). However, user involvement can also involve participation of individual users in developing their personal activation plans (Coenen-Hanegraaf et al, 1998). Of course, politicians and policy makers usually do not have this kind of user involvement in mind when talking about active and passive policies. Nevertheless, the issue is an important one, and we will deal with it separately later in this chapter.

The relation between passive and active policies

One of the issues raised in conceptualising activation concerns the issue of whether active social policies are a new generation of social policies or are more adequately conceived of as a transformation of existing policies. For some analysts, active policies are a new type of social policy, being developed and implemented alongside existing passive policies. In this context, passive policies are conceived as those that entitle people who are unemployed, or for other reasons lack sufficient financial resources, to some kind of income provision. Active policies, on the other hand, deal with participation rights and/or obligations, usually though not necessarily confined to labour-market participation. For others, the concept of active social policies denotes a transformation process through which social policies in general are phased out. Whereas 'traditional' social policies (designated as 'passive' ones) granted people a more or less unconditional right to an income, active policies are shifting emphasis from income entitlements to participation rights and obligations. From this perspective, active policies are not a separate type of social policy, but rather a reform of passive policies.

Both positions hold some degree of truth. On the one hand, active policies often are separate policies, existing legally and institutionally alongside income providing policies, very much like the traditional distinction between social security policies and labour-market policies. This is especially the case in nations with a long history of welfare state arrangements aiming at providing income protection. On the other hand, active policies are practically always linked in some way or another to passive policies, irrespective of whether the latter have a long history or are relatively new. Furthermore, unemployment benefits and social assistance for the unemployed have in many cases involved activation elements, of which the work test and the obligation to look for jobs are the most obvious examples.

Therefore, it might be useful to distinguish the activation objective underlying social policies on the one hand, from active and passive policies as specific kinds of social policies on the other. In this book, the concepts of 'passive' and 'active' social policies are used to distinguish types of social policies that reflect different 'welfare paradigms'. Whereas the main aim of passive social policies can be stated in terms of protection, compensation or indemnification, active policies' primary objective is to realise participation or activation (see van Berkel et al, 1999; Rosanvallon, 2000; Terpstra, 2000). Furthermore, both types of policy are based on different means and instruments to realise inclusion. Passive policies provide people with financial resources, without directly intervening in their participation in various kinds of activities. To a certain extent, passive policies include people into the system of consumption; which, one might justifiably claim, implies an indirect intervention into participation opportunities, since financial resources are an important precondition to participate in many of society's other systems. In addition, passive policies may be used as activation instruments in a more direct way, for example by varying levels of income replacement, making income compensation conditional on 'active behaviour', or by using them as mechanisms to reward or punish certain behaviour. Active policies, on the contrary, do not primarily deal with income resources, but with participation. Here, of course, a similar qualification should be added: insofar as policies promoting or enforcing participation are directed at labour-market participation, which they usually are, they will, when successful, influence people's financial resources. Furthermore, participation in activation programmes is usually rewarded with some sort of income, for example by providing access to passive policies.

In short, we cannot treat distinctions between passive policies, primarily aiming at income protection, and active policies, primarily aiming at promoting participation, as dichotomous from an activation perspective. Not least, because the very 'service' provided by passive policies (that is, income) is considered as an important motivator and activator[1]. Therefore, the interrelations between income protection schemes and policies aiming at promoting participation are an important issue in analysing activation. What matters in this context is whether we are looking at countries that have developed income protection schemes (that is, passive policies), or at countries where income protection schemes are absent or *in statu nascendi*.

In countries with developed income protection schemes, the activation approach can be introduced, not by developing separate active policies, but by reforming income protection schemes. There are numerous examples where the introduction of the activation approach takes the form of a *reduction* of benefit entitlements, for instance in the UK, Denmark and the Netherlands.

These measures are legitimised by stating that generous passive social policies make people passive, although recent research in Europe presents data that does not support this view (Gallie and Paugam, 2000). Decreasing the level of income protection is seen as an activation measure in itself, since it is thought to create incentives for labour-market participation and to reduce the poverty trap effects of social security.

When the introduction of the activation approach is accompanied by the development of active policies, in principle these can be *complementary* to passive policies. That is, income protection schemes remain unchanged, and, in addition, schemes and measures are being introduced specifically aimed at promoting participation in paid jobs or other forms of work.

However, in most cases the introduction of active policies does not leave income protection schemes unaffected. Firstly, sometimes the introduction of activating measures means that active social policies *replace* rather than complement passive social policies. In this case we should talk about 'work instead of benefit' policies rather than 'work for benefit' policies (Lødemel and Trickey, 2001). In practice, then, people should be offered a job through which they can generate an income, rather than some form of benefit in return for participation in some employability enhancing programme. Entitlements to benefits or social assistance are removed, and instead a formal right to participate in activation measures is introduced which, in the absence of alternative income resources, amounts to a practical obligation. Among other instances, this occurred in the Netherlands during the early 1990s, when young people's right to social assistance was 'replaced' by a right to participation in temporary, subsidised jobs through which they could gain work experience and earn an income. This was to increase their opportunities on the regular labour market.

Secondly, the right to income protection can be made *conditional* upon participation in activation programmes. This, for example, is what has been happening in the Nordic countries. People who, for whatever reason, are not interested in active social policy programmes, lose the right to passive social policies – that is, income protection – either partly or completely, temporarily or permanently.

Those countries where income protection schemes are non-existent, or which are in the process of developing systems of income provision, may be faced with a different situation. These countries may decide to develop their income protection schemes further and to adopt modes of activation that are similar to those mentioned above. However, they may also decide to introduce active social policies *instead of* passive social policies. For example, the French social assistance scheme, the Revenu Minimum d'Insertion (RMI), combines active and passive elements. That is, it provides income and aims at involving claimants in activation contracts. However, RMI excludes people under 25 years of age. The only way for the young unemployed to get an income is to participate in active social policies (Enjolras et al, 2001). Of course, the situation of the young unemployed French is different from that of the Dutch young unemployed. The Dutch saw their benefit rights being reduced or abolished as an effect of the activation approach, whereas the French did not have any social assistance entitlements before. In the Southern European countries, the issue about claimants who would have their cash benefits reduced or withdrawn for not participating in programmes does not exist or seems irrelevant. The theme here is rather the contrary: for those parts of the population which are not covered by social security arrangements, the only way to receive public financial support is via participation in activation programmes. Activation provides the only public means to be included, although often in a relatively weak position, into the system of income.

Countries differ with respect to their tradition of developing measures to promote participation. The Nordic countries are among those countries with a relatively long tradition in this respect. Active labour-market policies in Sweden, particularly, have been closely related to the commitment to maintain a high level of employment, preferably full employment (Therborn, 1986). In the Swedish tradition – and other countries followed what became known as the 'Swedish model' before Sweden was hit hard by unemployment around 1990 – active labour-market policies were adopted as an integral part of a policy to speed up structural change in the labour market. By means of job broking, job subsidisation and training measures, active labour-market policies were designed to stimulate labour demand or labour supply, and to improve the match between them as far back as the formation of the Swedish welfare state during the 1930s and 1940s (Johansson, 2001). Active labour-market policies involved public programmes which sought to qualify and (re)train participants in order to make them more attractive on the market and to help them find gainful employment.

The situation in the Southern European countries is completely different. In terms of modes of welfare regulation, the traditionally weak redistributive role of the state and the emphasis put on the family in producing welfare have created a completely different point of departure for the strengthening of the activation approach in social policies (Andreotti et al, 2001). Due to these historical differences, the current, European-wide emphasis on the active approach means different things in different welfare states. For some, the introduction of active measures as such may be a new phenomenon. For others, what is new is not so much the introduction of active measures as such, as the stronger links that are introduced between participation in activation measures and entitlements to income protection.

A typology of activation approaches

In order to elaborate various approaches of activation (see European Foundation of Working and Living Conditions, 1999) we have constructed a typology that represents four activation approaches. As many typologies, our typology of activation approaches is ideal–typical. Often, it will not be possible to reduce concrete activation debates and activation programmes to one of the approaches we distinguish, because they may combine elements derived from several approaches. However, the typology enables us to highlight dimensions that are important in analysing and characterising specific debates and programmes. Furthermore, it can be helpful in analysing the way activation is related to neighbouring concepts. For example, Drøpping et al (1999), in a discussion of the rise of the activation approach in the Nordic countries, mention active labour-market policies, the work approach, workfare and the work incentive approach as concepts that are somehow related to the active approach. We think that these related concepts can be conceived as sets of social policies reflecting specific activation approaches.

The first approach to activation is represented by what might be called the *autonomy optimists*. Adherents of this approach rely on people's own capacities and willingness to realise forms of inclusion in different systems on their own initiative and according to their own needs. In order to enable people to make use of their capacities and to act autonomously, society 'only' needs to provide them with sufficient means to meet basic needs. When these needs have been met, people will actively seek forms of inclusion for themselves: they do not need state support in the form of active policies. Advocates of this activation approach are in favour of unconditional minimum income schemes, of which a basic income or citizens' income is the most radical variety. More leftist oriented adherents of this approach sometimes advocate paid-work redistribution policies in order to create opportunities for labour-market participation.

The second activation approach is advocated by *welfare independence optimists*. Here, we find those who conceive of state intervention as a problem rather than a solution. Welfare independence optimists think that state intervention is the worst that can happen to people's initiative and to their role as active citizens. According to them (see, for example, Murray, 1994), welfare state arrangements immerse people in a culture of dependency, which will reproduce rather than relieve their exclusion from society. Therefore, the best that can happen to welfare state arrangements is their complete abolishment: a free, unregulated market will then provide people (especially 'the underclass') with enough opportunities and incentives to realise inclusion into paid work, income and a 'decent' family life.

Each of these activation approaches focus predominantly on the role of passive social policies and their effects on activation: a full unconditional basic income as a citizens' right on the one hand, and the abolition of income provisions guaranteed by the welfare state on the other. Whereas the former is based on the belief that income protection policies may have an activating effect because they may enhance people's autonomy to pursue an inclusive life by meeting their needs for sheer survival, the latter is based on the conviction that passive policies will produce passive people.

Among those who explicitly advocate active social policies we can also distinguish two ideal types. On the one hand, there are what might be called the *paternalism optimists*, who consider enforcing activation upon people who are unwilling to make use of participation opportunities to be in the interest of those targeted by these measures and, eventually, in that of society in general.

This form of 'enforced emancipation' stems from the early poverty laws and the workhouse tradition. It has been analysed by social scientists who have pointed out the controlling and disciplining functions of these arrangements (see the work of Foucault; also see De Swaan, 1996; Vranken et al, 1999). Currently, this activation approach influences many activation programmes in the EU countries (see Lødemel and Trickey, 2001).

At the other extreme are the *activation optimists*. They emphasise people's willingness to participate in and contribute to society, much like what the autonomy optimists are doing. However, the activation optimists are of the opinion that at least part of the target groups of social policies lack the resources to realise inclusion through participation, even when their financial needs have been met. Here active social policies enter the stage: they can 'lend people a hand' in fulfilling their participation needs.

In a closer analysis of these four ideal–typical activation approaches, different dimensions can be distinguished by which they can be classified. The activation approaches represent different views on the main forms of inclusion, on what constitutes a 'full citizen', and on the emancipation mechanisms that can bring about inclusion and 'full' citizenship. These different views result in different policy priorities. For the welfare independence optimists and the paternalism optimists the labour market and – especially for the welfare independence optimists – the family are the dominant systems of inclusion. A 'full' citizen is someone who manages to realise independence (from welfare state arrangements) through labour-market participation (or inclusion in the family). Therefore, the 'full' citizen in these activation approaches is highly marketised (or familialised). Whereas the welfare independence optimists are sceptical with respect to state intervention and advocate a free market as the most effective emancipation mechanism, paternalism optimists think that people should be supported in and, if necessary, forced to realise inclusion into (paid) work. Active policies are supposed to assist people in getting included; passive policies can be used as an incentive mechanism by transforming them into financial rewards for people's efforts to realise inclusion in the sense mentioned above. According to welfare independence optimists the state should not prescribe paths to 'full inclusion'. However, lack of alternative income resources will force people to realise inclusion either by finding a job or an earning partner. The paternalism optimists are more explicitly paternalistic in promoting emancipation. Those who are making efforts to realise the forms of inclusion prescribed by the state will receive financial support, whereas those who prefer other forms of inclusion will be left to their own (financial) devices.

For the autonomy optimists the emphasis is on income and consumption. By including people in these domains of society and taking away financial hardship, a sound base can be created on which they can and will develop inclusion in other systems. Therefore, the policy focus is on providing everyone with an income to meet basic needs, which is the dominant emancipation mechanism of the autonomy optimists. Active policies are often met with scepticism, because the autonomy optimists conceive of them as highly susceptible to paternalism. Policies aiming at paid-work redistribution, however, are popular among left-wing autonomy optimists. At the same time, many basic income adherents advocate a broad concept of work (Gorz, 1989). In the context of this concept of work, 'work' and 'inclusion' are not confined to regular employment only, as is often the case with the welfare independence optimists and the paternalism optimists. Autonomy optimists operate a more 'open' and differentiated citizenship concept in the sense that in their opinion, the state should enable inclusion without prescribing the exact forms inclusion should take. The autonomy optimists share this broad concept of work with (some of) the activation optimists. However, the latter consider income provision insufficient for realising inclusion into other systems. For the activation optimists, the 'full' citizen is someone who is included in some sort of activity. Supporting them in their inclusion ambitions through active policies is seen as an important activation mechanism: these policies should assist people, when and where necessary, in developing forms of participation. As far as the role of passive policies is concerned, activation optimists may tend towards views of the autonomy optimists, advocating some form of unconditional income provision, or towards the paternalism optimists, advocating a conditional income in return

Table 3.1: Characteristics of activation approaches

Activation approach	Main systems of inclusion and concept of 'full citizenship'	Emancipation mechanism	Role of passive policies
Welfare independence optimists	Labour market (marketised) and family (familialised)	Market and family; welfare state absent	Disincentive: should be abolished
Paternalism optimists	Labour market: labour-market participation and independence of social security	Paternalistic: supporting those who follow prescribed inclusion roads and discouraging/ enforcing the 'unwilling'	Income provision is conditional upon efforts to realise inclusion: desirable behaviour is rewarded and undesirable behaviour is punished
Autonomy optimists	Income: autonomy through relief from basic needs	Unconditional income	Offering resources to meet basic needs
Activation optimists	Active participation in various systems	Active policies	Unconditional or conditional (paternalistic: rewarding inclusion efforts, though in the context of a broad concept of work)

for their participation, which does not necessarily have to be labour-market participation.

Whatever their precise contents, by nature social policies intervene in the lives or biographies of the individuals these policies target, and therefore influence the relationship between the state and citizens or, more specifically, claimants of benefits and welfare. By granting people specific entitlements, social policies can enable people to reach the full citizenship status. By imposing certain obligations or responsibilities on them, social policies direct the way full citizenship should be realised. However, when analysing the impact of activation approaches on relations between citizens and the state, we should not only focus on the macro level of the design of activation schemes and programmes in general. To an important degree, these effects are also dependent on, created in, and the outcome of micro level, face-to-face interaction processes going on between policy consultants and clients, and the way these processes are structurated (see Eardley et al, 1996). Especially in the context of active social policies and activation programmes, policy interventions increasingly involve negotiations at the executive level. At the level of policy delivery the objectives of activation and the means through which these objectives should be reached are being made concrete and decided upon. This is accompanied by a process of 'contractualisation' (see, for example, Rosanvallon, 2000; Saraceno, 2002), which often results in agreements or contracts between consultants and clients regulating the rights and duties of both parties. The 'structured' character of these negotiations refers first to the fact that consultant–client interactions and negotiations are dependent on the instruments and resources active social policies make available. Secondly, it refers to the way power is distributed over the parties involved in the negotiations and the degree of asymmetry of this power distribution. These developments put increasing emphasis on what Lipsky (1980) has called the discretionary space of street-level bureaucrats. As Lipsky put it, these 'street level bureaucrats' hold the keys to a dimension of citizenship: their interactions with clients constitute a very important parameter in determining the way these policies *can* and actually *do* influence the quality of citizenship of unemployed and/or socially excluded people.

From the point of view of our typology of activation approaches, it is quite clear that two activation approaches constitute the most interesting cases for elaborating on the issue of citizen–state relations both at the level of policy design and policy delivery: those of the activation and the paternalism optimists. For it is these two approaches that attach explicit value to active policies and activation programmes, in which client–consultant interactions and their structuration have a strong impact on the outcomes of activation processes. Ideally, we can conceive of these activation approaches as representing two different ways of structuring citizen–state relations (also see Hvinden and Halvorsen, 2001). The paternalism optimists' activation approach represents an institution-centred or 'top-down' approach in structuring state–citizen relations whereas the activation optimists' approach structurates these relations in a 'bottom-up' or client-centred way. In top-down or institution-centred approaches, the aims of the activation process are predetermined in the targets set by active policies. The client may have a 'right' to be activated, but the aim of activation and the means that are used are beyond his or her influence. Top-down, institution-centred approaches in social policy are inherently paternalistic: clients have no active involvement in defining what constitutes exclusion or inclusion in their particular case, nor in determining ways out of exclusion and into types of inclusion. Of course, views of clients and consultants are not necessarily contradictory. However, it is well-known that they can be, for example in the case of those single parents with young children who want to give priority to raising their children, while active policies want them to (re)integrate into the labour market (see Levitas, 1998; Saraceno, 2002). Therefore, top-down approaches in active social policies come closest to treating clients as 'objects' of social policies. On the other hand, bottom-up or client-centred approaches grant clients autonomy in determining the aims and means of processes of activation. What constitutes full citizenship in concrete cases is not determined without the active involvement of clients themselves, and is therefore the result of a dialogue rather than a monologue. Bottom-up or client-centred approaches are sometimes also referred to as enabling or empowering. They do not enforce certain ways of 'leading a good life' (see Jordan, 1996), but support people by providing the conditions necessary for them to lead a 'good life' of their own choosing.

One final remark needs to be made in relation to the use of 'activation' and 'participation'. In this book, participation is used to refer to people's involvement or inclusion in certain systems of society. As was elaborated in Chapter Two, the number of systems and subsystems and, therefore, forms of participation is infinite, in principle. Here our main attention will go to participation in forms of work. Activation refers to attempts to promote inclusion, that is, participation in certain systems. In a social policy context, we are, of course, first of all interested in the resources, 'sticks and carrots' employed by governments to stimulate inclusion. However, this should not be interpreted as implying that we see government institutions as the 'subjects' and people dependent on benefits or social assistance as the 'objects' of activation. Furthermore, as was made clear in the description of activation approaches, activation programmes are not neutral with respect to the forms of inclusion and participation they want to achieve. This means, that in assessing the impact of activation on people's participation, we need to distinguish between types of participation at which activation programmes are aimed explicitly, and types of participation that are neglected or counteracted by them.

Activation and welfare state regimes

The introduction of active social policies and the increasing emphasis on activation is, one might hypothesise, conditioned by the welfare state regimes in which these processes take place, and at the same time influencing these welfare state regimes' characteristics. Although we do not intend to test these hypotheses here, we do briefly elaborate the relationships between activation and welfare state regimes.

It should be emphasised, of course, that the two most well-known welfare state typologies, those by Titmuss (1974) and Esping-Andersen (1990), were developed before active social policies were introduced on a large scale, and even before the concept of active social policies as such received the attention it does now. In other words, they are mainly typologies of income protection schemes. Nevertheless, this focus does not imply that activation is no issue in the regime types.

A closer look at Titmuss' typology (1974) shows that his 'residual welfare model' is based on the market and the family, which are considered to be the two 'natural' channels through which an individual's needs are properly met. Only when these break down should social welfare institutions come into play, and even then only temporarily. The true objective of the welfare state is to teach people how to do without. In terms of the typology of activation approaches we developed above, this model includes elements of both the welfare independence optimists and the paternalism optimists. In the context of the residual welfare model, active social policies would obviously have a highly obligatory character. Titmuss' second model, the 'industrial achievement–performance model', incorporates a significant role for social welfare institutions as adjuncts of the economy. It holds that social needs should be met on the basis of merit, work performance and productivity; and it is derived from various economic and psychological theories concerned with incentives, effort and reward. The outcome of important parts of the welfare system is mainly a result of labour-market performance (or the lack of it); distributions based on equality and need are of secondary importance only. Making entitlements to income protection conditional upon participation in activation schemes can be seen as another variant of the industrial achievement–performance model. Of course, there is a major difference with Titmuss' model. For although his model refers to work performance and productivity in the past, linking active and passive policies refers to work performance in the present. Rather than being established via the insured person's contributions, differentiation in income protection is being linked to the fulfilment of obligations. Titmuss' third model, the 'institutional redistributive model' of social policy, sees social welfare as a major integrated institution in society, providing universalistic services outside the market on principles of social equality and need. Activation in the context of this model would emphasise the entitlements to, rather than the responsibility or obligatory element of participation. In terms of our typology, we would expect elements of the activation approaches of the activation and autonomy optimists, although paternalistic elements need not necessarily be absent.

In a recent publication, Esping-Andersen related his well-known typology of welfare state regimes explicitly to efforts in the sphere of active policies (Esping-Andersen, 1999). In this book, a relation is suggested between regime types on the one hand and the relative importance attached to active policies on the other, based on the regulation mechanisms favoured by the various welfare regime types. Therefore, the clear commitment of the state to employment in the social democratic regime is reflected in relatively extensive activation programmes. According to Esping-Andersen, the social democratic approach to activation differs from the American, which is characterised by workfare (1999, p 80; italics omitted):

> Workfare in America implies that social benefits are conditional on accepting work whereas Nordic 'productivism' implies that the welfare state must guarantee that all people have the necessary resources and motivation to work (and that work is available).

However, the main elements of the social democratic welfare state – solidarity, universalism and decommodification – require high social expenditure levels, which can only be guaranteed when as many people as possible are in paid work and as few as possible are dependent on social transfers (Esping-Andersen, 1990). Increasing unemployment, then, will put the balance between high decommodification and high labour-market participation under pressure. This might be one of the reasons why Nordic active social policies have changed character during the 1990s, developing from more rights-oriented into more obligation-oriented policies. This shift from a more activation optimists' approach towards a more paternalistic activation approach makes the difference between 'Nordic productivism' and 'American workfare' less clear (see Kautto et al, 1999; Johansson, 2001; Lødemel and Trickey, 2001). More generally, the introduction of active social policies may contribute to a process of recommodification, especially when they are accompanied by measures to reduce benefit levels or to make benefits and social assistance more conditional.

As far as the other regime types, the conservative and the liberal welfare states, are concerned, Esping-Andersen (1999) states that they are characterised by a passive approach to employment management. Active policies are rather marginal, although for different reasons. In the liberal regime, which favours an activation approach with welfare independence optimists' elements, dealing with unemployment is left to the market, whereas in conservative welfare states unemployment management is left to the family (youth and female unemployment), or is dealt with by a reduction of labour supply.

In their study on unemployment in Europe, Gallie and Paugam (2000) developed an unemployment welfare regime typology closely resembling Esping-Andersen's, but added a fourth, the Southern European or sub-protective welfare regime. As far as the universalistic (social democratic) and liberal (minimal) regime types are concerned, Gallie and Paugam reached similar conclusions to Esping-Andersen with respect to the importance of active social policies in these regime types. In most Southern European or sub-protective welfare states, active policies are of limited importance. In employment-centred welfare states (Esping-Andersen's conservative regime excluding, however, the Southern European countries), active policies play a more significant role compared to the liberal and sub-protective regime types. In the view of Gallie and Paugam, governments of employment-centred welfare states see activation as an instrument of diminishing pressure on social assistance that is the result of gaps in their social insurance systems.

Why did activation emerge?

In addressing more closely the issue why activation policies emerged, developed and finally spread throughout the EU, we start by taking one step back and point to more general ideological positions and structural factors which have exercised influence on the origin of activation (Møller, 1999; Møller and Lind, 2000). Firstly, the primacy accorded to paid work is nothing new, though still highly relevant (Anthony, 1977; Weber, 1985). The mid-19th century's bourgeois revolutions in central Western Europe abolished most of the nobility's privileges and, by the same token, the significance of former aristocratic contempt for (manual) work. Correspondingly, some of the constitutional settlements introduced under the aegis of emergent bourgeois democracy included provisions with respect to the duty of individuals to maintain themselves, the duty of society to create work opportunities as far as possible, and even a duty to ensure maintenance by way of a last resort. The growing labour movements then followed up these developments, then as now, by turning the notion of a right to work into a fundamental demand. There is, therefore, a long-enduring element to the norm of both a right and a duty to work. There have been no basic changes on this score either in the transition from early industrialism to Fordism or in that from Fordism to post-Fordism. What is 'new' is only that over the last decade or so, an increasing number of EU member states have markedly sharpened the norm about work and activity.

A second contribution to the explanation of activation, is the industrial reserve army approach (Marx, 1971). Parts of the population are viewed as an industrial reserve army which at one period of time is drawn into the labour market and at the next pushed out again, depending upon the business cycle and changes in the demand for labour. The size and the composition of the industrial reserve army may vary, but its presence is important for capital accumulation since it has the function of keeping the price of labour down. Marx wrote about early industrial capitalism in Western Europe. Since then, the labour market and its regulation have changed much, among other things by the heterogeneity and segmentation of the labour force, a changed gender structure and strong unions. Nevertheless, recruitment among sections of the reserve army is also today of the utmost importance for capital's competitiveness. From this point of view, activation schemes can be considered as instruments in maintaining the employability of the reserve army.

A third framework which contributes to the explanation of the emergence of activation is what Jessop (1994) has identified as tendencies rooted in the crisis of Fordism and the Keynesian welfare state that might lead to a Schumpeterian workfare regime. These changes imply, among other things, that to secure the conditions for capital accumulation, the Schumpeterian workfare regime is supposed to enhance structural competitiveness through attempts to increase flexibility and permanent socio-economic innovation in open economies by intervening mainly on the supply side. And in order to secure the conditions for social reproduction, the Schumpeterian workfare regime subordinates social policy to the requirements of labour market flexibility.

Fourthly, political reactions to developments in society have their own impact on the emergence of activation. Frequently, these involve a shift of policies and other modes of regulation away from an emphasis on progressive redistribution, and away from freedom of choice and security of income for public benefit recipients towards larger emphasis on work incentives and concrete measures to bring people into employment.

These contributions to the explanation of the emergence of activation have their validity on a general level of analysis. They catch important elements of the neoliberal discourses, including important changes in social policy, which have gone over Europe during the last two decades or more. They contribute to the understanding of the shift from policies based on solidarity and equality to ideas about equality of opportunity and pressure on the weakest parts of the population to take responsibility for their own life. They cannot, however, be applied as tools for detailed explanations of the roads taken by various countries to activation, nor can they explain the specific time of emergence or the specific character of activation in the different nation states.

We do know that the emergence of activation in countries regionally and culturally akin, such as the UK, Sweden and Denmark, is far from identical. The Danish approach to activation is distinct because it constitutes a sudden and flagrant break with a century-old privilege for members of the unemployment funds to receive benefit as a *right* when unemployed. The only condition has been availability for the labour market; and this has always, by comparison with Swedish active labour-market policies, involved a narrow interpretation in terms of both geography and trade/skill; in other words, a generous reading of the condition. Compared to the Danish situation, the British road to activation was much more of a process than of a sudden break. During 20 years of Conservative government, entitlements, durations and benefits were frequently reduced, and gradually benefits became conditional upon some sort of 'activity'. The rights remained, but they were steadily cut down and, in the end, were of an almost formal character. New Labour has made New Deals; it is, however, a matter of dispute how much has changed for the unemployed, single mothers and disabled people (Grover and Steward, 1999).

When analysing the nation states one by one, it is most striking to observe the many different, often complementary – but sometimes contradictory – reasons and combinations of reasons for launching and further developing activation policies, such as:

- Reducing 'dependency' and 'dependency type behaviour' (for example, the UK and Norway);
- Enhancing inclusion into the domains of health, family, income, housing, and so on, via broader policies combating exclusion and not with an exclusive focus on the system of paid work only (for example, France and Portugal);
- Enhancing inclusion into the domain of paid labour via qualitative (supply side) improvements of the marginalised and excluded persons' general and specific work qualifications (for example, Denmark, the Netherlands, Belgium and Spain), and via job creation (the demand side) (for example, the Netherlands, Belgium and Spain);
- Legitimising the welfare state in the eyes of the tax payers (for example, Denmark);
- Maintaining political power, by giving concessions to the neoliberals on activation policy, the social democrats keep the liberal critics of the welfare state at arm's length (for example, Denmark and the Netherlands);
- Reducing (for example, Sweden, the UK and Germany) or increasing (for example France) social expenditures;
- Adapting national policies to European policies (for example, Portugal).

Some of these reasons relate directly to the activation approaches distinguished earlier in this chapter. They also reflect various degrees of concern as well as different answers to some of the main issues in welfare state reforms, mentioned in our introduction.

Several comments can be made regarding this (probably not exhaustive) list of reasons for the introduction of activation in general and active social policies in particular. First, legislation on activation is introduced and developed in many countries, in combination with other types of labour-market policies or social policy legislation. Consequently the official political legitimations and motives are often mixed with other policy motives. Secondly, and this is well-known from political sociology, the official rhetoric does not necessarily include all motives of policy makers. For example, in the Danish case, the support among (low income) tax payers vis-à-vis the welfare state is stated as a motive for activation only rarely, whereas the 'wellbeing' of the activated persons through their intended inclusion into paid labour is mentioned much more frequently. This combination of both official and explicit motives and intentions on the one hand, and unofficial, implicit and hidden ones on the other makes motives, intentions and objectives difficult subjects of analysis. Furthermore, political intentions may differ, as for example Foucault and Bourdieu have stated, from what is going on in practice. Therefore, and thirdly, the concrete implementation will always, more or less, differ from the officially stated goals/motives. This may be either because the official aims are less realistic or feasible and/or because the implementation of activation legislation in many European countries is a matter of regional or local authorities.

The introduction of activation: support, expenditure and institutional developments

Support for activation

One of the most striking phenomena of the introduction of the active approach is the widespread rhetorical support for it. Activation policies are among those rare policy issues that receive support from almost the entire political spectrum. It is concurrently being supported and justified by Anglo liberalism, Scandinavian socialism and French republicanism.

In the terminology of welfare state regimes, the active approach as it is currently being implemented in the social policies of many EU countries can be seen as a merging of liberal and social-democratic principles. The principle of obligatory activation is akin to classic liberal principles of 'something for something', 'help to self-help' and 'the individual's responsibility for her/his own life' (Møller, 1981). On the other hand, the principle of offering people participation opportunities and of redistributing work has a clear egalitarian, social-democratic background. The same goes for the emancipatory potential ascribed to labour-market participation. Nevertheless, it is quite clear that 'modern' social democracy has come to endorse the responsibility principle much more strongly than liberals have come to support redistribution principles. Both dimensions of the active approach have been developed most strongly by administrations led, at least in part, by social democrats. They launched a series of compulsory educational, training and other activation schemes of the 'food for work' type, sometimes for all categories of unemployed people, including drug addicts and psychiatric patients. 'Modern' social democracy has become one of the strongest advocates of introducing into social polity elements of the paternalism optimists' activation approach.

The issue of 'responsibility' is one of the fundamentals of the new social-democratic programme, which has been dubbed the 'third way'. Giddens, in a reply to the critics of this programme, describes this fundamental principle as follows:

> [The third way p]roposes to construct a new social contract, based on the theorem 'no rights without responsibilities'. Those who profit from social goods should both use them responsibly, and give something back to the wider social community in return. Seen as a feature of citizenship, 'no rights without responsibilities' has to apply to politicians as well as citizens, to the rich as well as the poor, to business corporations as much as the private individual. Left-of-centre governments should be prepared to act upon it in all these areas. (Giddens, 2000, p 52)

This does not mean, Giddens argues elsewhere in his book, that the third way has no attention for issues of inequality and redistribution. Nevertheless, by tying the redistribution of participation opportunities to the responsibility theorem, it is quite clear that the third way version of activation implies a social contract which introduces obligatory participation for those who do not voluntarily choose to participate in activation programmes.

The same tendencies are reflected in public opinion. Generally speaking, opinion surveys reveal that people in Western Europe remain supportive of decent welfare state provisions (for example, Svallfors and Taylor-Gooby, 1999). However, there is empirical evidence to show that this support is embedded in a discourse of mutual responsibilities of both the state and recipients of benefits and social assistance (Lødemel and Flaa, 1993; van Oorschot, 1996). Therefore, the theorem of the 'new social contract' seems to be endorsed by public opinion. At the same time, van Oorschot's study also reveals that this support may be based on a broader concept of work, of acting responsibly and fulfilling one's obligations, than that of the employment-centred politics of the third way.

Expenditures on activation

Table 3.2 presents data that can be interpreted in terms of the degree to which activation rhetoric is put into practice. It shows spending on active labour-

Table 3.2: Spending on active labour market policies as a percentage of GDP (1985-96)[2]

Welfare regime/country	1985	1990	1996	GDP share change 1985-96
Liberal				
UK	0.7	0.6	0.4	−43%
US	0.3	0.2	0.2	−33%
Social democratic/universalistic				
Sweden	2.1	1.7	2.4	+14%
Denmark	1.1	1.1	1.9	+73%
Conservative/employment-centred				
France	0.7	0.8	1.3	+86%
Germany	0.8	1.0	1.4	+75%
Belgium	1.3	1.2	1.5	+15%
Sub-protective				
Spain	0.3	0.8	0.7	+133%
Portugal	0.4	0.6	1.1	+175%
Italy	–	2.0	1.1	–
Hybrid				
Netherlands	1.3	1.2	1.4	+8%
EU average	0.9	0.9	1.2	+33%

Note: Countries studied by INPART in bold.

Source: Martin (1998)

market policies as a percentage of GDP. In this table, countries have been grouped into welfare state regimes to shed light on the degree to which different welfare regimes have been developing activation policies. Due to the 'hybrid' character of the Dutch welfare state (see Chapter One), the Netherlands is treated as a specific welfare regime type.

As might be expected, the social-democratic countries spend the largest share of their GDP on active policies, followed by the Netherlands and the employment-centred countries. The sub-protective welfare states perform 'better' than liberal states. In the period 1985-96, the sub-protective welfare states increased their spending as a percentage of GDP significantly, while the liberal welfare states decreased spending. In the period 1990-96, Spain and Italy show a decrease in relative spending on active policies, whereas Portugal has continued to increase its spending. On average, the EU countries increased their relative spending on active policies by one third between 1985 and 1996. According to the *Joint Employment Report 2000*, which compares the EU countries' performance and assesses these against the background of EU guidelines, activation is still increasing in the majority of EU member states (CEC, 2000).

Of course, expenditures on activation programmes are just one criterion in assessing the impact of the activation approach. Activation may have had its impact in other ways, for example in a reduction of benefit entitlements, in strengthening welfare recipients' obligations or in applying obligations more strictly. Therefore, even though the increase in expenditures on activation measures may not be very impressive, activation may still have affected the lives of the unemployed to an important extent.

The institutional context of activation

As was mentioned in section two when we discussed the impact of activation approaches on state–citizen relationships, activation analysis should not focus on the contents of social policies only. A second important level of analysis concerns the institutional context of the design, administration, implementation and delivery of social policies. Many countries in the EU are introducing institutional reforms, partly as a consequence of the increasing emphasis on activation in social policies. These reforms are taking place against various backgrounds. First of all, there is the growing recognition of the heterogeneity of target groups of activation, which challenges uniform, undifferentiated ways of managing problems of exclusion and poverty. Secondly, there is growing awareness that activation policies have to be adjusted to the diversity of regional and local labour markets. Finally, there is growing dissatisfaction with the effectiveness and quality of services of administration agencies and institutions.

Social policy interventions take place in very different individual circumstances and biographies. Even though poverty and unemployment risks are still unequally distributed over various population segments (the notion of a 'democratisation' of poverty, unemployment and social exclusion should be treated with care [see Beck, 1986; Geldof, 1999]), the assumption of the homogeneity of target groups of social policies, founded on the fact that they have some common features in terms of levels of qualification, ethnic background, age, and so on, needs qualification. This means that the starting point of interventions may be quite different, which is, of course, related to the multidimensional, temporal and biographical characteristics of social exclusion (see Chapter Two). The heterogeneity of target groups of active policies has gradually become more recognised by policy makers, specifically in countries that have a longer tradition of activation.

Consequently, two closely connecting processes are taking place: *individualisation* in approaching and dealing with the target groups of social policies, and *differentiation* of the instruments, measures and programmes that are available to stimulate participation and to increase the 'employability' of the unemployed. Individualisation in social policies can take different forms, which eventually may turn out to be different stages in a process of increasingly 'refining' individualisation.

A well-known form of individualisation is the distinction of several target groups, which are defined on the basis of demographic characteristics, since these are considered to be important in determining unemployed people's labour market position and because these can easily be identified. Policies distinguish target groups such as the young and the old, women, migrants, single parents, the low-qualified, long-term unemployed, and so on.

However, some have pointed out that these demographic characteristics are rather poor predictors of the likelihood of escaping from welfare state dependency and (re-)entering the labour market. For example, based on research on claiming periods of social assistance recipients in Germany, Leisering and Leibfried point out:

> Social characteristics do therefore correlate with the duration of claiming, but in each social group we found some people with both longer and shorter claiming periods. Thus these demographic categories can offer only a qualified explanation why some people managed to become independent of Social Assistance quickly and made no further claims during the period of almost six years which we observed, while others did not. (Leisering and Leibfried, 1999, p 84)

On the basis of their findings, Leisering and Leibfried draw the following conclusions. First, factors influencing exclusion and inclusion on an aggregate level are not necessarily relevant on an individual level. Secondly, other factors than those usually used in defining target groups turn out to be important in constituting people's employability or unemployability 'profiles'.

Based on similar experiences, several countries are developing more refined methods to distinguish categories of activation clients, and introducing profiling procedures and expert systems to determine the employability or labour-market distance of individual clients. On the basis of an assessment of clients' employability, decisions are being made about whether or not they will be subjected to an activation process, what instruments and schemes will be used, and what the aim of the activation process will be.

This development of tailor-making the delivery of activation is pursued even further in a form of individualisation, in which we see the introduction of an individual, client-centred approach where clients' needs and capacities are the starting points of activation rather than a predefined set of activation measures (Valkenburg et al, 2001; section two of this chapter). Originally, this approach was developed mainly in the context of activating groups of clients that never managed to enter existing activation programmes, or dropped out of them. Either because their situations are considered too complex for target group approaches, or because existing schemes are considered to be inadequate, a client-centred approach is considered to be the only way to develop successful activation programmes for these categories of clients (van Berkel et al, 1999).

Taking individual circumstances and backgrounds into account in activation processes, requires a differentiation of activation instruments. As Chapter Five elaborates, a variety of activation and labour-market inclusion programmes has been introduced in the EU member states. These include, among others, informing people of their participation opportunities and other forms of support in job finding; guidance and consultation; programmes for schooling, training and work experience; and a variety of forms of work ranging from 'regular' labour-market participation and self-employment via additional or subsidised job schemes to unpaid work.

Secondly, and partly in order to facilitate individualisation and differentiation, processes of *decentralisation* are taking place, increasing the role of regional, local or communal organisations and institutions in the administration and implementation of activation (OECD, 1998; see also Geddes and Benington, 2001). Granting local actors increased discretion in the design, implementation and delivery of active social policies is perceived as a condition to take into account local situations and to gear activation to the needs and circumstances of the target groups. However, decentralisation certainly does not automatically increase clients' autonomy or strengthen their position in the activation process. It can also make the treatment of clients highly dependent on local political circumstances, contribute to an increasing opacity of entitlements, and strengthen paternalism or even clientelism (Kazepov and Caputo, 1998).

Thirdly, decentralisation and an increase of local discretion are also being pursued to encourage local network formation, the development of *integrative approaches* in activation and institutional *decompartmentalisation*. This is most evident where institutions administering social security and labour-market policies are concerned: activation often implies closer linkages between social security policies and labour-market policies, also at the administrative level. Therefore besides this, other 'policy fields' and their institutions and organisations may become involved in active social policies as well, such as those operating in the fields of health, welfare, education, migration, the police, and so on. As an OECD report states:

One of the most important lessons from the experiences throughout the UK and Europe with local action to combat long-term unemployment is the need for effective collaboration or partnership working between all the agencies who have functions and responsibilities relating to this problem. Of course, the perception of what are the relevant agencies in this respect depends upon the conceptualisation of the problem – in particular, on how broad a range of factors is seen as influencing the prospects for unemployed people to obtain work. Substantial research has been undertaken around this issue and it is now widely acknowledged that a wide range of personal and social factors need to be addressed. (OECD, 1998, p 27)

Finally, processes of *privatisation* have created an institutional context in which private actors (private enterprises, non-governmental organisations [NGOs] and so on) are allowed to play a larger role in processes of activation (see De Koning et al, 1999). Advocates of this development expect, among other things, that privatisation will put an end to the monopoly of public employment services, and that this will contribute to efficiency and to an increase in the quality of activation services. At the same time, some fear that privatisation – in the sense of the marketisation and commercialisation of activation services – will reduce the efforts of institutions and organisations aimed at those that are considered to be relatively unemployable. According to these critics of privatisation, the costs involved in activating the relatively unemployable will stimulate private organisations to focus their attention on activating the most employable; and the public employment service, operating on a more competitive market, will be inclined to do the same to increase its competitiveness. Therefore, privatisation may put the activation of those most at risk of exclusion in jeopardy.

In summary, the development of active social policies has been accompanied by institutional reforms (also see Finn, 2000). In terms of the autonomy of citizens, these developments may involve serious risks, but also offer opportunities. They can be seen (and used) as instruments that refine institutional opportunities to enforce predefined obligations upon welfare claimants, and as mechanisms that reproduce rather than break unwanted exclusion. But they can also be seen (and used) as instruments in strengthening unemployed and poor people's active involvement in defining the means and objectives of social policy and activation interventions (see Jordan, 2000).

Notes

[1] The theory of human behaviour on which this consideration is based, however, is not unproblematic and has been criticised (see, for example, Taylor-Gooby, 2000).

[2] The paper on which this table is based described 'active labour market policies' as follows (Martin, 1998, p 6): "Active measures comprise a wide range of policies aiming at improving the access of the unemployed to the labour market and jobs, job-related skills and the functioning of the labour market. Spending on active measures is ... split

into five program areas: public employment services; labour market training; youth measures; subsidised employment; and measures for the disabled".

References

Andreotti, A., García, S., Hespanha, P., Kazepov, Y. and Mingione, E. (2001) 'Does a South European model exist? Some evidence of its presence', *Journal of European Area Studies*, vol 9, no 1, pp 43-63.

Anthony, P. (1977) *The ideology of work*, London: Tavistock.

Beck, U. (1986) *Risikogesellschaft. Auf dem Weg in eine andere Moderne*, Frankfurt am Maine: Suhrkamp.

Beck, U. (2000) *The brave new world of work*, Cambridge: Polity Press.

Coenen-Hanegraaf, M., Valkenburg, B., Ploeg, M. and Coenen, H. (1998) *Begeleid werken. Theorie en methodiek van een individuele, vraaggerichte benadering*, Utrecht: Van Arkel.

CEC (Commission of the European Communities) (2000) *Joint employment report 2000*, Brussels: CEC.

De Koning, J., Denys, J. and Walwel, U. (1999) *Deregulation in placement services: A comparative study for eight EU countries*, Brussels: CEC, DG-V.

De Swaan, A. (1996) *Zorg en de staat. Welzijn, onderwijs en gezondheidszorg in Europa en de Verenigde Staten in de nieuwe tijd*, Amsterdam: Bert Bakker.

Drøpping, J.A., Hvinden, B. and Vik, K. (1999) 'Activation policies in the Nordic Countries', in M. Kautto, M. Heikkilä, B. Hvinden, S. Marklund and N. Ploug (eds) *Nordic social policy. Changing welfare states*, London/New York, NY: Routledge, pp 133-59.

Eardley, T., Bradshaw, J., Ditch, J., Gough, I. and Whiteford, P. (1996) *Social assistance schemes in OECD countries: Volume 1, synthesis report*, DSS Research Report 46, London: HMSO.

Enjolras, B., Laville, J.L., Fraisse, L. and Trickey, H. (2001) 'Between subsidiarity and social assistance – the French republican route to activation', in I. Lødemel and H. Trickey (eds) *'An offer you can't refuse': Workfare in international perspective*, Bristol: The Policy Press, pp 71-103.

Esping-Andersen, G. (1990) *The three worlds of welfare capitalism*, Princeton, NJ: Princeton University Press.

Esping-Andersen, G. (1999) *Social foundations of postindustrial economies*, Oxford: Oxford University Press.

European Foundation for the Improvement of Living and Working Conditions (1999) *Linking welfare and work*, Dublin: European Foundation for the Improvement of Living and Working Conditions.

Finn, D. (2000) 'Welfare to work: the local dimension', *Journal of European Social Policy*, vol 10, no 1, pp 43-57.

Gallie, D. and Paugam, S. (eds) (2000) *Welfare regimes and the experience of unemployment in Europe*, Oxford: Oxford University Press.

Geddes, M. and Benington, J. (2001) *Local partnerships and social exclusion in the European Union. New forms of local social governance?*, London/New York, NY: Routledge.

Geldof, D. (1999) *Niet meer maar beter. Over zelfbeperking in de risicomaatschappij*, Leuven/Amersfoort: Acco.

Giddens, A. (2000) *The Third Way and its critics*, Cambridge: Polity Press.

Gorz, A. (1989) *Critique of economic reason*, London: Verso.

Gorz, A. (1999) *Reclaiming work. Beyond the wage-based society*, Cambridge: Polity Press.

Grover, C. and Steward, J. (1999) 'Market workfare: social security and competitiveness in the 1990s', *Journal of Social Policy*, vol 28, no 1, pp 73-96.

Hvinden, B. and Halvorsen, R. (2001) 'Emerging notions of active citizenship in Europe', Paper prepared for the Fifth ESA conference, Helsinki, Finland, 28 August-1 September.

Jessop, B. (1994) 'The transition to post-Fordism and the Schumpetarian welfare state', in R. Borrows and B. Loader (eds) *Towards a post-Fordist welfare state*, London: Routledge, pp 13-37.

Johansson, H. (2001) 'Activation policies in the Nordic welfare states. Arguments on the social democratic welfare regime', *Journal of European Area Studies*, vol 9, no 1, pp 63-79.

Jordan, B., James, S., Kay, H. and Redley, M. (1992) *Trapped in poverty? Labour market decisions in low-income households*, London/New York, NY: Routledge.

Jordan, B. (1996) *A theory of poverty and social exclusion*, Cambridge: Polity Press.

Jordan, B. (2000) *Social work and the third way. Tough love in social policy*, London: Sage Publications.

Kautto, M., Heikkilä, M., Hvinden, B., Marklund, S. and Ploug, N. (1999) *Nordic social policy. Changing welfare states*, London/New York, NY: Routledge.

Kazepov, Y. and Orientale Caputo, G. (1998) 'No organization, no services, no money. The poor and the excluded from welfare in Italy', in R. van Berkel, H. Coenen and R. Vlek (eds) *Beyond marginality? Social movements of social security claimants in the European Union*, Aldershot: Ashgate, pp 119-57.

Leisering, L. and Leibfried, S. (1999) *Time and poverty in Western welfare states. United Germany in perspective*, Cambridge: Cambridge University Press.

Levitas, R. (1998) *The inclusive society? Social exclusion and New Labour*, Basingstoke: Macmillan.

Lipsky, M. (1980) *Street-level bureaucracy. Dilemmas of the individual in public services*, New York, NY: Russell Sage Foundation.

Lister, R. (2000) 'Towards a citizens' welfare state: the 3 + 2 'R's' of welfare reform', Paper presented at the Social Policy Association Annual Conference, London, 18-20 July.

Lødemel, I. and Flaa, J. (1993) *Social puls*, Fafo-report 156, Oslo: Fafo.

Lødemel, I. and Trickey, H. (eds) (2001) *'An offer you can't refuse': Workfare in international perspective*, Bristol: The Policy Press.

Martin, J.P. (1998) *What works among active labour market policies: Evidence from OECD countries' experiences*, Labour Market and Social Policy Occasional Paper No 35, Paris: OECD.

Marx, K. (1971) *Kapitalen*, Copenhagen: Rhodos.

Møller, I.H. (1981) *Klassekamp og sociallovgivning, 1850-1970*, Copenhagen: Socialistiske Økonomers Forlag.

Møller, I.H. (1999) 'Trends in the Danish social mode of economic regulation', in J. Lind and I. Hornemann Møller (eds) *Inclusion and exclusion: Unemployment and non-standard employment in Europe*, Aldershot: Ashgate, pp 167-87.

Møller, I.H. and Lind, J. (2000) 'The labour market in process of change', *International Journal of Employment Studies*, vol 8, no 1, pp 155-95.

Murray, C. (1994) *Losing ground. American social policy 1950-1980*, New York, NY: Basic Books.

OECD (Organisation of Economic Co-operation Development) (1998) *Local management for more effective employment policies*, Paris: OECD.

Pahl, R. (1984) *Divisions of labour*, Oxford/Cambridge: Blackwell.

Roche, M. and van Berkel, R. (1997) *European citizenship and social exclusion*, Avebury: Aldershot.

Rosanvallon, P. (2000) *The new social question. Rethinking the welfare state*, Princeton, NJ: Princeton University Press.

Saraceno, C. (ed) (2002) *Social assistance dynamics in Europe: National and local poverty regimes*, Bristol: The Policy Press.

Svallfors, S. and Taylor-Gooby, P. (1999) *The end of the welfare state? Responses to state retrenchment*, London: Routledge.

Swift, P., Grant, G. and McGrath, M. (1994) *Participation in the social security system: Experiments in local consultation*, Aldershot: Avebury.

Taylor-Gooby, P. (ed) (2000) *Risk, trust and welfare*, Basingstoke: Macmillan.

Terpstra, J. (2000) 'Activering en bemiddeling van werklozen als onderdeel van sociale zekerheid. De moeizame weg naar een activerend stelsel', *Tijdschrift voor arbeid en participatie*, vol 21, no 4, pp 287-300.

Therborn, G. (1986) *Why some people are more unemployed than others. The strange paradox of growth and unemployment*, London: Verso.

Titmuss, R. (1974) *Social policy: An introduction*, London: Allen & Unwin.

Valkenburg, B., Lind, J. and van Berkel, R. (2001) 'Work and inclusion', *Transfer*, vol 7, no 1, pp 12-25.

van Berkel, R., Coenen, H. and Vlek, R. (1998) *Beyond marginality? Social movements of social security claimants in the European Union*, Aldershot: Ashgate.

van Berkel, R., Coenen, H. and Dekker, A. (1999) 'Regulating the unemployed: from protection to participation', in J. Lind and I. Hornemann Møller (eds) *Inclusion and exclusion: Unemployment and non-standard employment in Europe*, Aldershot: Ashgate, pp 89-111.

van Oorschot, W. (1996) *Nederland over sociale zekerheid en arbeid. Eerste resultaten van een uitgebreid onderzoek naar de publieke opinie*, WORC report 96.12.007/2, Tilburg: Tilburg University.

Vranken, J., Geldof, D. and Van Menxel, G. (1999) *Armoede en sociale uitsluiting. Jaarboek 1999*, Leuven/Amersfoort: Acco.

Weber, M. (1985) *The protestant ethic and the spirit of capitalism*, London: Unwin.

FOUR

The inclusive power of standard and non-standard work

Marisol García and Jan de Schampheleire

Introduction

This chapter examines the inclusive power of various types of work. It looks at some of the existing relevant national literature in Belgium, Denmark, the Netherlands, Portugal, Spain and the UK. Since most of the theoretical complexities involved in the term inclusion have been examined in Chapter Two, we now aim at an operationalisation of the relation between work and inclusion in a wider sense by incorporating the concept of *life chances*. By introducing the concept of 'life chances' we are emphasising the idea of generalised opportunity that comes not just from work, but also from education, collective activities, household sharing, life circle and concomitant age and gender opportunities. By incorporating these variables we intend to draw the outline of a readable picture of the way virtuous and vicious circles evolve in society in general and in people's trajectories in particular.

One striking observation extracted from a large part of sociological research is that it either takes the individual or the household as its points of reference. In fact, most research about employment takes an individual approach. People's life experiences however involve both dimensions. Despite the increasing number of single households in the six countries, the majority of households are still formed by more than one member. Even those who decide to live alone often have and enjoy close family and friendship relationships involving social reciprocity. This means that it is the pool of household resources – mainly income derived from work and property, but also social capital – which provides inclusion and not only the individual status provided by employment. Even if this pool of income and general resources pattern is more evident in the households of countries located in Southern Europe, this pattern is also present within households in the North (Pahl, 1984).

Taking these considerations into account, this chapter includes the two areas of sociological work: one focusing on individual work experience, the other on the household income from different types of work. In line with the former, the Weberian concept of 'life chances' in relation to work will guide the analysis of this chapter. Weber used the notion of life chances to indicate opportunities provided by the social structure. Later, Dahrendorf developed the concept as "the sum total of opportunities offered to the individual by his society" (1979, p 28). Life chances do not constitute attributes of individuals; rather, societies offer those chances to citizens. Life chances are restricted when social closure is enforced on a particular social group by the dominant group in a given society[1]. More specifically, life chances are functions of *options* and *ligatures*. A household notably bounds individual options. For example, a young couple might enhance their life chances by combining one partner's job in the formal labour market (which guarantees social rights for the household) with the other partner's job in the informal economy (which offers time flexibility for the household). In this conceptualisation, options, on the one hand, constitute possible choices: the more flexible the labour market the more choices available for a large number of people. Ligatures, on the other hand, are bonds: the more solid the social bonds the less danger of experiencing risk in times of hardship, such as when a person loses his work and is set on a downward road of exclusion. Bonds manifest themselves in the realisation of social networking and social reciprocity as well as in many types of emotional and material exchange among kin and community members. The importance of combining the two elements, warns Dahrendorf, is that "ligatures without options are oppressive, whereas options without bonds are meaningless" (1979, p 31).

We argue that work in general (not only work in the regular labour market) presents options and extends social bonds. Work, therefore, is a very important element of people's life chances and inclusion. In line with earlier chapters, inclusion is understood here as people's meaningful participation in a range of spheres or systems that have economic, political, social or cultural relevance. Individuals can then be understood to be included (or excluded) in many respects. Moreover, inclusion can be realised in several ways. For example, although someone might have no access to regular career possibilities, (s)he can nevertheless be included into many other systems, be valued in a non-working group and find meaning in what (s)he does. The inclusion of this person in work activity enlarges his/her life chances as a citizen and/or as a human being. However, whether or not individuals are in possession of what Weber calls 'appropriate chances or rights' constitutes a fundamental difference in the practice of full citizenship. These appropriate chances are social chances because they are secured by contract and sanctions (Dahrendorf, 1979, p 68). Following this, we would like to stress the differences between work that involves economic and social rights and that constitutes not only inclusion but also full economic and social citizenship,[2] and work that does *not* involve economic and social rights, but generates inclusion, voluntary unpaid work being a good example of this.

As Chapter Two of this volume argues, there are several degrees of inclusion into the work systems as well as in the different societal systems and subsystems. However, most recent literature tends to establish a hierarchy in which work in the formal labour market is considered of the highest possible value. This valorisation has been reinforced by the Fordist form of work integration in which participation in welfare institutions and even in decisions through trade unions and workers' representatives in parliaments has been considered of major importance for over three decades. In Europe, workers' sense of security at their work, the pursuit of satisfaction and the gains obtained through employment with economic rights has helped to meet people's expectations about citizenship (in Gallie, 2000, p 4). However, as was also pointed out in Chapter Two, INPART research has shown the relevance of widening the understanding of the different types of work that have been present during the Fordist era and thereafter, and their diverse capacity to generate inclusion. In order to grasp what the existing body of research can tell us on the different levels of inclusion offered by the different types of work, we compare standard and non-standard work. Given the huge amount of available research, our discussion, while risking incompleteness, aims at describing general tendencies.

Standard work is full-time work, fully and formally paid, and exercised during a lifelong career. It involves a contract and formal rights and obligations, is often considered the most inclusive, as it provides economic and social rights which support the holder of the job after the contract ends. Standard work corresponds to formal employment in the primary labour market[3].

All non-standard work forms deviate from the standard work characteristics in one or more ways:

(a) *Irregular work* (part-time work and fixed contracts): this is a deviation from standard work in the formal labour market that has developed mainly with the flexibilisation of employment.
(b) *Employment programme work* (all wage work that is partially or fully funded by a government employment plan): this is often work that takes place in the secondary labour market, although subsidies can be directed to the primary labour market in the form of tax exemptions to employers.
(c) *Targeted training* (applied education in a work environment).
(d) *Unpaid work* (neighbourhood work and voluntary work): this can take place within the kinship and friendship spheres. Often denominated community work.
(e) *Informal work* (paid work that is hidden from the state for tax, social security or labour law, but which is legal in all other aspects): a variation of this type is autonomous exchange work.

Of the five varieties (a), (b) and (c) generally involve a contract giving economic and social rights. The rights of part-time workers might however not be proportionally at the level of full-time workers. Targeted training and subsidised work involve some type of contract in which rights and obligations are clearly defined usually between the recipient and the institutions in charge of administering the work or training programme. On the other hand (d) either does not involve a contract or involves a contract with very limited social rights. Finally (e), by definition, is not formalised and therefore no contract is signed. These last two, (d) and (e), are better understood by applying notions such as social reciprocity. This is especially the case for autonomous exchange work.

Whereas standard and non-standard work can generate a social milieu in which the individual experiences inclusion, no 'appropriate chances' may be derived from non-standard work. In fact the crucial empirical question is the extent to which each of the non-standard forms of work enhances or reduces the likelihood of inclusion into standard work. Some research has argued against the idea that any job is better than no job because of the vicious circles into which a person can fall by constantly moving from bad jobs to social assistance and vice versa. The analysis of Atkinson (1998) and Paugam (1997) concludes that some jobs might lead to greater social and professional exclusion than social assistance itself. This conclusion has been supported by the ESOPO research[4]. It becomes apparent that forcing a person to take any job may have serious effects upon his/her skills, and hence the ability to stay in the labour market in the future. This is particularly true when the unskilled job is not protected by social security. Although this general argument needs to be qualified by considering specific biographies, "it appears that the risk of the revolving door mechanism is greater when the 'any job' rule is strictly enforced" (Saraceno, 2002, p 249). The revolving door mechanism takes place partly because the person cannot improve fully his/her capabilities and consequent 'life chances' when (s)he is subjected to unskilled, 'bad' jobs or when (s)he performs certain activation programmes' jobs or training activities which are rigidly framed and not suited to the individual cases. Therefore, a vicious circle develops by which the person loses the ability to perform socially and to pursue a path of sustained labour-market inclusion.

On the other hand, virtuous circles can develop from those personal trajectories in which there is improvement of personal capabilities through work that is non-standard, but can be part of a path into a job that offers long-time perspective and/or chances to improve the person's capabilities. In this case the person feels more in command over his or her life, and can build up life strategies either alone or in combination with other members of the household. Therefore, in this chapter we examine the inclusionary potential of different types of work by examining their ability to guide workers into virtuous or vicious circles. We argue that virtuous circles generate long perspective-working trajectories that increase people's life chances, whereas vicious circles do the opposite, putting people in situations of risk and vulnerability, and in the worst cases leading to exclusion from work, income opportunities and other societal systems. Virtuous circles develop more commonly when there is a combination of resources from more than one member of the household. For example, young people who stay in the parental house until their late twenties (and whose parents engage in both standard and non-standard work) can combine irregular badly paid jobs with university training leading to future advantageous income opportunities.

The interesting sociological analysis comes from the fact that household members combine different standard and non-standard forms of work creating a mixture of life chances. Therefore the stronger the family solidarity, the more probable is the profit from mixtures. This is often the case in the societies that conform to the *familistic regime*, in our sample Portugal and Spain[5]. On the other end, there are those societies in which there is prevalence of work established by contract, which means a more pronounced formalisation not only of employment, but of any type of work. This is the case in the countries that conform to the *social-democratic regime*, in our sample Denmark and, though less 'typical', the Netherlands. Belgium and the UK fall somewhere in between (they can be said to conform to the *conservative-corporatist* and *liberal regimes* respectively).

Two remarks based on empirical analysis must be made before we can analyse standard and non-standard work and their relation to life chances and inclusion. First, the mere possibility for comparing standard and non-standard work is a result of the 1980s and 1990s rise of non-standard work forms (Lind and Møller, 1999). On the levels of individuals and households, however, standard work and non-standard work make up a continuum. At least four elements contribute to this continuum:

• In the 1980s and 1990s much standard work has been partially disassembled with the introduction of pre-pension systems, leave systems and shorter or flexible working hours;
• Individual careers, before entering standard work, often involve one or more successive non-standard jobs;
• Within one and the same career period individuals can combine unpaid or informal work with standard work;
• Households – even more than individuals – mix standard and non-standard work forms, most prominently a (male) full-time job and a (female) part-time job.

Secondly, the type of work individuals perform, on the one hand, cannot be translated directly into life chances terms, on the other hand it has an important effect on people's construction of their own identities[6]. The most poetic version of the new reality of work and its effects on individual identity is offered by Richard Sennett (1998) in his portrait of the consequences that flexible and non-stable work has for the person's development of character and life meaning. Sennett shows, in his examination of individual work histories, the little or no importance companies give nowadays to the character of their employees. There is an increasing difficulty of constructing meaningful lives through work, while individual workers struggle with building affinitive, emphatic and solidaristic spheres within their households. The picture of the US's highly mobile labour force is coming closer to the European experience, even if the European labour market remains a more rigid system with strong emphasis on stability and economic rights. Therefore, in Europe, economic rights derived from employment are present only in formal employment though in varying degrees depending on whether the job involves a permanent or temporary contract[7].

Firstly, we provide an overview of the relative importance of standard and non-standard work forms in the countries under study, before looking at the inclusive power of standard work and compare it with its non-standard alternatives: irregular work; subsidised work and training; unpaid work; and informal work. As we mentioned earlier in this chapter, the focus is on general tendencies, rather than completeness.

The relative importance of standard and non-standard work

In the following tables differences in employment in the six countries are shown. Table 4.1 includes the *total* population, while Table 4.2 represents the female population only.

Table 4.1 shows that the impact of part-time work is less significant in the familistic welfare regime countries such as Portugal and Spain, where, on the other hand, self-employment is clearly more present. Therefore, self-employment in Portugal is three times higher than in Denmark. Social-democratic Denmark and the 'hybrid' welfare regime of the Netherlands (see Chapter One) present a contrast. The Netherlands especially has a very high level of part-time employment. In these countries, unemployment is also considerably lower, especially in comparison with Spain, the country that has registered the highest unemployment rate in the EU for years. In Spain, however, informal work is more present. Lastly, in only two of the six countries (Belgium and Spain) long-term unemployment is above 2%. In Denmark and the Netherlands, the levels of long-term unemployment are considerably lower. In these two countries the impact of activating policies designed and implemented by governmental institutions offers the unemployed ways of participating in work-related activities but not necessarily better chances to entering the primary labour market[8]. However, participants in those programmes are kept away

Table 4.1: Employment, unemployment and non-standard employment (1999)

	Denmark	Netherlands	Belgium	Portugal	Spain	UK
Employment rate	76.0	71.3	59.3	67.5	52.7	70.9
Unemployment	5.2	3.3	8.8	4.5	15.9	6.1
Long-term unemployment	1.1	1.2	5.0	1.7	7.3	1.8
Self-employed	7.2	14.7	17.9	28.4	17.1	12.1
Part-time work	21.6	39.8	20.3	10.9	8.1	24.8
Informal employment	low	low	med–high	high	high	med–low

Source: Employment in Europe (2001)

from the unemployment statistics. Whereas in Portugal, and to a lesser extent in the UK, the impact of government activation programmes was less significant, there has been a large proliferation of badly paid jobs in the formal and informal economy that have also had an apparent positive impact on the labour market and on keeping the file of the unemployed more under control than in Belgium, where unemployment benefit can in principle be obtained for an unlimited period (de Schampheleire and Vilrokx, 1998). In Spain, unemployment remains dramatically high partly due to rigidities in the labour market and partly to the perpetuation of a familistic culture[9], which have excluded young people and women from the labour market. This country shares with Portugal – and to a certain extent the UK – the limited impact of government activation programmes on the reduction of unemployment (García and Gómez, 1998, 2000).

Table 4.2 shows even greater contrasts. Denmark and the Netherlands, followed by the UK, present the highest employment rates. In practically all countries included, female part-time employment is almost double that of men. In the Netherlands especially, women's participation in part-time employment is considerable, while Portugal and Spain have the lowest rates. In all countries female unemployment is systematically higher than male unemployment. The same trend is to be observed for long-term unemployment. Female informal employment is – in line with total employment – low in Denmark and the Netherlands, high in Portugal and Spain and medium–high and medium–low in Belgium and the UK respectively.

Participation in standard work

In general the stable income supply and social security of standard work are strong facilitators of inclusion. However, since the 1980s and 1990s, with a stable or decreasing amount of formal work and an increasing amount of people participating in the labour market at each moment in time, the relative amount of standard jobs (full-time, lifelong career) decreased. Unequal participation in

Table 4.2: Female employment, unemployment and non-standard employment (1999)

	Denmark	Netherlands	Belgium	Portugal	Spain	UK
Employment rate	71.1	61.7	50.4	59.4	35.0	63.8
Unemployment	6.0	4.7	10.5	5.2	26.6	5.5
Long-term unemployment	1.3	1.6	6.1	2.0	14.5	1.3
Self-employed	4.4	12.5	16.0	27.2	15.3	7.7
Part-time work	34.7	69.0	40.2	16.7	16.9	44.5
Informal employment	low	low	med–high	high	high	med–low

Source: Employment in Europe (2001)

the labour market is most prominently related to education levels. In the 1980s and 1990s education levels have risen. The percentage of the population having reached at least upper secondary education has most notably risen in Belgium, Spain and Portugal: levels are 6–10% higher in the 25-29 than in the 30-34 age group (see Table 4.3). In the same period the required skill levels have also risen, both in recruitment and in actual job content (Gallie, 1996). The combined effect of growth in labour force and in education level has been more job opportunities for the many and less opportunities for the others.

In present recruitment policy, priority is given to formal education level rather than to tenure and knowledge by experience. In Portugal, the changeover to present-day systems is experienced with higher velocity than in other countries. One study (Oliviera, 1998) shows access to standard work to be highly dependent on individual mobility. Moreover, conversion in, for example, the wool sector and in mining mostly affects people between 30 and 40 years, who usually have acquired their skills in an informal way, and not the young people, who mostly have a higher level of education (Duarte, 1996).

The general increase of formal education level also leads to a displacement effect: workers with an appropriate skill level for certain jobs are pushed from these jobs by workers with a higher skill level. With subsequent workers working below their qualification level, the lowest level is particularly affected as it is pushed out of the regular labour market (for example, in the case of Belgium; see Simoens et al, 1997).

Differences in labour-market participation between education levels are to be found in all countries under study, with percentages differing between 18% and 30% (Table 4.4). The Netherlands and Belgium have the highest differences in participation, most notably for women's participation, with a difference of even around 40%. The differences become even more extreme when comparing the individual level to the household level.

It has been observed in the Netherlands and Belgium in particular, that there is a combined effect of the double income standard and the diminished labour

Table 4.3: Percentage of the population aged 25-59 having completed at least upper secondary education (1999)

	Denmark	Netherlands	Belgium	Portugal	Spain	UK
25-59	**81.1**	**66.2**	**60.2**	**22.0**	**37.7**	**63.5**
25-29	89.4	75.6	77.5	35.1	58.3	69.3
30-34	85.2	73.3	71.2	25.4	50.5	65.5
35-39	79.8	70.3	64.9	21.8	43.9	64.8
40-44	79.5	67.1	58.1	20.6	37.0	65.5
45-49	79.8	61.2	54.1	16.6	28.4	64.4
50-54	78.0	57.4	46.7	13.9	21.1	59.0
55-59	74.8	52.0	40.4	11.4	15.8	51.9

Source: Eurostat Yearbook (2000)

Table 4.4: Employment rates by age group and level of education (1997)

		Denmark	Nether-lands	Belgium	Portugal	Spain	UK
Men							
25-54	H	90.4	88.6	89.0	93.6	77.3	89.8
	M	83.4	81.9	79.0	82.1	66.9	81.2
	L	69.9	63.9	59.2	75.4	54.4	69.8
	Total	**82.7**	**77.7**	**74.5**	**78.6**	**61.3**	**78.3**
55-64	H	69.0	50.9	41.2	55.1	62.2	70.4
	M	53.0	36.1	30.7	48.6	43.1	66.8
	L	38.8	21.8	15.0	46.2	30.7	52.7
	Total	**51.4**	**31.4**	**22.0**	**46.8**	**33.5**	**59.4**
Women							
25-54	H	87.9	83.2	84.2	92.5	69.3	85.9
	M	77.0	70.4	66.8	76.7	51.4	74.0
	L	62.5	47.8	41.7	64.6	32.8	63.0
	Total	**77.0**	**65.1**	**62.6**	**69.9**	**43.4**	**71.3**
55-64	H	64.7	40.3	23.6	45.9	48.6	73.1
	M	45.9	24.8	18.5	42.8	27.0	64.7
	L	26.6	13.8	8.8	36.3	16.2	56.0
	Total	**41.2**	**19.8**	**12.4**	**37.0**	**18.0**	**60.2**

Source: Eurostat Yearbook (2000)

access of the low-qualified. With the increase of the income earned by the (most frequently male) main earner, the probability that the partner has a job and income increases (Van der Veen, 1997). Similarly, it can be observed that double incomes are to be found more often among the higher educated (Cantillon and Marx, 1995).

The inclusive effect of labour-market participation is, however, far from unambiguous. In general terms households particularly have a high labour-market participation when the partners are aged between age 25 and 50 (Eurostat Yearbook, 2000). As requirements for domestic work and childcare are usually also higher in this age period the adult members of the household come under pressure from other responsibilities or social activities. Differentiated according to education level, however, the double income and double labour-market participation is more interesting for the higher qualified; for them it is more profitable to delegate/externalise domestic work. In this respect too, the inclusive effect of double labour-market participation is clearer for the highly qualified.

Although there is a general observation of a positive link between inclusion and (both standard and non-standard) work, the negative effect of unemployment on inclusion is not as straightforward. Denmark has the most systematic studies differentiating between the economic, political, social and cultural level. Studies tackling the issue of political participation found small but systematic differences between the employed and the unemployed. The higher participation of the highly educated in particular is strongly reduced when being unemployed (Andersen et al, 1993). Membership of a political association is slightly lower among the unemployed; board membership, unsurprisingly, is dramatically lower (Fridberg, 1993). However, the level of cultural participation is the same for the unemployed and the employed. Differences in the nature of participation on the one hand depend on the available budget (the unemployed being more engaged in for example walking tours or reading library books) and, on the other, on education levels (the higher educated for example going more frequently to a theatre or a museum and the lower educated more frequently to a sports game) (Fridberg, 1989, 1994). Similarly, on the level of social contacts, studies do not always reflect a negative influence of unemployment on the quality of social contacts (Derks et al, 1995).

Irregular work

Irregular work covers part-time work and fixed term contracts. Obviously, this covers a wide area (see our introduction to this chapter) and here we can only make a very general overview of some of the research. From both an individual and a household perspective, there are two good reasons to engage in irregular work. First, irregular work can be welcomed in order to combine a formal wage job with domestic work. Second, employment chances can be higher if one is ready to accept irregular work. Although analytically distinct, the two reasons often mix in practice.

For households that already have an income based on one standard job, part-time and temporal work can be used to combine the extra income of a second job with the responsibilities of domestic work. There is a clear tendency for women to take up a part-time job in the household (see Table 4.2), reinforcing the different implication of men and women in domestic work. The care of children and other domestic responsibilities make the participation of women in the labour market focus on part-time work, because it permits the combination of childcare once maternity leave is over (Walby, 1997). In this respect, when combining domestic work with a formal job, irregular work is the only option. Nevertheless, the inclusive effect of certain forms of part-time work, including for example shift work and weekend work, is doubtful (Yeandle et al, 1999).

Part-time employment among men, although moderately rising, is not strongly linked with family responsibilities (Yeandle et al, 1999). In general, male employment is not strongly contingent on family situations. In all EU member states only 3% of all fathers work part-time (Yeandle et al, 1999). In Danish families with small children, the mothers are less involved in work outside the house, while the fathers work as many hours as men without children (Christoffersen, 1993; Holt, 1997). Similarly, in Belgian households fathers adapting their employment to the family situation are an exception (Glorieux et al, 2001).

Part-time employment also reflects gender stereotypes in the workplace, women being clustered in certain service jobs. This implies working in female-dominated occupations, in female-dominated businesses, and often for a female boss (Tijdens, 1999). All in all, as far as part-time work can operate in an inclusive way, it does this in a rather gender stereotyping way.

The relation between a worker's employment chances and his or her readiness to accept irregular work is also a bit ambiguous as the continuity of employment can be lower, while chances to find a job on the ordinary labour market can be higher. In Belgium, for example, a higher unemployment risk for part-time workers (women and men together) is observed (Holderbeke, 1996). The risk is also higher for women than for men (full-time and part-time together). Nevertheless, the unemployment risks for part-time working women show to be lower than for full-time working women. This could be due to high female part-time employment in specific tertiary and quaternary sectors that realise substantial productivity gains by employing part-time workers. The higher productivity (and relatively lower wages) for part-time workers would explain their lower unemployment risk.

Irregular work as the only alternative to unemployment has also particularly been observed in the UK (Cook, 1998). Between 1984 and 1994, while part-time work rose by 24%, it rose by 88% for male workers, and only 15% for women. However, in the group of part-time working men, 50% were under 25 years old (the majority being students). In the case of women, more than 50% were over 40 years old. In this way, many of the young Britons enter the labour market under biased conditions (Neathey and Hurstfield, 1995). Finally, it has been observed in the UK how employers tend to hire part-time workers, because they can increase the number of hours they work without incurring salary and benefit costs. If they hire a full-time worker they would have to pay overtime rates (Lucas, 1997). The majority of employers opt to hire part-time workers because they save costs (Dex and McCulloch, 1995).

The ambiguous relation between irregular work and employment chances on the ordinary labour market is most clear in the case of young people in Spain and in the UK. Young people have to accept irregular work if they want to have a chance on the labour market, while the inclusive effect of this type of work is also very limited. Spanish young people, who leave school at the age of 16 to enter the labour market do it under very precarious contract conditions. Another characteristic that defines precarious temporary contracts in relation to people that receive them is the lack of training, in many cases. Education is a central element in relation to job access. Young people with the highest levels of education occupy the most qualified jobs (Garrido Medina, 1996). On this point it is worth noting that it is not just a lack of training among some sectors of the population, but that to this big problem we must add the scarcity of qualified jobs (Martín Artiles, 1997).

In the UK in 1994, women between 55 and 59 years with low levels of education represented 52% of the total women working on an irregular basis. Women aged between 21 and 24 years under the same educational conditions represented 13% of the total (Walby, 1997). The precarious type of employment (basically very short time contracts without social rights) affecting many young Spanish people has meant that during the last decade different labour policies were directed toward the promotion of jobs for youth. At that time, temporary contracts proliferated as an element to include them in the labour market, reducing in this way the difficulties at the moment of finding that first job. Between 1990 and 1991 the minimum period for a temporary contract increased; consequently, minimum social rights also increased (closely related to the time factor) (Garrido, 1996).

In Denmark, the Netherlands and Belgium, contractual working conditions of irregular workers have improved, by and large, leading to workers' rights that come close to rights linked to standard work. Career chances on the other hand are quite limited. In the UK the basic rights to work, and related to part-time work, were not extended until February 1995, and still are deficient in comparison to standard work. In this way, it is difficult to look at part-time work as inclusive overall (Dex and McCulloch, 1995; Walby, 1997; Cook, 1998). A big barrier for qualification and work rights that flexitime workers have is presented by the legal obligation to work for the same employer for one year before getting statutory rights.

However, formal rights are not enough. In the Netherlands, workers in flexible jobs without stable contracts have a lot more trouble satisfying the requirements for receiving unemployment benefits than those who have definite contracts. In spite of these difficulties, the majority of the workers found in flexible jobs have legal insurance. Some categories of workers that work in a flexible way cannot accumulate rights or benefits during certain periods of time. On this point, many employers who hire temporary workers do not inform these workers on legal insurance, partly because they are not informed themselves (Baenen and Bosch, 1997).

All in all, one could propose that, from the perspective of double income households, irregular work can play an inclusive role when it is used as a supplementary source of income. As an income base, however, it is unsure and offers few prospects. From an individual point of view the reservations towards irregular work are even more clear: risks of poverty are quite real if one has to rely on this income source and the little social security it offers.

Employment programmes and training

Employment programmes are state-paid and focus on alternative ways of inclusion through work. In Denmark, Belgium and the Netherlands there are large-scale, institutionalised and funded measures for this type of work, together with non-governmental organisation (NGO) social economy projects. In the UK there are similar measures, but with much less coverage. In Portugal and Spain measures are limited to social economy projects linked to city councils following workers' strategies. Whereas in Spain cooperatives of workers are salient, autonomous employment is more common in Portugal. Until now social economy projects have often suffered from uncertain financial resources and very unequal results.

The advantages of employment programmes are quite clear, as they combine two goals with one action: unemployment is reduced, while demanded services are supplied. Most of the subsidised employment in the social profit sector is an expression of these goals. When the services are supplied to groups in danger of exclusion, the same groups are even helped twice. Local services are supplied in deprived city areas. Social enterprises recycle material or provide warm meals.

Problems with employment programmes are often related to those programmes that mainly or exclusively focus on the offer and demand sides of services, instead of analysing their implications for people's careers. One way of evaluating employment programmes, then, is to look at the access to regular employment that they give (see also Chapter Five).

In Denmark, most of the programmes for subsidised jobs focus eventually on regular employment. In fact the dominant point of view in this country is that participation in regular work is the best method of including excluded people. Subsidised jobs in the private sector achieve a better entry to long-term employment than jobs in the public sector. In one of these studies it was observed how 40-50% of the people who had participated in subsidised work or training had not improved their opportunities of getting regular employment (Bach et al, 1998). Another study showed how 7% of the unskilled long-term unemployed had never received an offer for a subsidised job, while 20% of them had not received such an offer since 1990 (SID and Det Regionale Arbejdsmarkedsraad, Arhus Amt, 1998).

Nevertheless, employment programmes most importantly should give workers a feeling of usefulness and direction in their lives. The latter could – but not necessarily should – imply access to regular employment. All in all, at least three policy elements are involved in helping people in making progress in their work, or in other terms, in developing their human capital:

- ameliorating the terms of employment;
- restricting subsidies to a limited period thereby promoting transfer to regular work;
- guidance or route counselling.

First, ameliorating the terms of employment has been a widespread practice in the Netherlands and Belgium. The Dutch Melkert 1 programme of the 1990s aimed typically for jobs in a regular employment environment. Nevertheless, participants often felt caught in a participation trap with low income, frustrated ambitions and a stigma from colleagues in 'real' jobs. In 1999 the Melkert 1 scheme was transformed into the so–called I/D-job scheme, which has more incentives for people to find jobs outside the scheme and which allows for a higher income ceiling, particularly for jobs targeted at scheme exit. A basic problem is that improvements in employment terms can sometimes be suspected of being *pro forma*. For example, Belgian PWA (Plaatselijk Werkgelegenheidsagentschap – local employment agency) jobs – which offer occasional service work for the very long-term unemployed – are legally defined as formal work while also foreseeing employment training. In practice, however, the PWA-workers remain unemployed and have very little social security.

Second, subsidy periods have been restricted. This can involve the subsidised individual's employment and the subsidised organisation. In Flemish WEP (Werkervaringsplan – work experience plan) projects, for example, young unemployed are given a one year contract in a Third System Organisation (a private organisation; see Chapter Five) in order to combine some work experience with small training programmes. Also, in insertion enterprises according to the Walloon formula, people are given an impetus in training or work experience, then launching them into another employment: the subsidy to the individual is temporal, while the subsidy period to the organisation is undefined. The subsidy can be temporary while the employment is permanent. Insertion enterprises according to the Flemish model are an example: here people have to be made competitive at the same time as their organisation has to become profitable. In the Belgian INPART research, the results of temporary subsidy systems combining work and training turned out to be quite motivating for the people involved (see Chapter Five of this volume). Insertion enterprises according to the Flemish model in particular actually use subsidies to increase people's human capital while giving them a contract for an undefined period. After all, temporary employment programmes require a lot of investment from the jobseekers that are addressed. They are asked to invest in training programmes and in new working skills – like managers of their own future career (Du Gay, 1999) – while their actual situation might be very uncertain.

Third, subsidised work programmes stress the importance of guidance. This has been a major improvement in employment programmes, since it involves focusing on the worker's needs instead of the mere coordination between offer and demand in employment. Nevertheless, in this respect too, policy can have an ambiguous nature. In Belgium, each person under 25 years of age who does not have a high school diploma and has been unemployed for five months is obliged to undergo intensive training. These young unemployed first go through a process of assessment after which an individual action plan is made which may contain several measures, such as practising job interviews, job-search training, vocational training or work experience (NAP Belgium, 1999). A similar approach is used in the Dutch comprehensive approach for young unemployed up to the age of 23. The Jobseekers' Employment Act stipulates that an individual action plan should be developed for the young unemployed as soon as they register as jobseekers. All young unemployed who have not found a job within a year after registration are offered an additional job (NAP the Netherlands, 2000). Both countries are now introducing similar approaches for older unemployed. Therefore, during 1999-2000 all Belgian unemployed aged 25-45 who have been unemployed for 12 months and do not hold a high school diploma will be offered guidance programmes. Looking at the Belgian and Dutch active measures, sanctions for declining activation offers have been introduced as well. Surprisingly, the National Action Plans (NAPs) of both countries leave this issue completely undebated (for a discussion of activation policies, see Chapter Three).

Unpaid work

From a citizen's perspective voluntary work offers the chance to feel appreciated. A great deal of social life is carried out in, and made possible by, the associative tissue, whether involving cultural, political or other activities. Certainly, belonging to a focus group or association may become the centre of one's social life. Every association attracts members with similar interests, beliefs or concerns, and in some instances sharing a common urban territory. From the societal perspective the voluntary sector is paying an increasing contribution in many areas in general and in social welfare in particular. Not only the people involved in voluntary work experience a sense of belonging and inclusion by the reinforcement of social bonds, but also the work carried out by some associations can contribute to other individuals' inclusion[10].

Each of the countries analysed are experiencing increased importance of voluntary work. For example, the Danish government has acknowledged that some of the serious social problems, such as homelessness and drug abuse problems, can be better worked out through the incorporation of voluntary work in the existing programmes. Therefore, voluntary work is gaining space in helping to deal with exclusion problems. On the one hand, those who are excluded (or are in danger of becoming excluded) can be engaged in voluntary work, and on the other hand, unpaid voluntary work is realising social needs in general or specifically helping excluded people in need. One of the few studies on the subject showed that people developing unpaid tasks have almost the same chances of getting ordinary employment or start training/education as those involved in other forms of activation. In recent years, there have been government attempts to give voluntary work a higher priority. Unpaid work has for many participants been accompanied by inclusion in social life, and even by inclusion in the regular labour market.

In the Netherlands, given the importance of voluntary work as a tool for social participation, a number of experiments have taken place under the Social Assistance Act of 1996: the Melkert 3, or Social Activation Scheme (see Chapter Five). The experiments primarily aim at stimulating labour-market participation and/or preventing or combating exclusion through participation in unpaid work. For some participants, the Melkert 3 scheme is considered as a step towards labour-market participation. Conversely, for others the reasons for participating in the programme are not directly related to the labour market. According to these participants, Melkert 3 is very useful in the creation and enlargement of social networks and as a satisfying way of spending one's time. Especially single mothers see the social activation scheme as a way to combine childcare tasks with activities outside the home.

In the UK, voluntary work has also been expanding within society. About 25% of the total British population do voluntary work each year. Time–budget studies (for example, Gershuny, 2000) show that the leisure time available to most people in Britain has substantially increased since the 1950s and that most choose to use time gained outside, rather than inside, the home. As in most countries, participation in voluntary organisations has increased considerably in the last decades, especially among the female population. However, although Britain possesses a good deal of volunteering, it is not a uniform society in terms of participation in organisational networks. This situation is polarising over time. In 1959, working class citizens participated to the same degree as the middle class, belonging on average to about 62% of voluntary associations. In 1990, this figure dropped to 45%. Volunteering, therefore, confronts the problem in Britain that the social capital gained from such activity is unevenly distributed, reinforcing rather than mitigating the social inequalities produced by unemployment (which hits the working class hardest). In practice, therefore, those not already possessing high skills are left to carry out marginal tasks, which do not require high levels of ability and are of minimal value in improving skill-levels or employment prospects.

In Portugal, a wide range of strategic services and support activities for day-to-day needs is provided neither by the state nor by the market but by common people and by voluntary organisations through voluntary and unpaid work. However, it was not until recently that researchers have shown an interest in voluntary work and the associative life in voluntary organisations. Research on unpaid work was mainly focused on housework, petty commerce and handicraft. In the area of welfare, the voluntary organisations are being increasingly supported and financed by the state to compensate for the gaps in public provision. This is the case for about 3,000 private non-profit institutions of social solidarity that are recognised as agencies of the Portuguese social protection system and combine voluntary unpaid work with professional work. Unfortunately, as in the British case, it seems that the opportunities for improving life chances through voluntary work are meagre. The participation inside voluntary organisations of technical personnel and of the beneficiaries or users is kept to a minimum, while the leaders tend to monopolise the most relevant jobs.

In Spain, voluntary work has expanded largely since the return of democratic institutions in the late 1970s. For years, the creation of voluntary associations developed without coordinated programmes. To coordinate the several policies around volunteering existing in this country, a legal framework (State Plans of Volunteers) was set up in 1997 with the purpose of establishing the necessary mechanisms and instruments so that volunteering benefits the people that volunteer, the organisations and the whole of society. As in the other societies examined, voluntary work has entered the areas of social services making an important contribution to the programmes against exclusion. Coordination is, however, in the hands of municipal councils who can either enhance or lessen the impact of voluntary work in society. Within this context, a debate exists about whether unpaid activities affect paid ones. Some sectors of the population see how unpaid activities cause disloyal competition to the formal sector. For example, one third of the population surveyed in a study for Catalonia perceived voluntary work as a threat to formal jobs.

In Belgium, 'empowerment' of low-income groups through voluntary work is an uncertain strategy. Whereas employment policies are very much oriented to reduce (or to solve) the high rate of unemployment, they are not so much concerned with underemployment or the unequal chances and incomes of different groups on the labour market. As a result, voluntary work by the unemployed receiving benefit is regarded very suspiciously.

Finally, the relation between unpaid work – in particular voluntary work – and inclusion has an ambiguous nature. In Denmark, the Netherlands and Belgium, primarily, voluntary work is reckoned as a way to gain work experience and esteem for the enlargement of social networks. By contrast, in Britain or Portugal for instance, the low possibilities that low-qualified and unemployed have in developing their skills limit their chances of finding a non-routine job. The Spanish case falls somewhere between the two.

Informal work

Informal activities have always existed. There is a variety of forms in which these activities occur in industrial societies in general and in Europe more specifically. Chapter Two of this volume distinguishes between several forms of informal work. In this chapter we concentrate on informal work as paid informal exchange, that is on work that is paid without being declared, including informal activities carried out by people who may be formally employed in the labour market. In the latter, an autonomous exchange work based on social reciprocity takes place. Both types can be seen as an expansion of survival strategies within a general frame of informalisation, in Europe since the 1980s, partly as a result of the general emergence of post-industrial societies (Mingione, 1991, p 88). However, the first type affects more the transformation of standard work into non-standard work. For the unemployed the informal economy is no doubt important in terms of expanding survival strategies and widening the scope for improving life chances. This is even more so if unemployment benefit or social benefit is insufficient or non-existent. For those that have access to social benefits it supplies a (necessary) supplementary income, while for those that have no access to such a benefit (refugees, marginal people) it supplies a basic revenue. Through prosumption and collective use of capital goods, it also helps to reduce consumption costs.

It would be misleading to interpret the expansion of informal work only in terms of the need for income of those who are employed in informal activities. It has been argued that informalisation of work has to be related to present social change and therefore it needs to be considered in relation to the effects of the uneven spread of advanced technologies over different geographical areas, and the exploitative use that corporate restructuring can make of informal work (Castells, 1989, in Mingione, 1991, p 90). However, as Mingione has argued, "the existence and diffusion of informal activities of various kinds in different contemporary societies do not *per se* imply social crisis or a new pattern of development" (1991, p 97). It could be argued that informal activities have been present all along in industrial society, as sectors of the economy that remained outside the regular labour market. For example, family business and self-employment although regulated have had more room for developing social reciprocity activities that were not incorporated as formal labour. What is particularly important is to stress the negative consequences of the unequal distribution of different kinds of work in society in general and within the household in particular. Therefore in some contexts, large numbers of non-standard jobs can have the counterpart of high levels of youth unemployment as parents take informal employment either as the primary source of income or as a complementary income while the young experience constraints in entering formal and informal labour markets. This fact has been observed in Southern Italy and in Spain. In these societies the interrelation becomes apparent between informal employment and compact kinship and community reciprocity relations in order to absorb the long time spent in working and self-provision activities (Mingione, 1991, pp 162-5). In Southern Europe in general, there has traditionally been a high tolerance of tax evasion and high levels of informal economy[11].

On the other hand, in many contexts the informal economy (meaning informal employment and undeclared activities) interconnects with the formal economy, creating networks of companies that fluctuate between formality and informality. Spain and the Netherlands were two such contexts in our study. In Spain research shows that the borders between formal and informal economy are in some cases very diffuse (Martinez and García, 1985; CC.OO, 1987). In this country it is possible to develop networks of small businesses that use self-employment, subcontracting and piecework in such a way that the informal and formal business completely intertwine (Alòs and Jódar, 1993; Jódar et al, 1994). The relevance of networks for the relation between formal and informal employment has been observed in other societies. For example, in the Netherlands, where informal activities influence profits made in the formal sector by subcontracting orders to informal entrepreneurs (Rath, 1995). Here, however, two salient types of informal employees have been observed. One type is composed of relatively well-educated workers who use informal employment as a stepping stone to a better position in the labour market. The other type represents immigrants with lower formal education for whom working in the informal economy becomes a dead-end-job (Kehla et al, 1997, p 44).

It is sometimes said that informal work is a result of economic crisis and increasing unemployment. In the UK, for example, it has been reported that many people who became unemployed in the last decade entered the informal economy (Parker, 1982). In this way, the informal economy may be considered a support for the unemployed (Robson, 1988). Similar data has been found for

Denmark, where there appears to be less cultural approval of tax avoidance (Mortensen, 1995). Spanish research has shown, however, that a distinction needs to be made between enterprises that had submerged as a result of financial constraints creating a vertical decentralisation model by which a network of businesses is generated on the one hand, and newly created enterprises, independently of other existing companies, on the other (Toharia and Muro, 1994). Whereas in the first case the background may be economic crisis, in the second this is not necessarily true. In both cases, however, a 'local system of companies' emerged, that is a network of companies and interconnections that are constituted in a locality with a clear activity specialisation. This local system is stable and involves a strong integration of both formal and informal enterprises and activities (Alòs and Jódar, 1993; Jódar et al, 1994). In his pioneering research Ray Pahl (1988) has demonstrated that, in the UK context, the unemployed have more trouble in getting involved in informal activities than those who work or are closely related to the formal labour market. Therefore the conclusion to be drawn is that informal employment is primarily a means of accumulating advantage for those already in employment and that the number of regular 'working claimants' accounts for a very small proportion of all informal employees (EIU, 1982; Pahl, 1984; Howe, 1990; Warde, 1990; Morris, 1994). However, with the increasing numbers of unemployed workers a traditionally Fordist productive economy like the UK has experienced an expansion of informal, badly paid jobs.

Our research has identified the need to distinguish between different categories of unemployed due to the significant variations in their participation in informal employment. Morris (1995) argues that the short-term or temporary unemployed are much more included into the subsystem of informal work than the long-term unemployed, perhaps because the short-term or temporary unemployed retain many of the contacts, resources and skills which they have gained from their formal employment. However, it is not only the extent of participation that is important to consider when examining the relationship between employment status and informal employment. There is also the issue of the nature or quality of the informal employment undertaken.

From the point of view of the household, however, informal work cannot be seen as a general compensation for formal work. As a matter of fact, households that are involved in formal work profit most by supplementary informal work. Access to informal work varies a lot among the unemployed, due to differences in neighbourhood opportunities and in family and acquaintance networks (Pahl, 1984). Formal work connections prove to be the best instruments to have a good access to informal work. Short-term unemployed usually have an access to their former formal work and continue to have some access to the informal work it offers. Long-term unemployed, however, lose this access, together with the informal resources it can offer. Therefore, as was pointed out in Chapter Two, there is an unequal distribution of inclusion between unemployed and employed into the subsystem of informal work, as demonstrated by Pahl (1984). Finally, the question is what type of informal activities people engage in. In the Spanish context, the formally employed have more access to, and embark on more autonomous non-routine activities, profiting from both formal and informal work. The unemployed, on the other hand, are more orientated towards routine work and monotonous informal work (VV.AA, 1991).

Informal employment, therefore, is not solely a response to economic circumstances and indeed, when households are in financial crises, the most common responses are either to cut back on expenditure or to seek income-generating activities. In a study of Kirkcaldy, Main (1994) examines how respondents deal with financial crises in the British context. Non-labour-market responses are most frequently mentioned. For example, the most popular strategy is to cut back on luxuries, followed by cutting back on necessities, giving up holidays, receiving financial help from family and/or friends, working overtime, taking a second job, the partner taking a second job. The implication, therefore, is that labour-market responses such as informal employment are not a primary coping strategy adopted by people when dealing with a financial crisis. Instead, their principal response is to reduce expenditure rather than try to generate more income. Consequently, even if the unemployed engage in informal employment for economic motivations primarily, this does not make informal employment a principal coping strategy used by the unemployed. Any additional income received, moreover, is likely to come from kinship networks as loans or gifts rather than from informal employment (Morris, 1993). In contrasting European contexts, such as Portugal where deruralisation has taken place much later than in the UK and in an uneven form, other coping strategies are present, such as investing in primary solidarity networks. (This is clearly shown in Chapter Six of this volume.)

The informalisation thesis that emphasises a new organisation of work based on the reorganisation of institutions related to the introduction of new technologies, on the one hand, and on the expansion of a large variety of economic activities interrelated with and functional to the global economy on the other hand needs, therefore, to be empirically tested. Different societies respond in different ways to informal work practices. Often informal practices are only functional to local economies. In many other instances there is a well-developed web of organised production involving both formal and informal work. In Denmark, where studies have assessed the value of this economy to be 3% of its GNP, it was found that more than half of the total Danish population does not want to be involved in moonlighting work, while only 38% were willing to do so if they have the opportunity (Mortensen, 1995). In Spain and Portugal, estimates varied. However, in some localities and activities, employment has flourished in the informal sector. For example, it is estimated that in Spain one in five of the self-employed workers is operating within the irregular market (Toharia, 1994). The widespread practice of informal employment in Portugal and Spain that traditionally developed around particular types of work organisation, mainly self-employment (see endnote 11), more recently can partly be explained in relation to labour-market changes in which the section of workers in informal employment without associated economic rights expanded after the industrial restructuring of the late 1970s, generating a division between 'insiders' (or workers with economic rights) and 'outsiders' (workers in precarious jobs and in the informal economy without rights associated with the job). While little creation of permanent, well-protected jobs occurs in these countries, employment has flourished in the informal sector. This sector is estimated to be about 25% of GDP in Portugal and Spain (*The Economist*, 1987). In Belgium, it has been estimated that the informal economy represents between 10% and 15% of GNP, putting this country close to the Southern European societies in terms of informalisation of employment and activities. Finally, in the UK estimates are between 6% and 10% (European Commission, 1995).

Moreover, there are other implications of the expansion of informal work. For informalisation is also an instrument of exercising power. Although it is presented as a way to generate autonomy within the rhetoric on the virtues of the new organisation of work, the fact is that informalisation disaggregates people in a complex web of tasks to be done under considerable time-pressure: 'we are all victims of time and place'. In this context there is an absence of the 'other' as a real face-to-face connection with those whom lack of agreement or even conflict needs to be acknowledged. The use of 'us' becomes more symbolic than real as there is little common identity developed among workers who develop superficial communities (Sennett, 2001). Not only the absence of accompanying economic rights renders the recipients highly vulnerable to all sorts of abuse and exploitation, there is also an increasing difficulty for the worker to envisage a way out of informal work, with the danger of falling into a vicious circle of vulnerability.

There is, then, the danger of carrying all too positive consequences of inclusion into the system of informal economy such as, for example, the Third Italy[12], as models for economic development applicable to other societies. Therefore, the well-developed network of enterprises embedded into a relatively prosperous community life becomes an ideal type from which most experiences deviate to a large extent. On the one hand, it can be argued that the informal economy offers considerable room for inclusion as it often operates within systems of social networks. On the other hand, extensive research illustrates the need to evaluate the human, social and political costs of some types of informal work before considering them as potential instruments for national policies (Narotzky, 2001).

However, the question remains: how is one to measure the inclusive value of social networks within the informal sector? How are informal social networks structured in different social systems, and how exclusive or inclusive are those networks? As we pointed out earlier in this chapter, it is crucially important to find out who is included and excluded in each particular context, and the extent to which informal networks enhance or mitigate processes of disqualification and disaffiliation (Madanipour et al, 1998) leading to a deterioration of life chances.

Conclusion

In our review of standard work and its 'alternatives', the inclusive effects of work have appeared to be moderate but systematic. Standard work offers very clear advantages, in terms of both inclusion into a system of consumption and income maintenance, as well as inclusion into social networks. Whether or not they are in the Fordist system of production or regionally bound small and medium-sized enterprises, workers benefit from continuity and career perspectives in standard work. There are also, of course, badly paid standard jobs that, being the sole source of income, can cause problems for households. Furthermore, low job sovereignty and long or irregular working hours can seriously jeopardise meeting individual and family needs. Households with two adults working full-time are the most prominent in experiencing time–budget problems. In this respect, the aim for higher consumption standards reduces time available for family life and for participation in the cultural and political spheres. Children and households *in se* are clearly negatively affected by this life pattern.

Alternative work formulas such as part-time work and informal services can offer more possibilities in bringing equilibrium to paid work and domestic work, and to broad-spectrum social and local contacts. In Northern Europe at least, the working conditions for part-time workers have been improved, offering in principle a social protection proportionally comparable to full-time work. In comparison to standard work, however, a large part of non-standard work forms offer less sovereignty and are less remunerated. Similarly, the more interesting forms of voluntary work or informal work are more often carried out by people who already have a standard job. In this sense, the alternative possibilities of inclusion are 'pirated' by those who do not need them the most. Non-standard work forms might also give little access to the career possibilities standard jobs are offering. In this way liberty is gained at a very high price. Lack of perspective is most prominently found among the unemployed working on a voluntary basis and in subsidised employment programmes. With this lack of perspective it is quite embarrassing that in the political discourse on flexibility and activation job-seekers and subsidised workers are expected to be the entrepreneurs of their own careers (Du Gay, 1999).

The most obvious conclusion, then, is that different types of work and employment can be situated on a continuum: on the one side, well-paid standard work, offering the easiest access to inclusion; on the other, precarious, badly paid and unprotected work that gives very limited possibilities for inclusion. We have, however, tried to portray the creation of virtuous circles in which a person can start with a non-standard job and find paths to move from conditions of insecurity and vulnerability into conditions of security and inclusion with institutional help.

For this latter purpose it might then be useful to distinguish two sides of inclusion. On the one side, the cooperation of family and kin solidarity, the pooling of income within the household, the impact of institutional measures, as well as the support of voluntary work, prevent people in conditions of economic vulnerability from following a desperate and dramatic career towards exclusion with no return. In this sense resources provided by income opportunities and social networks developed within the informal economy offer ways of inclusion in communitarian terms. Nonetheless, real options must be available for individuals to build up enhancing trajectories, since community bonds without options can be oppressive (something that feminists have realised for a long time).

On the other side, however, all formally paid work – whether standard or non-standard – clearly offers a widening of people's action possibilities. In this respect the inclusive effect of irregular, informal and subsidised work is very clear. Full inclusion via work, however, also requires enduring relations within the work sphere, which non-standard work forms have difficulties in offering. A sense of belonging and identification is needed. In general, and since workers do the same tasks but in different working conditions, solidarity between workers is diminished (Vilrokx, 1999). Bonds to work – as Sennett (1998) explains – involve a compromise that is able to assume differences over time. To repeat the point made at the beginning of this chapter: *options without bonds become meaningless*.

All in all this stresses the importance of people's identity and long-term perspectives. People can sometimes gain more resources in situations where they are less well-off in terms of formal pay and social security. INPART has shown that virtuous circles can develop when people have the possibility to engage in work that they choose, even if they earn little momentarily (the case in the Netherlands), or when they have been involved in training programmes that are according to their needs and aspirations and therefore provide possibilities for action and enhance capabilities (as we observed in Belgium). The bonds that make the work experience not only inclusive, but also enduring are well-portrayed in this book's study of Spanish cooperatives (Chapter Seven). There the reader will see that for inclusion responsibilities count as much as rights. Sennet (1998) wonders, as we do, if the crucial question in feeling part of society is: "Who needs me?"

Notes

[1] An example in the job market could be the closure exercised by the trade unions in defence of long-standing male workers against the entrance of women and young workers in some societies.

[2] In his classic work, *Citizenship and social class and other essays* (1950), T.H. Marshall set forth the compelling argument that all citizens are of equal worth and therefore universally entitled to a minimum standard of living. Linking civil citizenship with social welfare and with work, Marshall maintained that the universal provision of education, health, social security and welfare benefits leads to the development of full citizenship.

[3] These categories were established in Chapter Two.

[4] ESOPO stands for Evaluation of Social Policies against Social Exclusion at the Local Urban Level. The results of this comparative research that analysed minimum income policies in thirteen European cities have been published in Saraceno (2002).

[5] For a more detailed analysis of the characteristics that entail this welfare regime, see Andreotti et al (2001).

[6] There is a current debate in both academic and policy making circles concerning the increasing diversification of work and employment. A segment of this debate concerns the transformation of work-related identities (Sträth and Wagner, 2000). This debate is important because it touches one of the objectives of this chapter, which is to reflect on the inclusionary power of work.

[7] There is a wide literature on social rights and work. One of the authors defending the importance of extending economic rights attached to work in order to create decent work and living conditions is Amartya Sen; for a synthesis of her position see Sen (2000). The following chapters in this book will explore the consequences of some types of non-standard work for the lives of workers and their families.

[8] In both countries (as will be discussed later in this chapter; see also Chapter Five) activation programmes provide opportunities for increasing self-esteem and new opportunities to learn as well as inclusion in social networks. In Denmark the participants in activation programmes who were placed in the private sector proved to be more successful in getting a job in the primary labour market or entering further education than those placed in the public sector (Hansen et al, 1998). In the Netherlands, the evaluation of activation programmes showed that although initially some recipients could profit by the programme according to expectations, the longer they participated in the programme the more critical (s)he became, as by participating in the programmes they felt excluded from entering the primary labour market (van Berkel et al, 1998).

[9] Rigid labour laws protected male workers who were heads of the family, undermining the possibilities of employment for women and young people. The high rates of female and youth unemployment and their exclusion from the labour market has been functional to maintaining the system and reinforced the familistic culture (see Andreotti et al, 2001).

[10] The ESOPO research conducted by Saraceno (2002) shows that the role played by third sector institutions in local policies against poverty is becoming more salient. This is happening due to the fact that there is an extended challenge of social integration in all cities included in the study to create comprehensive public intervention as well as to establish new relationships between the institutionalised, bureaucratic forms of public action and more flexible, informal ways of dealing with social problems. However, the large variety of third sector institutions call for caution in drawing mechanistic

conclusions about the place and role of the third sector in the local welfare mix (see Saraceno, 2002, pp 35-81).

[11] In these countries the informal sector has historically been linked to the existence of a large proportion of self-employed workers, micro enterprises and subsistence economies. The increase in unemployment these countries experienced during the 1980s propelled the expansion of the informal sector even more (see Pugliese, 1993).

[12] The Third Italy model has been elaborated on the basis of the work of Bagnasco (1977). The analysts of this model identify the existence of an industrially defused region within a network of medium-size towns located mainly in the Emilia-Romagna region. The type of industries are small and medium size that, in combination with self-employment, have developed cooperation among them as well as life chances for families and communities. This context has generated continuous growth and redistribution (see Bagnasco, 1977).

References

Alòs, R. and Jódar, P. (1993) 'Estudi de l´economia sumergida a la industria textil', Unpublished paper, Barcelona: CERES.

Alòs, R. and Jódar, P. (1997) 'La descetralizació productiva, motor de sistemas locals d'empresa. Esutdí de dos casos: Mataró l Santa Coloma de Gramanet', in Papers No 51, pp 137-47.

Andersen, J. et al (1993) *Medborgerskab. Demokrati og politisk deltagelse*, Copenhagen: Systime.

Andreotti, A., Garcia, S., Hespanha, P., Kazepov, Y. and Mingione, E. (2001) 'Does a South European model exist? Some evidence of its presence', *Journal of European Area Studies*, vol 9, no 1, pp 43-63.

Atkinson, A. (1998) 'Social exclusion, poverty and unemployment', in A.B. Atkinson and J. Hills (eds) *Exclusion, employment and opportunity*, CASE Paper 4, London: London School of Economics and Political Science, pp 1-20.

Bach, H., Larsen, J.A. and Rosdahl, A. (1998) 'Langtidsledige i tre kommuner', *SFI Rapport*, vol 98, no 9, Copenhagen: Socialforskningsinstituttet.

Baenen, N. and Bosch, L. (1997) *Sociale zekerheid ook voor flexibele arbeidskrachten? Ontwikkelingen op het terrein van flexibilisering en effecten op sociale zekerheid*, Zoetermeer: EIM.

Bagnasco, A. (1977) *Tre Italie: La problematica territoriale dello sviluppo italiano*, Bologna: Il Mulino.

Bourdieu, P. (ed) (1999) *The weight of the world: Social suffering in contemporary society*, Cambridge: Polity Press.

Cantillon, B. and Marx, I. (1995) 'De nieuwe sociale kwestie', *Samenleving en Politiek*, no 7, pp 28-34.

Castells, M. (1989) *The informational city*, Oxford: Basil Blackwell.

CC.OO. (1987) *Mujeres y economía sumergida*, Madrid: Secretaria de la Mujer de Comisiones Obreras.

Christoffersen, M. (1993) *Familiens ændring – en statistisk belysning af familieforholdene*, vol 93, no 3, Copenhagen: Socialforskningsinstituttet.

Cook, J. (1998) 'Flexible employment – implications for gender and citizenship in the European Union', *New Political Economy*, vol 3, no 2, pp 261-77.

Dahrendorf, R. (1979) *Life chances*, London: Weidenfeld and Nicolson.

de Schampheleire, J. and Vilrokx, J. (1998) *Research on inclusion and exclusion*, Belgian INPART WP2 Report.

Derks, A., Elchardus, M., Glorieux, I. and Pelleriaux, K. (1995) 'Wordt vervolgd', *Tijdschrift van het Steunpunt Werkgelegenheid, Arbeid en Vorming*, no 2-3, pp 66-8.

Dex, S. and McCulloch, A. (1995) *Flexible employment in Britain: A statistical analysis*, Equal Opportunities Commission Research Discussion Series No 15, Manchester: EOC.

Duarte, A.M. (1996) *Desemprego e reconstrução de identidades. O caso dos mineiros do pejão*, Research Report, Lisbon: JNICT.

Du Gay, P. (1999) 'In the name of "globalisation": enterprising up nations, organisations and individuals', in P. Leisink (ed) *Globalization and labour relations*, Cheltenham: Edward Elgar, pp 78-93.

EIU (Economist Intelligence Unit) (1982) *Coping with unemployment: The effects on the unemployed themselves*, London: Economist Intelligence Unit.

European Commission, Directorate-General for Employment and Social Affairs (2001) *Employment in Europe*, Brussels: EC.

European Commission, Directorate-General V (1995) *Communication of the Commission on undeclared work*, Brussels: EC.

Eurostat (2001) *Eurostat Yearbook*, Brussels: EC.

Fridberg, T. (1989) 'Danskerne og kulturen', *SFI Rapport*, vol 89, no 8, Copenhagen: Socialforskningsinstituttet.

Fridberg, T. (1994) 'Kultur- og fritidsaktiviteter 1993', *SFI Rapport*, vol 94, no 6, Copenhagen: Socialforskningsinstituttet.

Gallie, D. (1996) 'Skill, gender and the quality of employment ', in R. Crompton, D. Gallie and K. Purcell (eds) *Changing forms of employment. Organisations, skills and gender*, London: Routledge, pp 133-59.

Gallie, D. (2000) *The quality of working life: Is Scandinavia different?*, Working Paper 2000/154, Madrid: Centreo de Estudios Avanzados en Ciencias Sociales, Instituto Juan March de Estudios e Investigaciones.

García, M. and Gómez, A. (1998) *Research on inclusion and exclusion*, Spanish INPART WP2 Report.

García, M. and Gómez, A. (2000) 'Activerend sociaal beleid en arbeidsmarktregulering in Spanje', *Tijdschrift voor Arbeid en Participatie*, vol 21, no 2/3, pp 208-20.

Garrido, M. (1996) *Paro juvenil o deseigualdad*, Geneva: ILO.

Gershuny, J. (2000) *Changing times: Work and leisure in postindustrial society*, Oxford: Oxford University Press.

Glorieux, I., Koelet, S. and Moens, M. (2001) 'Hoe besteden Vlamingen hun tijd?', *Tijdschrift van het Steunpunt Werkgelegenheid, Arbeid en Vorming*, no 1-2, pp 198-201.

Hansen, H., Lind, J. and Møller, I. (1998) *Research on inclusion and exclusion*, Danish INPART WP2 Report.

Holderbeke, F. (1996) '(G)een risicogroep? De positie van laaggeschoolden in de werkgelegenheid', *Nieuwsbrief van het steunpunt WAV*, no 3, pp 6-13.

Holt, H. (1997) 'Tilpasning mellem arbejdsliv og familieliv i Danmark', in J. Bonke (ed) *Dilemmaet arbejdsliv – familieliv i Norden*, *SFI-rapport*, vol 97, no 5, Copenhagen: Socialforskningsinstituttet.

Howe, L. (1990) *Being unemployed in Northern Ireland: An ethnographic study*, Cambridge: Cambridge University Press.

Jódar, P., Madariaga, S., Martori, J.C. and Mendoza, R. (1994) *Estudi sobre el sector de la confecció a Santa Coloma de Gramanet*, Santa Coloma de Gramanet: Grameimpuls.

Kehla, J., Engbersen, G. and Snel, E. (1997) *Pier 80. Een onderzoek naar informaliteit op de markt*, The Hague: VUGA.

Lind, J. and Møller, I (1999) *The labour market in process of change?*, CID Studies No 22, Copenhagen: CID.

Lucas, R. (1997) 'Youth, gender and part-time work – students in the labour process', *Work, Employment and Society*, vol 11, no 4, pp 595-614.

Madanipour, A., Cars, G. and Allen, J. (eds) (1998) *Social exclusion in European cities. Processes, experiences and responses*, Regional Policy and Development Series, London: Jessica Kingsley Publishers.

Main, B. (1994) 'The labour market: friend or foe?', in M. Anderson, F. Bechhofer and J. Gershuny (eds) *The social and political economy of the household*, Oxford: Oxford University Press.

Marshall, T.H. (1950) *Citizenship and social class and other essays*, Cambridge: Cambridge University Press.

Martín Artiles (1997) *Memòria de la investigació:Accès dels joves a l'ocupació. Resultats i conclusions*, Barcelona: Universitat Autònoma de Barcelona.

Martínez, E. and García, M. (1985) *La economía sumergida en la Comunidad Valenciana*, Revista: Papeles de Economía.

Marx, I. (2000) 'Met een subsidie aan het werk. Wat leert evaluatieonderzoek?', *CSB-berichten*, vol 2000, no 6, Antwerp: Centrum voor Sociaal Beleid, Antwerp University.

Mingione, E. (1991) *Fragmented societies*, Oxford: Basil Blackwell.

Mortensen, N. (ed) (1995) *Social integration and marginalisation*, Copenhagen: Samfundslitteratur.

Morris, L. (1993) 'Is there a British underclass?', *International Journal of Urban and Regional Research*, vol 17, no 3, pp 404-12.

Morris, L. (1994) 'Informal aspects of social divisions', *International Journal of Urban and Regional Research*, vol 18, no 1, pp 112-26.

Morris, L. (1995) *Social divisions: Economic decline and social structural change*, London: UCL Press.

Mortensen, N. (1995) 'Mapping system integration and social integration', in N. Mortensen (ed) *Social integration and marginalisation*, Copenhagen: Samfundslitteratur.

Narotzky, S. (2001) 'El afecto y el trabajo', *Archipielago*, no 48, pp 73-7.

Neathey, F. and Hurstfield, J. (1995) *Flexibility in practice: Women's employment and pay in retail and finance*, Equal Opportunities Commission Research Discussion Series No 15, Manchester: EOC.

Oliveira, L. (1998) *Inserção profissional. O caso da reestruturação dos lanifícios da Covilhã*, Lisbon: Edições Cosmos.

Pahl, R. (1984) *Divisions of labour*, Oxford: Basil Blackwell.

Pahl, R. (1988) 'Some remarks on informal work, social polarisation and the social structure', *International Journal of Urban and Regional Research*, vol 12, no 2, pp 247-66.

Parker, H. (1982) 'Social security foments the black economy', *Economic Affairs*, vol 3, pp 32-5.

Paugam, S. (1997) *Integration, précarité et risque d'exclusion des salariées*, December, no 19, Paris: Fondation Nationale des Sciences Politiques, CNRS, Observatoire sociologique du changement.

Pugliese, E. (1993) *Sociología della disoccupazione*, Bologna: Il Mulino.

Rath, J. (1995) 'Beunhazen van buiten: de informele economie als bastaardsfeer van sociale integratie', in G. Engbersen and R. Gabriëls (eds) *Sferen van integratie. Naar een gedifferentieerd allochtonenbeleid*, Meppel: Boom, pp 74-110.

Robson, B.T. (1988) *Those inner cities: Reconciling the social and economic aims of urban policy*, Oxford: Clarendon Press.

Saraceno, C. (ed) (2002) *Social assistance dynamics in Europe: National and local poverty regimes*, Bristol: The Policy Press.

Sen, A. (2000) 'Work and rights', *International Labour Review*, vol 139, no 2, pp 119-28.

Sennett, R. (1998) *The corrosion of character. The personal consequences of work in the new capitalism*, New York, NY: W.W. Norton & Company.

Sennett, R. (2001) 'La flexibilidad laboral', *Archipielago*, no 48, pp 29-36.

Simoens, P., Denys, J. and Denolf, L. (1997) *Les entreprises et le recrutement en Belgique. 1996*, Brussels: Upedi.

Sträth, B. and Wagner, P. (2000) 'After full employment: theoretical and political implications', in B. Sträth (ed) *After full employment: European discussion on work and flexibility*, Brussels: PIE-Peter Lang, pp 261-78.

Tijdens, K. (1999) 'Flexibilisering in het Nederlandse bedrijfsleven. Ontwikkelingen in de jaren negentig', *Bedrijfskunde*, vol 71, no 3, pp 50-8.

Toharia, L. and Muro, J. (1994) 'El empleo irregular en 1993', *Informe FOESSA 1994*, Madrid: Fundación FOESSA, pp 1369-94.

van Berkel, R., Tholen, C. and Valkenburg, B. (1998) *Research on inclusion and exclusion*, Dutch INPART WP2 Report.

Van der Veen, R. (1997) 'Basic income in the Netherlands', *Citizen's Income Bulletin*, no 23, pp 11-13.

Vilrokx, J. (1999) 'Towards the denaturing of class relations', in P. Leisink (ed) *Globalization and labour relations*, Cheltenham: Edward Elgar, pp 57-77.

VV.AA. (1991) *Estudios de economía del trabajo en España. El problema del paro*, Madrid: Centro de Publicaciones del Ministerio de Trabajo y Seguridad Social.

Walby, S. (1997) *Gender transformations*, London: Routledge.

Warde, A. (1990) 'Household work strategies and forms of labour: conceptual and empirical issues', *Work, Employment and Society*, vol 4, no 4, pp 495-515.

Weber, M. (1978) *Economy and society*, Berkely, CA: University of California Press.

Yeandle, S., Gore, T. and Herrington, A. (1999) *Employment, family and community activities: A new balance for women and men*, Dublin: European Foundation for the Improvement of Living and Working Conditions.

FIVE

Inclusion through participation? Active social policies in the EU and empirical observations from case studies into types of work

Henning Hansen, Pedro Hespanha, Carlos Machado and Rik van Berkel

Introduction

Much has been written in this book about the inclusionary and exclusionary potential of work and of special schemes directed at activating people through work (Chapters Two to Four). It was noted repeatedly that social policies – or, to be more precise, activation policies – are driven by the assumption that unemployment is directly linked to exclusion. This assumption is then used to justify that work and welfare systems prioritise employment to pursue inclusion. Rather than promoting inclusion in a wider variety of systems, for example types of work and participation outside the labour market, increasing economic independence by labour-market participation and decreasing social benefit dependency are in many cases the main objectives of these policies.

It was an important objective of our research to shed light on the validity of these assertions by confronting them with the experiences of participants in different types of work and activation schemes. This chapter (and the two that follow it) presents the main results of our case studies into types of work, and in the process reveals the inclusion and exclusion opportunities and risks of various forms of work and participation. Chapter Six analyses these results in terms of what they show about the relations between inclusion in, and exclusion from, various systems of society. Chapter Seven elaborates on one specific case study, an activation programme aimed at 'entrepreneurial activation' which differs considerably from the mainstream activation programmes in the EU. So that overlap of chapters does not occur, this chapter will pay no specific attention to this scheme.

The case studies themselves were not designed as a systematic evaluation of activation programmes and schemes. Types of work, rather than activation programmes, were the central focus of the case studies. These are, of course, closely connected, which explains why various case studies dealt with these programmes. Besides, we also primarily focused on labour-market participation as the 'participation' or 'inclusion standard', and on types of work (voluntary and informal work) that, in most EU countries, do not play a significant role in social policies aimed at promoting inclusion. Secondly, the case studies as a whole were not designed as a large-scale quantitative investigation testing precisely defined hypotheses and aiming at statistical representation, although some of the national case studies fitted this design. The overall aim of the case studies was to map and analyse the diversity of people's experiences, both within and across the types of work being investigated. In order to achieve this objective and to respect the various backgrounds of the partners in the project from a methodologically pluralist point of view, a mix of quantitative and qualitative research methods was used (see Chapter One). Therefore, we did not try to standardise research methods. However, irrespective of whether case studies used surveys or in-depth interviews, a degree of standardisation was reached by using similar items in developing questionnaires. In other words, by using a common framework for the conceptualisation and operation of the concepts of inclusion, exclusion and work (cf Chapter Two), we tried to attain comparable and valid results. Thirdly, in studying the inclusionary and exclusionary potentials of types of work, a 'double perspective' was used. That is, we studied these potentials both from a participant and an 'outsider' point of view (explained in Chapter Two when we referred to subjective and objective approaches of inclusion and exclusion). Not only did we try to find out to what degree inclusion in certain systems (types of work) stimulates or prevents inclusion into other systems (an issue that is treated more systematically in Chapter Six), we were also interested in participants' own experiences and evaluations of the inclusionary and exclusionary potentials of the types of work under observation: to what degree do these types of work meet people's needs in terms of inclusion (or, for that matter, exclusion)?

We distinguished four types of work and participation in the case studies (see Chapter Two, where these types of work and participation have been introduced):

1. The primary labour market;
2. The secondary labour market (a concept that refers here to temporary or permanent subsidised job schemes for unemployed people);
3. Unpaid/informal work;
4. Participation in training and education schemes for the unemployed.

Table 5.1 presents an overview of the case studies, the methodology used and the number of respondents involved in the case studies.

This chapter is structured as follows. To enable the contextualisation of our findings, we begin by paying attention to active social policies in the EU in general, and in the six countries that were involved in the INPART research in particular. This section then elaborates on two types of activation programmes mainly: subsidised employment programmes for unemployed people (the

Table 5.1: INPART research framework: case studies, methods and number of respondents

	Primary labour market	Secondary labour market	Unpaid work	Training and education
Belgium		Local and social economy activities within Third System Organisations *Survey (218)*		Education and work-training in Third System Organisations *Survey (297)*
Denmark	Types of paid work *In-depth interviews and survey (284)*	Activation: subsidised work *In-depth interviews and survey (267)*	Voluntary work *In-depth interviews and survey (22)*	Activation: educational projects *In-depth interviews and survey (39)*
The Netherlands		Subsidised work: Melkert *In-depth interviews (25)*	Unpaid work: Social activation *In-depth interviews(20)*	
Portugal		Occupational programmes *In-depth interviews (20)*		Measure 2, INTEGRAR subprogramme *In-depth interviews (20)*
Spain		Capitalisation of unemployment benefits scheme *In-depth interviews (100)*		
UK	Part-time work *In-depth interviews (23)*		Unpaid (and informal paid) work *Survey (125)*	

'secondary labour market' as we call it in this book), and education and training schemes. This is followed by an elaboration of the types of work under investigation in the case studies. The results of the case studies are then presented, analysing what our findings tell us about the inclusionary and exclusionary potentials of various types of work.

Active social policies in six EU countries: a general overview

Since the Luxembourg Summit that took place in November 1997, all EU member states have agreed to implement a common strategy to fight unemployment, built on four pillars:

- employability;
- entrepreneurship;
- adaptability;
- equal opportunities.

It was developed through a set of guidelines that every member state must follow and convert into an annual National Action Plan (NAP) for Employment.

Although unemployment can be seen as a 'European problem', specific characteristics of the different labour markets are recognised (in terms of employment and unemployment rates, of education and skills of the labour force, of job security and flexibility, of sustainability of labour-market systems, and so on). In addition, these characteristics determine the solutions and the priorities set by each national government. Being a result of a new form of European regulation based on guidelines, benchmarks and systematic monitoring – the so-called 'open method' of coordination – the Luxembourg process provides each member state with a large margin of manoeuvre for the implementation of the strategy according to their particular economic and social situation both in terms of priorities, goals, target groups, resource allocation, timing, and programme contents and duration, as well as in terms of political and ideological foundations of state intervention. However, efforts have been made to make each member state's NAP consistent with the European strategy: targets and deadlines should be clear and quantifiable, peer evaluation of the compliance with the common targets of guidelines was instituted, mechanisms of control such as EC recommendations were created.

A recent overview of member states' employment performance, which coincides with the midpoint in the European strategy implementation, acknowledged that employment had increased in all member states. However, progress was uneven. Employment rates were steadily rising, and in some member states already exceeded the EU target of 70%, but the increase was much less visible in terms of full-time equivalents. In addition, younger people were turning increasingly to the labour market while older workers still tend to exit prematurely. Unemployment has been falling almost everywhere, and some labour markets were showing signs of emerging 'bottlenecks', yet some member states still show worryingly high levels of long-term unemployment and youth unemployment; and regional disparities in unemployment still persist (CEC, 2000a, p 20).

Employability, one of the four pillars of the strategy, remains the most prominent action area. Analysis of the general objective of increasing access to a good job is divided into different principles and goals:

- a preventive approach (in order to combat youth and long-term unemployment and the increased numbers of unemployed persons participating in active measures);
- tax and benefits reform (in order to promote the creation of new jobs);
- the extension and improvement of education and training systems (including

the implementation of lifelong learning and new technology apprenticeship systems);
• the reduction of early school leaving;
• the inclusion of disadvantaged groups into the labour market.

All of these goals, and specifically those related to the move towards more active and preventive policies, have been integrated and implemented by the six countries involved in INPART, albeit at varying rates by different levels of compliance, as a recent assessment of national performances showed (CEC, 2000a).

With respect to implementation of the preventive approach, the best results according to the EC were achieved through the UK's Jobseeker's Allowance. The UK's strategy for tackling youth unemployment includes "new active labour-market policies, the largest of which is the 'New Deal for Young People'" (CEC, 2000a). Based on a strong component of workfare (compulsory attendance), this kind of policy offers employment or training with appropriate support to unemployed young people before they descend into long-term unemployment. Denmark scores 'fairly well' regarding the low rate of young unemployment inflow to long-term unemployment (10%) and 'extremely well' regarding the adult rate (4%). Priority has been given to the improvement of efficiency and quality of activation and to the reduction of possible disincentive effects of early activation on those unemployed having a good chance of finding a job by themselves. In the Netherlands, the preventive approach provides the young unemployed with an individual action plan as well as a subsidised job to those unable to find a job within 12 months. A high rate of inflow to long-term unemployment calls for an improvement of the efficiency of the first stage (individual action plan) and a review of possible disincentive effects on the second stage (subsidised jobs). Portugal and Spain have made progress in implementing earlier intervention measures, but rates of long-term unemployment inflow still remain high. In Belgium, implementation has been unequal both regionally and by target groups; as a result, reduction of rates of inflow progresses slowly (CEC, 2000a, 2001a).

With respect to progress in active labour-market policies, each member state seems to have complied with the common target of raising the number of unemployed persons participating in active labour-market measures to a level of at least 20% (Portugal and the UK being the least effective performers). In terms of expenditure (see also Chapter Three), almost all the countries increased their share of active measures in total national labour-market spending, but training and some other traditional human resource measures saw their relative weight in the total active measures decline (CEC, 2000a, 2001a).

A large set of policies are being deployed to enhance, via demand policies, the participation of unemployed people in the labour market – and, by supply policies, to increase their employability – in the six countries, covering different forms of participation and assuming distinct regulatory positions. In our research, four main forms of participation were distinguished: in the primary labour market; in the secondary labour market; in unpaid/informal work; in education and training. Each of these is dependent on the regulatory strength of the specific policies in terms of legal enforcement, degree of compliance, and social legitimacy.

For the purpose of this chapter we have selected only those policies related to subsidised work and to education and training, as these areas are considered particularly relevant for testing the activation issues.

Subsidised participation

Subsidised participation is a type of policy targeted at unemployed and disabled people who have difficulties in participating, or are unable to participate, in productive activities without subsidies from national or local authorities. The target groups are placed in jobs which, in principle, could be performed by regular employees and the working conditions are often similar to regular conditions. The jobs are mostly additional and subsidised by public funds. Due to a lack of economic profitability they would (in principle) not have been created in the absence of public support, and members of the target groups would not have occupied them without help from the employment authorities. In some countries, for example the Netherlands and Denmark, there is a debate about whether all additional jobs are really additional or would have been established anyway. The target groups are mostly long-term and/or low-skilled unemployed or disabled persons who are unable to get a job on their own. We will deal here with the following categories of subsidised participation:

- job placements in the private sector;
- job placements in the public sector or non-governmental organisations (NGOs);
- sheltered jobs;
- insertion enterprises;
- self-employment.

Job placements in the private sector

This category of subsidised participation normally involves additional jobs in a private firm for a limited period of time. All of the six INPART-studied countries have schemes for private job placements.

Usually the purpose of the schemes is reinsertion and enrolment into the labour market. A common feature is wage subsidisation for additional jobs during a period of time (for example six to twelve months). Another form of subsidy is a reduction of the employers' social contributions.

The target groups differ slightly in the different countries. However, the long-term unemployed are generally considered to be the main target group. In some countries the young unemployed and recipients of social assistance/ subsistence allowance are particular target groups.

Job placement in the public sector and NGOs

Job placements in the public sector and NGOs are the most frequent form of subsidised participation. Mostly they involve additional jobs for a limited period of time. This kind of scheme exists in all six participating countries.

The general purpose is, again, reinsertion and enrolment of long-term unemployed people into the secondary labour market. In some schemes, the purpose is activation, but without ambitions of reinsertion into the primary labour market. In general, the reinsertion ambitions of job placements in the public sector are lower than in the private sector. These schemes often have the purpose of meeting social needs or of improving the quality of services. The target groups are normally long-term unemployed and receivers of social assistance benefits. Compared to the target groups of job placement in the private sector, the target groups of public job placements are, generally speaking, the more vulnerable and underprivileged; that is, the very long-term unemployed.

In general, job placement schemes in the public sector and NGOs consist of work and activation in additional jobs or functions. Often, they are jobs in 'soft' areas such as social service, environmental and cultural institutions or social and humanitarian organisations/NGOs. These are areas where subsidisation of employment will have limited consequences for private firms and competition.

Sheltered employment

Most countries have special participation schemes for specific groups of disabled people, often called 'sheltered jobs'. There are a lot of similarities between job placements and sheltered jobs, but the target groups are different. Job placements are meant for able-bodied, unemployed people, while sheltered jobs are for disabled people.

The general purpose of sheltered jobs is reinsertion into employment. They can be jobs on the primary labour market in the private or public sector on special terms according to the disability. However, they can also be special jobs in firms/organisations separated from the regular labour market: sheltered workshops.

Insertion enterprises

In most countries new initiatives are being taken, by both the state and civil society, that function as a platform for marginal workers to enter the labour market. Created under different legal forms (most often as cooperatives or associations), insertion enterprises are societal undertakings aiming to provide training, temporary jobs and job-training activities to their members and clients.

There are various ways to establish and organise insertion enterprises. In Belgium, the insertion enterprises are temporarily subsidised companies that give priority to employment with the legal obligation of having (after three years in full-time-equivalents) at least 30% of people belonging to target groups (the low-skilled) among their employees. In Spain support is provided by fiscal payments and reduction of social contributions. In Portugal training grants are supplied through the insertion enterprises at a level of 70% of the minimum wage.

The general target group is people who are most excluded and have very little access to the labour market.

Self-employment

Self-employment has become a very common form of subsidised work. It has several advantages. It involves work in the private sector, and, at a later stage, the self-employed may be able to provide employment to the unemployed. Self-employment could also be an innovative measure where new products and services are invented and produced. All countries now have self-employment schemes to offer unemployed people.

The general purpose of self-employment schemes is to give the unemployed an opportunity of starting their own enterprise. Moreover, it is hoped that these initiatives will have an employment 'spin-off' effect when the new companies are able to employ other unemployed.

The general form of subsidy to unemployed people who want to be self-employed is by granting them a special benefit instead of unemployment benefit for a certain period, for example, two to three years. There are several modalities of special benefits, including the Spanish capitalisation of unemployment benefits (see Chapter Seven). During the period of support the unemployed person does not have to be available for other kinds of work.

Education and training

In the context of labour-market policies, education emerges as a central instrument for participation, since uneducated and low-skilled workers run a higher risk of becoming unemployed. Moreover, as the demand for low-skilled labour is diminishing, education is seen to be essential for future employment and employability. Therefore, the widespread growth of the number of low-skilled unemployed calls for a steady and increasing development of education, particularly at local level.

It is currently assumed that the separation between education and vocational training is becoming less and less clear. In spite of an emerging general diversification trend in education systems in recent years, there still seems to be a lack of strategic integration of basic education, vocational education and vocational training in different countries aimed at increasing the level of performance of human capital, and improving the opportunities for inclusion into the labour market[1].

Since 1998, the European Employment Strategy has been pressing member states to make their systems of education and training more coherent and more able to improve 'employability'. Together with social partners they are called upon to promote the development of a skilled workforce by adopting comprehensive strategies for lifelong learning, improving initial education, reducing the drop-out rate and developing agreements to increase training provisions. For those categories of persons more vulnerable to unemployment or marginalisation in the labour market, a preventive approach based on individualised assistance and early action has been extended at national level.

Activation is the other key concept in this strategy. Targeted at 20% of the unemployed people, it involves training actions (representing near half of all the participants in active labour-market policies) and a wide range of other measures. However, evaluation results indicate that measures focused on training alone are less efficient than those that combine both work and training (CEC, 2000a).

Since the Lisbon summit in March 2000, particular attention has been given to disadvantaged groups. Positive discrimination in favour of the socially disadvantaged has emerged as a new goal for those facing the increasing risk of being excluded from the use of the new tools in the emerging knowledge-based economy and society. It became clear that the EU assumes a commitment to a socially cohesive Europe, not only in its own right, but also as a factor of economic competitiveness. This included specific goals on education and training as unquestionable tools for combating marginalisation and exclusion; tackling educational disadvantage being one of the eight core challenges according to the Commission (CEC, 2000a, p 2, 2001b, 2001c)[2]. Other developments in education and training refer to an increase in autonomy for those involved in programmes, as well as decentralisation and diversification of education and training systems.

Experience has shown that the most decentralised systems are also the most flexible, the quickest to adapt to changes in the labour market, and hence more able to develop new forms of social partnership. There has been evidence of a decentralisation trend in several countries during the last decade, such as Belgium and Spain where funding as well as definition of objectives are totally decentralised. In Denmark and the Netherlands the definition of objectives and vocational training and education funding are not completely decentralised. In the UK, since the mid-1980s, the competencies of the national authorities have been reinforced vis-à-vis private initiative through decisions on training objectives, the accreditation of occupational standards, the criteria for quality assessment and the resources for public and private training institutions. Finally, in Portugal vocational training and education programmes are nationally funded, although in some of them objectives are defined at a decentralised level.

As an outcome of the trend towards diversification of the educational curricula, described earlier in the chapter, new technological courses were created within secondary education. However, the perception of the risks generated by an excessive specialisation has held governments back from following this diversification trend more openly. Acknowledgement of the need for good preparation and certification of young persons aiming to enter the labour market has led some countries to create vocational courses outside the education system and outside the vocational training system. In Spain, training schools were set up in the 1990s offering two-year courses. In Portugal, training schools offer three-year courses and further job training. They were instituted in the 1980s by social partners (local authorities, employer associations and trade unions) and partly funded through the European Social Fund.

We now turn to a more detailed analysis of the specific and innovative measures in education and training in order to reduce the risk of marginalisation from the labour market in the countries under investigation. Young people, unemployed adults, and employed adults constitute the broader social categories to be covered by new training policies.

Young people

A particular concern is devoted to inexperienced young people, since any delay in the normal age of inclusion into the labour market is considered to increase the risk of unemployment. A number of innovative measures have been taken, and specific targets have been set in the framework of the European Employment Strategy.

Almost all of the six countries are undergoing a strategy of coordination of the different phases of education and training, both in terms of curricula and certification of formal and informal learning. Specific actions on early school leavers (and ethnic minorities, immigrants), focusing on providing additional or special training within flexible curricula have been taken in countries like Belgium, Spain and Portugal (the latter two having particular problems in this area). This includes offering a second chance to people who have not completed basic education or training.

Some measures aim to include young unemployed people into a first temporary job, and to give them work experience and an introduction to the labour market. Very commonly, training and employment under an alternating scheme are combined in order to ease the inclusion of trainees into working life, and simultaneously to develop skills and attitudes in work contexts. A combination of job training and formal education has been used. In Belgium, for instance, a part-time scheme for young people aged between 15 and 18 years old was promoted ('convention premier emploi jeune'). A similar solution (the workshop schools and apprenticeship centres programme) has been adopted in Spain and in Portugal. In Spain, tutoring is a key approach for young people under the Social Guarantee Programmes covering several areas like basic education, career planning, job orientation and training, complementary counselling and training. It is targeted at students over 16 years of age who are in danger of dropping out of the mandatory secondary education or equivalent studies.

Activation of youngsters is an outstanding concern in some countries, such as Denmark. This concern gives rise to specific measures for young people without education. They are encouraged or even forced to attend vocational training courses or to follow an individual education plan. A similar scheme emerged in the UK with the New Deal policies. After six months of unemployment, young people are obliged to choose among several options, one of them being to follow full-time vocational education. In other countries, such as Portugal, compulsion is not so strong and incentive measures are still dominant (pre-apprenticeship grants, level 1 certification awards).

In general, training measures are aimed at making the inclusion of young people into working life easier, and at reducing the number of people that are incorporated in the labour market without a suitable basic education. The cooperation of employer associations and companies in the implementation of measures trying to combine training and employment, such as job training, is quite crucial. For that reason governments or local authorities look for partnerships as a precondition of success. Nevertheless, INPART suggests that companies often appear to be reluctant in assuming such responsibilities whenever governments try to involve employers in enrolling young people, as was reported for Belgium. The lack of cooperation of firms in sharing the costs of the Portuguese apprenticeship programme was also reported.

Unemployed adults

Long-term unemployed workers increasingly share with young people the major part of the resources available for training activities. However, the impact of those activities on the employability of the adults, is weaker than the impact on young people's employability when we take into account the proportion of those trainees that remain unemployed one year after the end of the training activity.

In almost all countries, training courses have been adapted to the particular unemployment condition of the trainees (unemployment duration, welfare status, sector of activity, education, gender, and so on). Continuous training and retraining courses also play an important role, especially for workers in economic sectors in the course of restructuring where the risk of becoming unemployed is high. In Spain, for instance, they involved almost 15% of the waged workers in 1996. In the Netherlands, some training activities were organised by the public employment services together with branches of industry.

Special modalities of training for unemployed workers include training courses, job training, training and employment and substitutional jobs associated to educational leave.

Employed adults

Training programmes and incentives are not confined to unemployed adults. Those in occupation can also benefit from policies to improve employability, reinforce competence and qualifications and encourage labour-market participation, such as training courses, training grants, and 'training while working'.

Lifelong learning is a new key concept associated with adult education. The recent *Memorandum on lifelong learning* (CEC, 2000b) has launched a debate on needed strategies and practical ways to foster lifelong learning for all, and the EC included this new objective in the guidelines for the member states in the framework of the European Employment Strategy. Member states are required to develop comprehensive and coherent strategies for lifelong learning, covering all the different education and training systems and involving the main actors and social partners in order to share responsibilities and negotiate on education and training measures for adult workers. In this framework various measures have been adopted to implement a lifelong learning strategy. Some are targeted precisely at employed adult workers, such as:

- increased opportunities for skilled workers to obtain qualifications in the field of new technologies;
- participation of more unskilled workers in training measures within companies;
- assistance for older workers to continue training;
- the possibility of job rotation for employees undergoing training;
- development of distance learning and adult education;
- development of on-the-job training;
- recognition of experience;
- introduction of individual learning accounts (CEC, 2001d, p 12).

The absence of coordination between the various stages and sectors of education and training, in particular within national governments and between the various other actors, is a major obstacle to the development of comprehensive and coherent lifelong learning strategies (CEC, 2001d, p 15). Denmark, the Netherlands and the UK are reported to be the best performers, by putting in place the main building blocks for national lifelong learning strategies. Despite its efforts, Belgium has not yet fully achieved a strategy to tie to the first group, whereas Spain and Portugal have the least comprehensive and coherent approaches to lifelong learning (CEC, 2001d, p 17).

In this field, for instance, the EC associates best practices with the Learning and Skills Councils in the UK as coherent structures which will help underpin lifelong learning. Further examples are provided by the training courses for disadvantaged groups (including older workers) and job rotation in Belgium, and the mechanisms for the recognition of prior and work-based learning by several countries, notably Belgium, the Netherlands, Denmark and Portugal. However, it is recognised that such tools need to be developed in a more systematic manner to ease movement between different learning systems.

Types of work and the case studies

In the following section, we provide a short description of the types of work under observation in the case studies, with special emphasis on those case studies that dealt with activation programmes. This description deals with the situation during the period in which we carried out our case studies. Since activation programmes change frequently, our descriptions can in some instances differ from what may constitute the current situation.

Primary labour market

Two case studies focused on primary labour-market participation (in the way this concept is used in this book). Of course, the primary labour market is highly differentiated: processes of labour-market flexibility have eroded the notion of a 'regular' or 'standard' job. Nevertheless, social policies often cling to an undifferentiated concept of primary labour-market participation as the best and most desirable form of participation in society.

The Danish case study into primary labour-market participation conducted a survey among a sample of employed people drawn from the national labour-force register. No selection criteria were used with respect to the nature of jobs within this labour-market segment, so that the sample includes, as a result, a variety of jobs in the primary labour market.

The UK case study into this type of work focused on part-time work (less than 30 hours a week), an increasingly regular way of labour-market participation, especially for women, even though often considered as an irregular type of paid work (see Chapter Four), because employment rights of part-time workers can differ considerably from those of full-time workers, for example. This was specifically the case in the UK in the pre-Blair period, during which the UK was exempt from the Social Protocol of the 1992 Maastricht Treaty. Consequently, many of the employment rights directives developed in the EU were not applied in the UK.

Secondary labour market: subsidised work

The secondary labour market (as defined in this book) is a product of active policies, and can involve quite different kinds of programmes, as was shown in the previous section.

The Belgian case study focused on local economy initiatives undertaken by so-called Third System Organisations. These organisations aim to provide goods and services to the local community, and therefore undertake economic activities at the local level. Contrary to private enterprises, profit maximisation or profit generation is not their basic objective. These organisations play an increasingly important role in active policies, since they give particular attention to the problems of disadvantaged persons or groups, either by placing them into the labour market or by providing services (or a combination of both). They are normally subsidised by the state, but may also raise funds from donations or non-commercial loans. Third System Organisations are often involved in partnerships with public or private companies. In some cases, they are born out of specific groups' or communities' needs (for example, special retraining activities for African or Arab women in suburban areas). It should be emphasised that contrary to many nationally implemented active social policies, some of these local initiatives try to develop bottom-up approaches where individual demands are the starting point of labour-market inclusion interventions.

Methodologically speaking, the local initiatives are a mix of three ingredients: a job offer, a training programme, and individual guidance and assistance. The ways these ingredients are mixed and receive attention in specific programmes are an important aspect of the contextualisation of this type of work. Here, we will focus on the more 'work-oriented' projects (the more 'training-oriented' projects will be described under the heading of 'Training and education'). Within the 'work-oriented' projects, we can distinguish the following types of programmes:

- *Work experience:* various kinds of temporary work contracts, combining paid-job experience with preceding or supplementary training. The basis of the payment for training hours is the social benefit, for working hours it is the sectoral minimum wage. Participation usually lasts one to two years.
- *Insertion enterprises:* low-skilled or long-term unemployed people work temporarily on a subsidised contract. These enterprises, though primarily concerned with social and environmental needs, have to be economically profitable. Participation may be permanent, but wage subsidies of the participants are not.
- *Social enterprises:* work with no explicit perspective on an increase in skills or productivity. Most people involved are very long-term unemployed (more than five years) or have been dependent on the subsistence minimum. Work is subsidised at a moderate level but continuously; participation may be permanent.

Both the work-experience projects and the insertion enterprises are meant to prepare people for primary labour-market participation. The case study investigated 25 initiatives in the Antwerp, Liège, Mons and Ghent areas, and Brussels.

One of the Danish case studies involved a survey among a group of activated people dependent on unemployment benefits or social assistance. Although activation of both groups is regulated by different laws in Denmark, the activation programmes are quite similar. Here, we will deal with work-oriented programmes. Work-oriented activation programmes include the following:

- Job training, which may be with private or public employers. Pay and other working conditions should be according to collective agreements applicable to the sector. Employers receive a wage subsidy for each recruited unemployed person. After six months of having received subsidies, a private employer has to employ the unemployed worker without receiving any further subsidy, or should offer the unemployed training.

- Individual job training also involves a temporary job at a private company, a public institution or a semi-public organisation. The employer receives a wage subsidy which may last longer than one year. Conditions in individual job training are rather flexible and working time is set individually. The wage is a special project allowance and should not exceed the maximum rate of unemployment benefits.
- Pool jobs are public sector jobs of up to three years duration for persons who have been unemployed for a period of one year. The main aim of this scheme is to create more permanent jobs to meet social needs or improve the quality of existing services.

With the exception of those involved in job training in the private sector, where no income ceiling exists, the participants in these schemes may not earn more than the maximum rate of unemployment benefits. When full-time wages exceed this limit, working hours are reduced accordingly. Although participation periods may be shorter or longer, the programmes are designed to increase opportunities for inclusion within the primary labour market.

The Dutch case study dealt with the 'extra employment for the long-term unemployed scheme' – or Melkert 1 – introduced in 1995. The aim of this scheme – which has been modified since the completion of our case study – was to enlarge the availability of low-skilled and low-paid jobs in the labour market, while, at the same time, to improve the quality of public services. The jobs were targeted at people who have been unemployed for at least one year. Participation may be permanent, though primary labour-market exit is increasingly being emphasised. Wages were set at a minimum of 100% and a maximum of 120% of the nationally set minimum wage, on the basis of a regular full-time working week. Other labour conditions depended on the collective agreement applicable to the sector in which the Melkert 1 worker was employed. Melkert 1 jobs were fully subsidised. This case study focused on a group of Melkert 1 participants in the city of Rotterdam, which employed over 10% of all Dutch Melkert 1 workers.

The Portuguese case study focused on the Occupational Programmes for Unemployed People (POC) that are oriented towards people receiving unemployment benefits or the unemployed in economic need. POCs provide short-duration (less than one year) occupational activities, mainly in areas such as the environment, culture or social support. According to official documents, POCs were created to combat demoralisation and marginalisation tendencies among the unemployed, and to contribute to their inclusion through a socially useful occupation. The programmes are not targeted at job creation or at including participants in productive jobs in the labour market. Recipients of an unemployment or social security benefit are obliged to accept a POC job offer, or else lose their benefit entitlements. For young people without any formal labour-market experience and consequently without any social benefits, the POC income may be very attractive. POC placements entitle recipients to a complementary income of 20% of the unemployment benefit, plus transportation, meals and costs for accident insurance.

Finally, the Spanish Capitalisation of Unemployment Benefits Scheme has the least characteristics of a secondary labour-market programme. In fact, subsidies are provided to create jobs in the primary labour market. Therefore, of all job schemes presented in this section, the Spanish scheme resembles primary labour-market participation most. The scheme stimulates the creation of jobs that are located in the social economy sector (see Chapter Seven of this volume). The general idea of the capitalisation process is that workers can receive in one time the total value of their unemployment benefit entitlements. Contrary to most other schemes discussed in this section, the Spanish scheme is not targeted at the long-term unemployed. The reason for that is simple: the longer people are unemployed, the more of their unemployment benefit entitlements will have been consumed, and the less interesting it is for them to capitalise their unemployment benefits. Furthermore, since the scheme only involves people that are entitled to unemployment benefits, their labour-market attachment, compared to schemes targeted at social assistance recipients, is relatively strong.

Unpaid work

The case studies presented here involve different degrees of 'social policy relatedness'. The UK case study, mainly concerned with unpaid work but also involving some informal paid work, focused attention on working and unemployed people's strategies of doing, and making use of, informal work to get work for themselves – or for others – done. The promotion of informal and unpaid work is often seen as problematic since governments may harness it either to reduce welfare expenditure by trimming social services and emphasising individual responsibilities, or to cut back on social rights. However, unpaid and informal work can also be promoted and analysed from an 'assisted self-help' approach, an approach that was used explicitly in the UK case study.

The Danish study involved a group of unemployed people that, on their own initiative, began to participate in voluntary work and received permission from benefit agencies to do so. They were still receiving benefits. They might be called 'self-activated', since they found this voluntary work themselves. Their participation seldom takes place in the social policy context of qualifying for labour-market participation. There is even some truth that this group of people does not necessarily have major difficulties in finding a regular job. Generally, they have been unemployed for a relatively short term.

In contrast to the UK and Danish case studies, the Dutch case study concerned a specific activating social policy scheme, targeted at the long-term unemployed on social assistance and aimed at increasing inclusion by stimulating and supporting their involvement in unpaid activities. The case study focused on one of the experiments in the context of the 'Social Activation' scheme. This scheme targets a group of 'hard-core' unemployed people that have been subjected to creaming-off processes by previous activation measures. In other words, social activation was designed to be a 'participation safety-net system' for people who, for whatever reasons, fell out of, or did not manage to get access to, the other activation subsystems. Social activation is *not* a job scheme. Participants are engaged in unpaid activities while remaining social assistance recipients. Local discretion in designing experiments is quite large, which means that these experiments may differ in various aspects. Our case study focused on the largest and one of the earliest social activation experiments, the experiment in the city of Rotterdam. Some of the main characteristics of the Rotterdam social activation experiment were as follows:

- Labour-market participation is no objective of the experiment. Re-entering the labour-market is considered to be a positive 'side-effect'.
- Participation in the project is voluntary. If people do not want to participate, they will not be sanctioned in any way.
- The activation methodology promoted by the experiment is 'bottom-up' or client-centred, starting with an assessment of people's capacities, wishes, ambitions, and so on. This is followed by a process of finding or developing appropriate participation opportunities.
- Participants are released from the obligation to apply for jobs. People who belong to the scheme's target group but do not want to participate remain under this obligation.
- Participants in the project that are involved in socially useful activities receive a small reimbursement of expenses (a maximum of €45 a month).

Training and education

Like the 'secondary labour market' case studies, all studies focusing on training and education relate directly to active social policy initiatives. Training and education are practically always aimed at increasing the qualifications or 'human capital' of the unemployed in order to improve their labour-market chances. However, training and education activities can also be seen as types of participation in themselves, for they may provide participants with new social networks, useful activities, status ('trainee' or 'student'), and so on. In the case studies, training and education initiatives have been investigated from both perspectives.

The Belgian study looked at some Third System Organisation initiatives which, though primarily oriented towards training, may also involve elements of work or work experience. Three kinds of programmes were distinguished:

- *Alternating learning:* primarily focused on young school drop-outs (aged 15-21), these programmes give young people the opportunity to learn and to acquire skills in a workshop environment for a maximum period of four years. Participants receive an income that is derived from the minimum wage for young people.

• *Vocational training:* Third System Organisations facilitate the participation in vocational training of people who are not registered as unemployed or of people facing individual problems. Programme duration is between one and three years. Participants remain on social benefits.

• *Training enterprises:* resembling the alternating learning programmes, training enterprises also involve learning in a workshop environment. However, the target group of these programmes is not as homogeneous as the case of alternating learning. Furthermore, the participation period is shorter, nine to 18 months. Participants receive social benefits plus remuneration. Individual guidance and route counselling are typical for these programmes.

As we mentioned earlier, the Danish case study involved a group of activated unemployed. Here, we focus on the education/training part of Danish activation policies. These training and education schemes either take place in the ordinary educational and training system or are organised as part of special, tailor-made programmes. Unemployed persons participating in these schemes may receive a trainee allowance. As a main rule, no allowance will be granted to participants in medium- or higher-level education programmes. Participation in vocational training programmes is another option in the context of these schemes. Young people (under 25) on unemployment benefits who have not completed a formal education or training programme are treated differently from other unemployed persons. After six months of unemployment, their benefits are reduced to 50%, and they have the right and obligation to participate in education or training for at least 18 months.

Finally, the Portuguese case study on training and education focused on the so-called Measure 2 of the Integrar Sub-Programme. This programme was adopted in 1994 under the second EU Support Framework through the programmes 'Improving the Quality of Life and Social Cohesion', and 'Health and Social Integration'. Its core aim was to create, through training and employment measures, conditions for a stronger inclusion of marginalised groups in the economy and society. Measure 2 is directed at the vocational inclusion of the long-term unemployed by promoting informative sessions, vocational guidance and training courses. Priority is given to low-skilled unemployed women who have difficulties finding a job, persons unemployed for more than two years and those who are not receiving unemployment benefits (neither contributory benefits nor social assistance), as well as to recipients of the Guaranteed Minimum Income.

Types of participation and inclusion opportunities and risks

The empirical evidence from the case studies makes it quite clear, that the relationship between types of work and experiences of inclusion and exclusion is a complex issue. First, there is no clear dichotomy between inclusion and exclusion, as we already concluded from our theoretical elaboration of the concepts in Chapter Two. Secondly, equating having a paid job with inclusion is as much a simplification as is equating unemployment with exclusion.

On a general level, we cannot make sense of the contribution of participation in types of work to inclusion (or the risks they entail in terms of exclusion) without taking into consideration the following factors (which we will elaborate in more detail in the concluding section):

• The characteristics of the *participants*, in terms of the social context they live in, their biography, needs and ambitions;
• The characteristics of the *specific work involved*, in terms of the resources it does or does not provide to participants (for example, income, career opportunities, access to social networks, 'in-work welfare');
• The characteristics of the *policy context in general* and, in the case of activation programmes, characteristics of the *activation approach* (see Chapter Three of this volume) on which these programmes are based.

Of course, this does not prevent us from analysing types of work and activation programmes in terms of the risks and opportunities they embody with respect to their inclusionary and exclusionary potentials. However, in the end, it will be the fit between the resources a specific type of work offers to participants, and the needs of the participant involved, that will determine whether or not, to what degree and in what respect that type of work will contribute to his or her (wanted) inclusion or (unwanted) exclusion.

All (sub)types of work that were investigated in the case studies revealed both opportunities and risks in terms of their potential contribution to the inclusion of participants in those types of work. In this section, we explore these opportunities and risks at the level of the four types of work distinguished in our research. In doing so, we unavoidably abstract from a lot of characteristics of the work and activities people are participating in. The heterogeneity between and within types of work is much richer than can be captured by any typology. Nevertheless, our typology suffices to substantiate the main conclusion we reached in analysing our empirical data, namely that the impact of participation in types of work (or, for that matter, of not participating in types of work) in terms of experiences of inclusion and exclusion is much more complicated than is revealed in debates on activation and the 'employment is the royal road to inclusion' slogan underlying many active social policies.

Participation in the primary labour market

There is widespread recognition that paid labour in the primary labour market is still a main contributor to inclusion. This is reflected in the strategies and policies deployed in national and cross-national EU social policies nowadays. Not only is it seen as giving individuals and families access to decent living conditions resulting from the acquisition of financial resources, but also allowing them to participate in other systems of society. Paid work in the primary labour market, in this sense, is considered as a privileged way of inclusion that, among others, enlarges social networks, reduces the risk of poverty and allows access to many other activities (for example, inclusion into the systems of culture, sport, leisure, and so on).

Of course, emphasising the dominance of paid work in policies of inclusion is not plain rhetoric. For example, Table 5.2 reveals that the risk of poverty of unemployed people is considerably larger than of the employed.

However, the latter statement needs to be measured carefully. First of all, the figures in Table 5.2 reveal as much, or as little, about the intrinsic qualities of paid work in the primary labour market as they do about the intrinsic qualities of social security systems in the different countries. In other words, different poverty rates among employed and unemployed people can not only be interpreted as an argument in favour of the dominance of paid work, but also as the result of prioritising employment in policies. Furthermore, we can look at these figures from the opposite perspective and conclude that employment does not always prevent poverty, or that unemployment does not necessarily make people poor.

In emphasising the importance of employment as the 'royal road to inclusion', we should take into account that the 'world of employment' has changed dramatically. The UK case study into part-time work makes this point quite clear. It shows that we are far from an equal treatment of different groups of workers, even though the UK has been changing its policies regarding this issue considerably since Tony Blair's Labour mandate (end of the 1990s). This situation not only causes different inclusionary potentials of different types of paid jobs in the primary labour market. It also makes sure that different groups of workers are protected – in terms of social security rights – in different

Table 5.2: Poverty rate for the employed and unemployed population between 16-64 years of age (data for beginning of 1990s)

	Total	Unemployed	Employed
Belgium	4.6	9.2	0.7
Denmark	4.0	9.8	2.8
Norway	4.4	11.5	3.2
Netherlands	6.9	12.8	3.8
Germany	6.3	13.1	3.7
Sweden	6.6	16.8	5.2
Spain	13.1	18.4	7.5
Australia	12.5	31.4	5.4
Canada	12.3	32.8	7.6
UK	14.5	38.9	4.1
US	19.1	42.7	13.8

Source: Luxembourg Income Study (LIS), cited in de Lathouwer and Thirion (1999, p 10)

degrees against risks that may occur in the future, such as unemployment, illness and old age. As one might conclude from the UK study, this type of work offered the (female) respondents partial security: a moderate income, social interactions outside the private sphere of the family, and a certain degree of flexibility and autonomy to match paid work with the prioritised mother role. At the same time, part-time work excluded them from opportunities to choose the job they would like to do, from certain employment rights, from long-term security and from the means which could let them take part in leisure and cultural activities. Their vulnerability in terms of poverty can be illustrated by the fact that a quarter of the respondents were also claiming in-work benefits and almost half of them earned incomes below the National Insurance threshold. At the same time, this does not imply that these women would be better off in full-time jobs. Even though people working part-time may not have the same degree of security and social protection as full-time workers, working full-time might prevent them from being included in other respects, for example, in being able to take care of their children in the way they want to or have to. As a matter of fact, all respondents but one had been working full-time prior to having children. Therefore, for the women in this case study part-time employment is a strategy to combine various forms of inclusion (work and family).

A similar story concerns the participation in 'non-occupational' work and in social networks. Anticipating a more systematic comparison of the results of the Danish case studies among groups of employed and unemployed people in Chapter Six, it is clear that employed people are more firmly included into work and employment, including voluntary work, moonlighting, helping friends and DIY activities. The UK case study into informal work, comprising household work, DIY activities and mutual aid, revealed that this type of work is more frequent among wage earners than among unemployed low-income households. Nevertheless, the unemployed are not absent in these activities. As far as inclusion into social networks is concerned, the Danish data is interesting as well. Comparing the employed and unemployed with respect to inclusion in and exclusion from social networks, a more diverse picture arises. More details are presented in the next chapter, where it will become clear that our results do not verify that the employed are unequivocally better off in terms of their inclusion into social networks than the unemployed.

From these observations wider implications for social policies can be derived, to which we will return in Chapter Nine. Generally, they show that we need to qualify the policy assumption that, in terms of inclusion, unemployment is 'the' problem for which employment is 'the' solution. This may be so for politicians and policy makers, but it is definitely not the case for all unemployed and employed people. Of course, employment will make people independent or at least partially independent from social benefits and social assistance. That is, however, at worst something completely different from inclusion, and, at best, only one aspect of inclusion, namely inclusion into the system of income/consumption. This does not mean that we want to return to a situation of 'romanticising unemployment', as some have been criticised of doing during the 1970s and 1980s. However, 'romanticising employment', as seems to be fashionable nowadays, has serious drawbacks as well.

Participation in the secondary labour market

A 'lower-tier' alternative to primary labour-market participation is what we have called secondary labour-market participation. As was elaborated earlier in this chapter, in this context we speak about job- and work-related activation schemes, usually targeted at long-term, low-qualified or low-productive unemployed people. As far as participation in this labour-market segment is concerned, the case studies show that the success of activation schemes in the sense of providing a positive feeling of inclusion depends on a number of factors. Although these schemes may offer an income or income improvement, independence of social security, social contacts and self-confidence, the schemes also involve some serious exclusion risks.

The small sample of subsidised employment schemes covered by our case studies displays great variety. From these, the respondents in the case study of the Spanish Capitalisation of Unemployment Benefits scheme seem to be the best-off in terms of inclusion into the systems of work and income/consumption (but not necessarily as far as inclusion into other systems is concerned; see Chapters Six and Seven). Furthermore, compared to participants in the other schemes, these participants were already better-off before starting their participation. On average, they were better-qualified, had a more stable labour-market history, and were short-term unemployed. This can partly be explained by the nature of the programme itself, which makes its classification as a secondary labour-market scheme rather inadequate. Rather than providing activation opportunities after people have been unemployed for some time, the Spanish scheme provides these opportunities the moment people are threatened with unemployment. Furthermore, the scheme aims at supporting people financially in creating or maintaining employment in the primary labour market.

In the other case studies we could observe that, within the same type of work (subsidised employment), different results were obtained. In general we can conclude that these schemes do provide resources and opportunities for (partial) inclusion. They offer people an income independent from benefit transfers or even any income at all, for example in the case of the Portuguese POC scheme where some of the participants were not entitled to social security. They also can provide people with some income improvement, although this is often quite limited for reasons elaborated below. For example, the POC respondents considered the personal remuneration in the context of the scheme an important effect of participating. However, only about 30% of the Danish participants reported income improvement. A group of approximately similar size reported that their income situation actually deteriorated.

Respondents also reported positive consequences for participation in social life. Forty per cent of the Danish activated respondents reported that their social life had improved since their participation in the schemes. Of the Belgian respondents in work-related activation schemes, even 62% reported positive effects in this respect. Some Dutch participants in the Melkert 1 scheme told us that increasing self-confidence and relief from feelings of shame or marginalisation, related to unemployment, contributed positively to social interactions with others. More generally, participants in the activation schemes reported instances of improvements of feelings of wellbeing and personal development. For example, several Dutch respondents mentioned increased assertiveness and social and functional skills. The Belgian respondents felt more positive, were less affected by feelings of boredom and uselessness, and felt in a better position to contribute to society. Danish respondents evaluated participation positively with respect to feeling more responsible, leading a more exciting life, having new opportunities for self-expression and feeling part of society; even though, as in the Belgian and Danish cases, experiences may vary over different schemes. Taking the Danish case study as an example, 51% of the respondents in pool jobs got more self-respect since entering the scheme, compared to 60% of those in job-training schemes and 67% of those in individual job-training schemes. Participation contributed to an increase in the respect from others to a smaller degree. Of the participants in the job-pool scheme, 33% gained respect from others, compared to 47% of job-training participants and 62% of individual job-training participants.

The respondents also pointed out serious exclusion risks or inclusion flaws of the schemes. Partially, the exclusionary risks detected are related to the objective of the social policy in which schemes are embedded. Many measures are limited in time and fragmented, aimed at achieving (consequently) limited objectives. In the case of temporary measures, the most important issue is, of course, what happens after the termination of participation. Since these schemes are designed to be stepping-stones to the primary labour market, their inclusionary potential is highly dependent upon the realisation of labour-market participation. Obviously, the risks of stigmatisation and feelings of exclusion increase significantly when participants do not reach a sustainable, permanent and stable situation of employment. The fear of being trapped in an 'activation recycling' process was latent, especially among participants that had already been participating in other schemes. For example, almost half of the Belgian respondents had been enrolled in other activation schemes before entering the current one. And although 82% of the Belgian participants in work-related activation schemes consider their activities as useful for getting a job, 80% think it will be difficult to find a job in the future. Many of the Portuguese POC respondents reported similar experiences. By the stage of our second interview, 75% had completed participation. Of these, 60% were still unemployed. This can raise problems of demoralisation, loss of prospects and stigmatisation. At the same time, the Portuguese POC case also showed that prior labour-market experiences may influence the evaluation of temporary activation schemes: a succession of bad jobs and spells of unemployment seems to make the precariousness of the POCs more acceptable for some participants.

Of course, permanent schemes offer more sustainable forms of employment. However, this does not necessarily correspond with sustainable forms of inclusion. The two examples of permanent schemes we studied, the Dutch Melkert 1 scheme and the Belgian Social Enterprise scheme, revealed several exclusion risks, which accounts for the fact that quite a few participants in these schemes longed for a job on the primary labour market (72% of the Melkert 1 respondents) or, at least, some other job (30% of the Belgian Social Enterprise respondents). The exclusion risks relate, among other things, to their weak or marginal position in the labour market and also to income improvement opportunities. For example, after five years of participation, Melkert 1 workers reach the income ceiling of the scheme. From then on, no income improvement is possible, not even by working overtime.

Another issue in this respect is the status of the participants. Whereas status differences for participants in temporary schemes may be acceptable because there is the expectation – or the hope – of finding a regular job in the near future, status differences for permanent scheme participants may at some point become unacceptable and turn into an important motive for leaving the scheme. For example, only a minority of Social Enterprise respondents reported that recognition from their social environment had increased. Some Melkert 1 workers decided not to inform people in their social networks about their participation in the scheme, because of the low status attributed to the programme. Melkert 1 participants also reported 'in-company' status differences, which were experienced as particularly unjust in cases where they did the same tasks and shared the same responsibilities as regular workers. Some respondents in this case study experience difficulties in relations with 'regular' colleagues: 36% say they are confronted with condescending and stigmatising comments, are treated with contempt and asked to do tasks the respondents experience as inferior. Therefore, in both cases of permanent schemes, the experience of participants was that they were employed in jobs that offer little prospects. When they realise that opportunities of participation in the primary labour market hardly turn up, participation leaves them feeling resigned.

A final issue we would like to mention concerns the match between people's skills and abilities and the characteristics of their jobs. In the Belgian case, for example, nearly half of the population in working programmes affirmed they were doing tasks which did not correspond to their level of qualification. The same complaint was made by Melkert 1 respondents, a majority of whom were critical of the degree of development offered to them in the context of the scheme. Many reported under-utilisation of their skills and competencies, and a lack of opportunities to realise their participation ambitions.

Therefore, even though they carry out their jobs in different policy contexts, participants in temporary and permanent schemes both are confronted with a potential lack of future prospects. Many of them experience lack of support, either in entering the primary labour market after temporary schemes are finished or in improving their situation when enrolled in permanent ones. Therefore, their inclusion is weak in several respects, such as income, labour-market position and status. Both Dutch and Portuguese respondents reported that once they were placed in the scheme, no one cared for them anymore. These and similar schemes seem to be oriented towards realising placements in the short term, rather than towards offering opportunities and support for more long-term, sustainable activation and inclusion processes.

Participation in unpaid and informal work

Whereas the promotion of secondary labour-market participation is entirely subject to active social policies, the opposite can be said of unpaid and informal work. Supportive policies that enhance and reward this type of work, and guide people in finding a job afterwards if that is what they want, are practically absent from European social policy. Traditionally, social policies were even repressive in their attitudes towards participation in unpaid and informal work by the unemployed. Quite frequently, unemployed people were not allowed to engage in voluntary work, as this was considered as an obstacle to their labour-market availability. However, in contrast to this approach of unemployed volunteers, in two out of three case studies dealing with unpaid and informal work – the Dutch and the Danish – a more lenient attitude towards (groups of) unemployed people engaged in voluntary work was observed.

The case studies clearly show that unpaid work has inclusionary potentials, at least for parts of the unemployed population. Furthermore, the Dutch case illustrates the impact social policies themselves can have on the inclusionary potential of unpaid work, for example by offering a (small) financial remuneration, recognition, guidance and support, access to free courses, and so on.

Informal work, as studied in the UK case study, is often seen as a strategy to deal with financial hardship and to get domestic tasks done in a relatively cheap way, at least in monetary terms. However, only 14% of the respondents in this case study reported that they carried out domestic tasks using household or do-it-yourself work (the most frequent forms of informal activity) for purely economic reasons. In the vast majority of cases, this is the preferred coping strategy. At the same time, lower-income households are more likely to run up against limits in expanding the quantity of tasks carried out in this way. In addition, they are less likely to possess the required combination of money, tools, knowledge, practical skills and physical ability.

Many of the respondents from the Dutch case study started participating in voluntary work to get, or stay in what they saw as a temporary or permanent 'good alternative' for a job, to prevent social isolation, or as a stepping stone towards a paid job. As far as the latter is concerned, this strategy turns out to be successful in a significant number of cases. Of the 7,000 people that participated in the Social Activation scheme in Rotterdam during the period 1995-2001, about one quarter managed to find a job on the primary or the secondary labour market, or to enter other labour-market inclusion programmes. A considerable group of job finders was offered a job in the institution or organisation where they were doing their voluntary work.

From the Danish volunteers we do know that – compared to the employed, unemployed and activated people in the case study – greater emphasis is placed on the immaterial meanings of work, such as respect and work content, rather than material ones, such as money and self-support. Whether this merely reflects their current situation as unemployed volunteers or deeper cultural orientations is a question we cannot answer.

Obviously, without additional measures, unpaid work as a source for inclusion is almost by nature limited to immaterial aspects. It may offer status and respect, social networks, personal development and meaningful activities for the participants. These immaterial aspects can be quite meaningful. We already pointed at preference as an important motive of the respondents in the UK case study. Reasons for preferring informal work are ease, choice, higher quality or individualisation of the end product (that is, adjusting the end product to personal preferences), and pleasure. For most respondents, informal work is a way of engaging in meaningful and productive activity for the benefit of both themselves and others. For these households, informal work is the preferred means of satisfying their needs and maintaining a reasonable quality of life. In this respect it contributes to various forms of inclusion. In addition, the Danish volunteers scored highest of all groups surveyed in the Danish case studies on an index of inclusion in social networks. Furthermore, they are the most satisfied with their social networks. For the respondents from the Dutch Social Activation scheme, inclusion into social networks seems to be more problematic than for their Danish volunteer colleagues. Of the Dutch respondents, 20% report shortcomings in their participation in social networks. A third of them were not fully satisfied with the extent or quality of their social networks. Partly, this will be due to the fact that the Dutch volunteers studied constitute a more vulnerable group of unemployed than the Danish volunteers that were interviewed. Nevertheless, the Dutch respondents also point to positive effects in this respect, either because of their engagement in unpaid activities or as a result of the support and guidance they receive from Social Activation consultants. These positives include diminished feelings of shame in social interactions, have something to talk about in social interactions, and the distraction that participation offers from social problems, among other things.

The participants in the Dutch Social Activation programme mentioned some additional contributions that unpaid work made to their experiences of inclusion. Firstly, they experienced an increase in respect, status and recognition from the municipal social services, from social activation consultants and sometimes also from their social environment. Secondly, some reported increased autonomy and independence, for example in the way their activation process developed. Social Activation gives them more room to determine the content and speed of the activation process than is often the case with other programmes. The voluntary nature of participation, and the fact that participants may be released from the obligation to apply for jobs temporarily, strengthens feelings of autonomy and independence. Thirdly, most respondents report that they go through a process of personal development. Here, as in other aspects, the inclusionary potential of unpaid work depends much on the degree to which respondents' wishes and ambitions in this respect are satisfied. For example, when unpaid activities offer too little or too much challenge, they can contribute to feelings of uselessness or of being involved in threatening situations respectively, which both can have a negative impact on experiences of inclusion.

Of course, in terms of access to income and consumption and of realising a situation of autonomy from welfare-state arrangements and institutions, unpaid work does not have much to offer. This may be considered an important exclusion risk of this type of work. Therefore, even though the Dutch volunteers expressed satisfaction with the small remuneration they receive (a monthly maximum of €45), some consider it quite low given the time and energy they invest and the responsibilities they have. This might also explain why the Danish volunteers expressed dissatisfaction with their income situation more frequently than the employed, unemployed and activated groups of people. However, they also claimed to be very satisfied more often with their present standard of living. Of course, we should not isolate people's statements regarding their income situation from the social context in which these statements are formulated. Some of the Dutch participants told us that they were not yet ready to accept a paid job, whereas others estimated their labour-market opportunities to be very low due to age, qualifications or health, or as limited to jobs that would not offer them much income improvement anyway.

Contrary to secondary labour-market programmes, our case studies into unpaid work did not reveal many experiences of stigmatisation of unemployed people. A reason for this can be found in the fact that our case studies did not deal with forms of compulsory participation in unpaid work. Furthermore, and contrary to several secondary labour-market programmes we studied, the unpaid activities carried out by unemployed people cannot be distinguished from unpaid work done by other categories of unpaid workers. Finally, secondary labour-market schemes often limit work tasks to low-skilled or low-productive work. Similar limitations did not exist where unpaid work was concerned. The degree to which participants in activating social policies or their tasks can be clearly 'identified' influences the risk of stigmatisation. This does not mean, of course, that unpaid workers did not report experiences of stigmatisation. However, in these circumstances processes of stigmatisation were likely to be directed at unpaid workers as such, and not specifically at unemployed voluntary workers.

Participation in training and education schemes

The training and education schemes we investigated were designed to prepare people for labour-market participation. Consequently, their labour-market inclusionary potential is highly dependent on people's opportunities to get a job after completion of the training period. Even though the profile of the participants in these schemes was on average younger than participants in the secondary labour-market schemes, there is a clear risk of 'educational recycling'.

Some of the training and education programmes we studied focused on young people and school drop-outs. Others targeted older unemployed people. The Portuguese case study, being the only one where respondents were interviewed both during and after the training programme, provides some insight into the post-programme labour-market situation. Respondents were much more positive during the training than afterwards since many of them had not been able to find a paid job. During the second interview, half of the respondents were enrolled in another training course, a quarter were unemployed without being involved in a new programme. The final quarter had succeeded in finding a job, often subsidised in the context of an activation programme. In some cases, problems in finding training posts for the participants during the training programme had jeopardised the effects of the scheme in terms of employability.

From the Belgian and Danish case studies data is available on respondents' expectations as to employment after the programme. Half of the Danish participants in educational programmes think it will be easy to find a job in their trade; the other half expect more difficulties. Three quarters of the respondents claim to have a brighter view on the future since having been enrolled in activation, and this makes them more optimistic than those in the work-oriented programmes. Similar results were found in the Belgian case studies. At the same time, over one third of the Belgian respondents feared that they would remain in activation programmes; here it should be remembered that almost half had been enrolled in an activation programme before. Not surprisingly, expectations were less optimistic among older age groups. Of course, we have to put the optimism among respondents in perspective, as the results of the Portuguese case study underline. If participation in these schemes raises people's expectations to be able to find a job, frustrations are likely to occur when inclusion into the labour market fails.

Despite these considerations, training and education schemes also have an inclusionary potential: they may offer people new skills, social contacts, status, meaningful activities, even income improvement in some cases. In this sense, participation in training schemes may contribute positively to people's inclusion. Sometimes training and education programmes recognise this explicitly, as in the Portuguese case where stimulating participation in social networks was considered to be a separate objective of the training programme, apart from labour-market inclusion. The Portuguese respondents reported that the programme did indeed contribute, as it aimed to do, to their ability to strengthen social networks in a quantitative or qualitative way. Of the Danish respondents, 56% experienced that participation had improved their social life. And of the Belgian respondents, two thirds stated that participation enlarged their networks.

For the participants in the Portuguese education and training programme, the training benefit was considered a way of relieving their economic difficulties. Of the Danish respondents, two thirds expressed satisfaction with their present standard of living, although this figure makes them the least satisfied among the surveyed Danish activated persons. The fact that satisfaction with standard of living should not be simply attributed to the activation programmes as such, is made clear by the fact that only a quarter of the respondents claimed that their income situation improved after having started their participation.

Finally, a majority of respondents reported positive effects in terms of general wellbeing (self-respect, brighter view of the future, recognition), and of feeling useful and being actively involved in society.

Conclusions

In this chapter we explored the inclusionary and exclusionary potentials of paid work in the primary labour market, work in the secondary labour market (subsidised employment), unpaid and informal work, and education and training. On the basis of our case studies we can draw the following conclusions.

First, it is clear that all types of work have potential for (wanted) inclusion and involve (unwanted) exclusion risks. At the same time, the types of work we distinguished are an abstraction from the 'real' forms of work that people are participating in: the variety *within* types of work is as great as those *across* them. Table 5.3 divides some of the results from the Belgian case studies into work-oriented and education-oriented activation schemes, and clearly shows this variety.

Therefore, from an inclusion point of view, there is no reason why social policies should a priori exclude certain types of work. At the same time, they should acknowledge the variety within types of work. The assumption that primary labour-market participation should be prioritised in activation policies because it will always contribute more to inclusion than any other type of work needs qualification.

Secondly, the inclusionary and exclusionary potentials of types of work in terms of resources offered to or withheld from participants are not simply 'inherent qualities' of those types of work, but are, at least partly, subject to policies, such as the employment rights of part-time and secondary labour-market workers, the recognition of unpaid and informal work, income ceilings of people working in subsidised jobs, career opportunities of participants in activation schemes, among others. In other words, policies *matter* when it comes to the inclusionary potential of types of work.

Thirdly, whether or not a certain type of work will contribute to an individual's inclusion, not only depends on the (policy mediated) resources that that type of work offers, but also on the resources that individual needs to fulfil his or her preferences for inclusion. Inclusion can mean quite different things to different people. For some, it will mean income improvement and being financially independent from welfare state arrangements. For others it will mean being able to combine household responsibilities with some outdoor activity. For others, it will mean being involved in challenging and useful activities that encourage self-esteem and self-respect. Therefore, the issue whether *potential* opportunities for wanted inclusion or risks of unwanted exclusion of types of work will be *real* opportunities and risks, also depends on people's needs and preferences in terms of inclusion. Broadly speaking, the better the fit between

Table 5.3: Inclusionary effects of local activities on participants in the Belgian case studies of Third System Organisations (*)

	Education oriented			Work oriented		
	AL	**VT**	**TE**	**WEP**	**IE**	**SE**
Being more optimistic		+	(+)			−
Giving a sense to personal life	−	(+)	+			
Feeling good and self-esteem		+		(+)	−	
Enlarging social networks			(+)			−
Contribution to society		− −	++	(++)		
Attitude to work	(++)	−		+		
Recognition	+	−	(++)	++	− −	−
Learning values and priorities in life			+	(+)		
Being active	−	+	− −		−	−
Inclusion in the group			+			−
Atmosphere in the activity	−		+		−	− −
Employability	++	+				− −
Job satisfaction					+	

Notes: AL=alternative learning; VT=vocational training; TE=training enterprise; WEP=work experience project; IE=insertion enterprise; SE=social enterprise.
(*) Significant deviations from average scores. The + or ++ between brackets demarcate the highest positive value found in each of the categories. ++/− −: scores are more than a factor 1.25 respectively less than a factor 0.75 times the average; +: scores are in between 1.10 and 1.25 times the average; −: scores are in between 0.75 and 0.9 times the average.

Source: INPART Belgium Research

the individual's needs in terms of inclusion and the resources and rights provided by a type of work, the more that type of work will contribute to the individual's inclusion. At the same time, we need to recognise the temporal aspect of processes of activation and inclusion. What can pass a 'fitting test' at one moment of the inclusion and activation process, can turn out to be a serious mismatch at other moments.

This brings us back to our general conclusion. The central issue whether or not a certain type of work will contribute to a person's experiences of inclusion depends on the fit between the policy-mediated resources offered by that type of work and the resources required by those people. From this point of view, social policy's contribution to promoting inclusion can be twofold. First, social policy can influence the resources that types of work offer to their participants, thereby influencing the inclusionary potential of these types of work. Secondly, social policy can, as a core objective of activation programmes, improve the match between these resources on the one hand and the resources people need on the other. (These issues are explored in detail in Chapter Nine.) We conclude this chapter by pointing out some core issues in this matching process. In line with our general conclusion, these issues can be seen as resources that concrete types of work may or may not offer. On the other hand, people will depend on these resources to various extents depending on what inclusion means to them, that is, their needs and preferences in terms of inclusion.

The first core issue is *income*. This can mean different things in different situations. It can mean getting access to any income at all, as was the case for some of the Portuguese respondents. As Chapter Three has described, in some welfare states participation in activation schemes is the only option for some groups of people to get access to formally recognised income. It can also mean realising a situation of (partial) independence from welfare-state arrangements or welfare-state institutions. And finally, it can mean income improvement, or the prospect to realise income improvement in the near future.

The second issue is *autonomy*. Here, different issues can be at stake. Autonomy first of all can mean (as we have just pointed out) independence from welfare-state arrangements or institutions and from rules and regulations attached to receiving social benefits. It can also relate to the activation process, referring to the degree to which activated people have a say in defining the problems activation should solve and in determining the means and objectives of the process of activation. Finally, autonomy has to do with the characteristics of participation and of types of work, for example in terms of the nature and variety of working tasks, the number or scheduling of working hours, and so on.

The third issue concerns *personal development* and *career opportunities*. Participation and activation are learning processes in which people acquire new skills and competencies, and often develop new needs and preferences to engage in new challenges. Types of participation and activation can vary considerably in the degree to which they encourage these developments and offer resources to meet career or other types of needs and preferences that participants may have. Our case studies clearly show that it is not evident for activation programmes to be organised explicitly as learning processes, and to be springboards rather than participation traps.

The fourth core issue concerns *status* and *recognition*. For many people status and recognition, or the lack of it, are important attributes of types of work. To an important extent, status and recognition are shaped by social policies. In principle, the status and recognition people can derive from activities may have far-reaching consequences both for their personal wellbeing and for their social interactions. It can influence their social interactions with colleagues and management at work, with social security authorities or consultants and with friends and relatives all of which, of course, are recursively related to people's self-esteem, self-confidence and self-respect.

By interpreting activation policies as mediating between people's needs in terms of wanted inclusion and the resources offered by types of work, the guidance and support offered by activation schemes become important issues as well. In this context, activation or participation schemes may operate according to a 'plug-and-play' philosophy, in which little care is given to participants before, during and after placement, or according to a more human resource management philosophy, in which more intensive and tailor-made guidance and support are offered. This does not imply that all people actually need guidance and support. Whereas some are very well able themselves to mobilise resources, others experience themselves as completely dependent on 'third parties' to do this. The availability of the right 'dose' of guidance and support may therefore become an important determinant in increasing the inclusionary potential of types of work. This is specifically the case for long-term unemployed people who are or have been confronted with several and severe problems.

The latter points to a more general issue. To a varying degree, people depend on work (in the broad sense of the term outlined in Chapter Three) and activation. They may have access to other kinds of resources to realise inclusion, for example, family support or support from social networks. And they may prioritise other types of work than primary labour-market participation. However, the same social policies that increasingly emphasise the importance of, and each citizen's responsibility to, participate on the labour market, erode or at least threaten the role of alternative security providers such as the family, mutual aid, and so on, as well as the inclusionary potential of types of participation outside the labour market. For these policies not only increase the pressure on large parts of the population to find paid work, they also decrease the legitimacy of, and recognition for, being engaged in other types of work (for example, child raising by single mothers or voluntary and informal work by the unemployed).

Notes

[1] Taking as an example the upper secondary students who were taking a vocational training and education programme in 1995-96, we can see that they account, on average, for 58% of the total but there are large differences across countries. In some countries, such as Denmark, the UK and Belgium, this percentage rises to 70%. In others, such as Spain and Portugal, general education predominates and students in the vocational stream account only for 38% and 29% respectively (CEC, 2001a). As far as initial training is concerned, the differences are stronger. The various forms in which it takes place – in schools, in enterprises or in both (dual system, 'alternance') – depend on the relative influence of the labour market or the government in the design of programmes. Some countries are more liberal and training is predominantly steered by the market; some are more corporatist and the training is dualised; and others are more state regulated and training is offered by state schools.

[2] "Large pockets of illiteracy remain in some areas, which, if not tackled appropriately, will irremediably place less educated workers at a disadvantage in the information and knowledge-based society" (CEC, 2000a, p 39).

References

CEC (Commission of the European Communities) (2000a) *Joint employment report 2000*, Brussels: CEC.

CEC (2000b) *A memorandum on lifelong learning*, SEC (2000) 1832, Brussels: CEC.

CEC (2001a) 'Recommendation of the 19th January 2001 on the implementation of Member States' employment policies (2201/64/EC)', *Official Journal of the European Communities*, 24 January, vol 44, pp 27-38.

CEC (2001b) *Assessment of the implementation of the 2001 employment guidelines. Supporting document to the joint employment report 2001*, SEC (2001) 438, Commission Services Paper, Brussels: CEC.

CEC (2001c) *Draft joint report on social inclusion* (COM/2001/565), Brussels: CEC (europa.eu.int/comm/employment_social/news/2001/oct/i01_1395_en.html).

CEC (2001d) *European report on education and training in employment policies*, Brussels: Education and Culture Directorate-General.

de Lathouwer, L. and Thirion, A. (1999) 'Unemployment traps in Belgium', Paper for the IUAP workshop, 10 June 1999, Antwerp: Centrum voor Sociaal Beleid, UFSIA.

SIX

Patterns of exclusion/inclusion and people's strategies

Iver Hornemann Møller and Pedro Hespanha

Introduction

As Chapter Two has already explained, it is central to our understanding of the concepts of exclusion, inclusion and marginalisation that *differentiation comes before exclusion*. We begin with differentiating five major systems:

- work;
- income/consumption;
- the social network;
- the cultural system;
- the political system.

Within this framework different understandings and conceptualisations of differentiation into subsystems will also be applied. For example, the system of social networks can be further differentiated into subsystems. These include not only the nuclear and the extended family, but also various networks of friends – at work, in associations and at other places, neighbours, and so on – and between the various types of support a person may receive from the networks (economic, emotional, educational, and so on).

Our most central empirical focus is on the general questions about the relations between the different (sub)systems (Chapter Two): how far can one predict a person's position within other (sub)systems from her/his position within one specific (sub)system?

Within this more general formulation several specific issues about the relations between systems are dealt with in both theoretical and empirical terms. Theories are tested by our empirical data, upon which we attempt to formulate new hypotheses. The empirical analyses will first of all be based on the INPART data; other observations, however, when they can shed new light on the INPART observations or give them a broader perspective are also referred to.

More specifically, this chapter focuses on two main issues. The first is about *patterns of inclusion and exclusion*. In an overview of the different (sub)systems, what are then the most general and important patterns of inclusion and exclusion? Our attempt to discern these involves three patterns and four themes.

Patterns

1 A comparison of patterns of inclusion/exclusion between a group of employed persons on one side, and a group of unemployed/activated persons on the other.
2 Patterns of inclusion/exclusion among the groups of unemployed and activated.
3 Patterns of relations between any single individual's inclusion/exclusion into or from the various systems.

Themes

1   To what extent do our data support the dominant European labour-market theme about 'the royal road to inclusion'? That is, that inclusion into the system of employment in the sense of paid work is, if not the only, then the most important way to inclusion also into other systems.
2.1   The prevalence of other *virtuous circles*, where strong inclusion within one system is associated with strong inclusion within several other systems.
2.2   The prevalence of *vicious circles*, where a marginal position within or exclusion from one system is associated with marginalisation or exclusion from other systems.

Together 1, 2.1 and 2.2 will test the full Matthew principle, "Whoever has will be given more.... Whoever does not have, even what he has will be taken from him" (St Matthew's Gospel 13:12; see also Chapter Two). In operational terms, this means the prevalence of both vicious circles and virtuous circles where the former refers to situations where exclusion or marginalisation from one system is followed by exclusion or marginalisation from another, and the latter to situations where a strong position in one system is followed by strong positions in other systems. As was elaborated in Chapter Two, Niklas Luhmann claims that inclusion into one system is seldom linked to inclusion into other systems, while exclusion from one system probably often does involve exclusion from other systems. Therefore, Luhmann predicts the prevalence of vicious circles but the absence of virtuous circles. This Luhmannian hypothesis about the 'half Matthew principle' will also be tested.

3 The prevalence of *patterns of compensation*: to what extent is unwanted exclusion and marginalisation from one system 'compensated' by inclusion into other systems?

4   Is the prevalence of a rather *strong* position within one system *associated* with exclusion from other systems as a consequence of limited economic resources or shortage of time?

As we discuss in greater detail later in this chapter, one of the most outstanding results is that only a small number of associations between individuals' positions within the different systems can be observed (pattern 3). Despite the fact that the number of associations – positive and negative – between individuals' exclusion from and inclusion into different systems is rather small, the associations when present are also often relatively low (with most other systems' associations with the system of consumption/income as the only – and most important – exception).

Moreover, the presence of virtuous circles (theme 2.1) is moderate when measured by 'the length' of the circles; that is, the number of systems included in each circle. Furthermore, we cannot find any support either for a pattern of vicious circles (theme 2.2) or, in contrast, for the hypothesis that unwanted exclusion from one system is 'compensated' by inclusion into other systems (theme 3).

These main empirical conclusions, which show little 'automatic' effects of inclusion into and exclusion from one system on inclusion into or exclusion from other systems, contends that this absence of a relationship is something that is often practically acknowledged by people in contemporary societies. To some extent our data supports this understanding, since they suggest that most people react accordingly and, rather than rely on 'automatic' inclusion and exclusion, try to develop their own strategies to pursue exclusion from and inclusion into their preferred systems. In the second part of this chapter we elaborate on this issue and focus on the various *strategies* every person applies to attain her/his personal preferences for inclusion, exclusion and marginalisation (for example, when an individual wants to leave a burdensome family or to retire from the labour market, which implies taking an excluded or marginalised position vis-à-vis these systems).

Patterns of inclusion and exclusion

When dealing with patterns of inclusion, marginalisation and exclusion it is important to bear in mind from the outset what groups or individuals are to be focused upon. When we observe, for example, that within the system of consumption/income, employed persons as a group are better-off than the group of unemployed, this observation does not, of course, imply that within this system each employed individual is better-off than any unemployed individual. And when it is observed that the group of employed people have a better position within several (sub)systems than the group of unemployed it does not mean that *the same employed persons individually* have better positions within all the (sub)systems than any unemployed, nor that *the same unemployed persons* all have weaker positions within all (sub)systems than any employed.

Let us then focus on the most outstanding results from analyses of our empirical data about patterns of exclusion and inclusion.

The unemployed/activated persons compared with the employed

The first type of pattern of exclusion and inclusion involves a comparison between the unemployed and activated persons on the one side and the employed persons on the other side (pattern 1). However, only one of the national INPART case studies – the Danish study – allows us to make such comparisons. An important result from the Danish study, which covers the five different systems mentioned in the introduction, is that employed persons are better-off than the unemployed and activated persons within the systems of:

*   work/employment, including partaking in voluntary work, moonlighting, doing favours for friends, and DIY work;
*   consumption/income;
*   politics, including political associations, movements and democratic associations (for example, day care institutions, school boards and tenants' organisations)[1].

There seem, however, to be more diverse tendencies so far as the following systems are concerned:

*   leisure-time;
*   social networks.

There does appear, however, to be a polarisation in leisure-time systems. A relatively large group of unemployed persons spend more time on leisure-time activities (including activities in non-political associations) than the employed and activated persons. At the same time, however, there is also a relatively large group of (other) unemployed who are rather less or not at all involved in leisure-time activities, certainly less so than the employed and activated persons.

In addition, as far as the system of social networks is concerned, it is not possible to point to one group which is unequivocally better off than the two others:

(a) When further differentiating the system of social networks into subsystems, it is observed that employed persons more often live within nuclear families than the unemployed and the activated.
(b) However, employed persons have less frequent contact with friends and with the non-cohabiting part of the family.
(c) Feelings of loneliness are, on the other hand, more widespread among the unemployed and the activated persons than among the employed.
(d) Since it is often observed, for example by Gallie (1999), that the proportion of friends who are unemployed is higher among the unemployed than among

employed persons, it is not surprising that the Danish study found that the quality of the network is better for the employed as far as financial support is concerned (responses were limited to 'the possibilities for borrowing money').

(e) The better quality of the employed persons' network, however, also and more remarkably includes emotional support (responses were limited to 'someone to comfort you when needed').

(f) All in all, the employed persons express more satisfaction with their social network (a mixed quality and quantity dimension) than the unemployed and the activated persons.

Several of these findings are in line with the results of Gallie's analyses (Gallie, 1999, 2000). Following the sequence of the findings above, correspondence is first observed concerning (a) where Gallie, based on a major survey (1996) in 15 EU countries, found that, whereas 32% of those in work in the EU were single, this was the case for 48% of the unemployed.

With regard to (b), Gallie concluded that "there is no evidence then of any general collapse of social networks accompanying unemployment. Rather, unemployment seems to increase the frequency of contact with relatives and friends" (1999, p 146). Also, in line with the Danish INPART study, he found that, with regard to (d) a higher proportion among the employed could rely on someone to lend them money. However, in respect of (e), the Danish data contrast with those of Gallie, who reports that the unemployed were as likely to receive support if they were depressed as other people. As for (c) and (f), data are not comparable.

The Danish observations also correspond with a recent analysis of data from the 1995 Norwegian survey of living conditions (Statistik sentralbyrå, 1996). Here it is argued that persons who are excluded from, or have a marginalised position within, the labour market are involved in as many types of informal social relations as those in normal employment conditions. The labour market does not appear to have any overall significance as a mediator of social affiliation. Ensuring a satisfactory income for people is a more important measure for creating affiliation than wage labour (Johannessen, 1998). The importance of inclusion into the system of consumption/income is discussed in greater detail later in this chapter when we deal with the relatively greater importance of income compared to paid employment for inclusion into several other systems.

As far as 'the royal road to inclusion' is concerned (theme 1), it is clear from the Danish data that inclusion into paid employment is followed by inclusion into the system of consumption/income and the political system only, but not by inclusion into the leisure-time system and the social networks system.

The unemployed and activated persons

The second type of patterns of exclusion and inclusion looks at the degree to which unemployed and activated persons – without making comparisons with other groups of persons – are excluded from or included into the various systems and subsystems.

A most important result is that the Belgian and the Danish studies both show that activated persons are quite likely to be performing voluntary work (around one third of the Belgian activated and a little more than one fifth of activated Danes). The unemployed and activated Belgians and Danes are rarely socially isolated; they are seldom culturally excluded; they are rarely politically excluded and quite often they consider themselves to have a relatively fair or, at least for shorter spells of unemployment, a tolerable position within the system of consumption/income.

In general, however, the UK and Portuguese data suggest that the situation is rather different in those countries. Unemployed persons there often consider themselves to have a marginal position within, or to be excluded from, the system of consumption/income. So it seems, for the part-time employed UK women and for the activated Portuguese women in our study, that their prior levels of living when unemployed have been so low (or the present alternative unemployment allowances so meagre) that the additional money from part-time employment and activation is by far the most important and overshadowing effect even of their weak inclusion into the system of paid work/activity.

For the UK, moreover, it is evident that the low rates of pay associated with part-time employment, combined with the hardship of work circumstances or unemployment benefits, childcare costs and the expense of social activities, resulted in many of the women in our study not being able to take part in social life as much as they wanted to. And in some extreme low-income cases it resulted in exclusion from everyday activities such as going out, going on holiday or 'even just being able to treat yourself sometimes'.

For Portugal, the activated women explained that, given economic hardship, spending on social contacts and participation in formal social activities such as local associations were eliminated or reduced to a minimum. The same applied to inclusion into the cultural system and sometimes even encompassed the health system.

> "Many times I have had to give up going to the doctor ... because I have to contribute my share of the payment of the medicine and I needed the money for other things."

Consequently, receiving a cash benefit when activated was crucial to increase the family budget.

However, on the inclusion side, the Portuguese study revealed evidence of general inclusion into the extended family system, by way of daily family relationships. Furthermore, it seems to be rather usual to find people who help their relatives and neighbours by doing farmwork, needlework, mending clothes or helping with other occasional jobs, such as moving or painting the house. The Portuguese study also registered some inclusion into the system of politics.

In the Netherlands too, activated workers perceive their economic situation as troublesome, and the wages are a source of much dissatisfaction. One of the most important criticisms is that, after years (sic!) of participation in the scheme, hardly a single participant has experienced any financial improvement.

> "Relatives and acquaintances think that I make good money because I work. But they don't know that I earn little.... When I go on holidays I have to borrow money from my daughter."

Although some of the activated Dutch mentioned financial constraints as an explanation for not being included into sports, culture and other leisure-time activities, most of the respondents were more or less included into the cheaper parts of, or free activities within, these systems: watching football, free pop concerts, creative activities, and so on. The study also showed that the majority of the activated were somewhat included into the political system.

For most of the activated Dutch persons activation did not change their social networks. However, during the first part of the activation period some participants enlarged their network but it later contracted again, partly as a consequence of stigmatisation (low payment and 'not real work'; see Chapter Five).

The Spanish data underline a strong degree of inclusion into the extended family system and therefore, together with the Portuguese evidence, sustain Paugam's conclusion, that in Southern Europe, the extended family is a prime foundation for social affiliation (Paugam, 1996).

Gallie's results again support some of the above mentioned observations. From surveys of 15 EU countries, he concludes that there were marked differences in the extent to which the unemployed found it difficult to manage financially, and points out that Belgium, Denmark and the Netherlands were among the countries where the unemployed were less likely to report financial hardship (Gallie, 1999). In another EU research project encompassing seven EU countries including Denmark and the Netherlands, he found that participation in associative life was much higher in Northern than in Southern Europe. Even so, in all countries unemployment was negatively associated with this type of participation (Gallie, 2000).

From patterns 1 and 2 of exclusion/inclusion, it is possible to infer two more general and important conclusions, both of which relate to 'the royal road to inclusion' (theme 1). Firstly, no evidence was found to support the research in the interwar period, which strongly suggested that unemployment led to the collapse of people's social networks (Jahoda et al, 1975). Secondly, income seems to be of relative greater importance than work for the inclusion of people into other (sub)systems. The second observation is further confirmed when we turn to our third and final pattern of exclusion/inclusion.

Relations between individuals' inclusion in and exclusion from different systems

The search for a consistent set of relations between individuals' inclusion in and exclusion from different systems is our third approach to the study of patterns of exclusion/inclusion. We are able to identify empirical evidence to test the position from St Matthew's Gospel: that those persons who have a good/bad position within one (sub)system also have a good/bad position within one or more of the other (sub)systems (themes 2.1 and 2.2). We shall also be able to shed some light on theme 3 concerning compensation (the supposition that unwanted exclusion and marginalisation is 'compensated' by inclusion into other systems).

Several INPART case studies point to positive and sometimes also causal relations between *two* systems: that inclusion within one system is associated with inclusion into another system and vice versa, so far as marginalisation and exclusion are concerned.

One of the most prevalent associations is that a process of inclusion into paid work often leads to increased inclusion into the system of consumption/income. For example, the UK study demonstrates that working part time provides some people with an essential income, without which they would not be able to afford necessities let alone leisure activities.

Let us stop for a moment. It can be argued in support of 'the royal road to inclusion' (theme 1) that inclusion into paid work is often followed by a stronger position in the system of income/consumption and in that way inclusion into paid work, via higher income, enhances the likelihood of a stronger position in other systems as well. It should be realised, however, that although paid work often leads to higher income/consumption, income/consumption and work in other ways are two quite different notions. The concept of paid work includes many other dimensions than income (for example, 'doing things together with other people', making a time structure, self-respect, respect from others, contribution to society, and so on). Income is only one part of the concept of paid work, and conversely, you may also have an income without doing paid work.

Several INPART case studies indeed show a direct relationship between the amount of income on one side and inclusion into the cultural system, the leisure-time system, the social network system and other systems and subsystems on the other. For example, the Belgian data show that people with economic constraints – that is, with difficulties in making ends meet – participated less, and expressed a stronger desire for further inclusion, in the cultural system and the leisure-time system than those who could afford it. The Belgian data, in general, along with that from Portugal and, in part, the Netherlands, also lead to the conclusion that lack of income or more broadly of economic resources quite often may hamper the degree of participation in the cultural sphere, social networks, leisure-time activities and other systems and subsystems.

The Danish study shows that there are some – although, in general, remarkably weak – partial associations between the five systems identified by the study. However, the associations to the system of consumption/income are again those that stand out overall. Table 6.1 illustrates this, and uses gamma coefficients as indicators of negative and positive associations between the five systems.

Without postulating causality, which often goes 'both ways' and which is also contingent on the interaction between one or more intermediate variables, it is clear that the system of consumption/income shows by far the strongest associations with the other systems – both the system of employment, the system of social networks and the system of politics – though not with the system of leisure-time. Despite acknowledging that the Danish observations are the only set of data in the INPART project which give us more representative comparisons of the importance of inclusion into one system for inclusion into other systems, and without postulating monocausality, it is striking that inclusion into the system of consumption/income seems to be of more importance for inclusion into other systems than 'paid employment as the royal road to inclusion' (theme 1)[2]. So, these observations further support the results of the two previous approaches and further undermine the theme about 'the royal road to inclusion'. As was mentioned earlier, binary relationships may or may not be a result of one-way causal relations; but by definition they never include more than two subsystems.

Table 6.1: Correlations between positions of employed, unemployed and activated persons within different systems, gamma coefficients (1999)

	System of consumption/ income	System of social networks	System of politics	Leisure-time system
System of work:				
Employed	+0.404	+0.094	+0.052	+0.011
Activated	+0.017	+0.021	+0.057	-0.046
System of consumption/income:				
Employed		+0.146	+0.272	-0.058
Activated		+0.298	+0.225	+0.049
Unemployed		+0.291	+0.209	+0.036
System of social networks:				
Employed			+0.103	+0.054
Activated			+0.203	+0.017
Unemployed			+0.135	+0.106
System of politics:				
Employed				+0.076
Activated				+0.147
Unemployed				+0.281

Strength of correlations: 0.3 and higher: strong; around +/-0.2: moderate; in between –0.1 and +0.1: weak.

The Danish study – one of the two INPART case studies which systematically focused on relations between the same individuals' positions (strong or weak) within *more than two systems* – provides some evidence, albeit somewhat limited, particularly among the employed, for the presence of virtuous circles. That is, whereby inclusion in one system leads to inclusion in others (theme 2.1). However, the same data also indicate that these tendencies are restricted in scope – that the length, so to say, of the virtuous circles is limited. This is because one cannot observe any individual at all who has a strong position in all five systems and even those people who have a strong position in four systems are in fact very few (see Table 6.2).

The Danish study also shows that there is almost no tendency to vicious circles (theme 2.2), whereby people who are marginalised or excluded from one system would be marginalised or excluded from most other systems (Table 6.3).

The Portuguese study is the only other study that has provided information about the prevalence of vicious and virtuous circles. While the Danish data are quantitative and based on a nationwide survey, all the Portuguese data came from in-depth interviews using a life trajectory perspective. In general, the

Table 6.2: Number of systems where one has a strong position, Danish case studies

	Employed	Activated	Unemployed
None	13%	28%	37%
I system	25%	39%	26%
2 systems	37%	21%	28%
3 systems	25%	10%	7%
4 systems	1%	2%	2%
Total	101%	100%	100%
No of respondents	187	269	121

Table 6.3: Number of systems where one is marginalised or excluded, Danish case studies

	Employed	Activated	Unemployed
None	68%	50%	44%
I system	27%	26%	30%
2 systems	4%	17%	14%
3 systems	1%	6%	9%
4 systems	–	1%	3%
Total	100%	100%	100%
No of respondents	187	269	121

results from the two data sets support each other and thereby add to the INPART study's validity.

The main deviation relates to inclusion in the social network system. In Portugal, the pervasive prevalence of the extended family system frequently plays a decisive role as a stepping stone to inclusion into other systems and subsystems. These systems are, in particular:

- the system of consumption/income (sharing land, homes, clothes and food);
- the leisure-time system;
- the cultural subsystems (in particular its low cost elements);
- the system of work (informal and formal paid work).

The Portuguese extended family – particularly prevalent in rural areas where the data were collected – often functions as the first link in virtuous circles:

> "I see my parents every day, my parents and my brothers and sisters.... We also see a lot of my uncles and aunts, my father's brother and sisters. We visit a lot, we often go to their place and they often come to ours. We meet at the weekends and have meals together and then we all go to the cafe together. It is a good thing for families to be close."

The Portuguese data do not stem from a representative sample; we cannot, therefore, measure their representativeness. We can say only that these and other data (for example, Paugam, 1996) point to the significant inclusionary potential of the extended family as often a very important and first link in a chain leading to virtuous circles (theme 2.1). However, the data also reveal that the extended family does not always foster inclusion into other systems. A few of the interviewed women reported chauvinist husbands who, in combination with stricter norms about what is decent female behaviour, impose restrictions on their inclusion into leisure-time and cultural activities as well.

> "It is like I don't feel right. I'm used to being at home.... Only if my husband goes, then I go along too."

All in all, while acknowledging that data on virtuous and vicious circles encompassing more than two systems are available for only two of the six countries under observation, one can draw some more general conclusions:

- With the very important exception of the inclusionary potential of the Portuguese extended family, there are no tendencies to *significant* accumulation of either good or bad situations. These observations are contrary both to the 'full St Matthew's principle' and the 'half St Matthew's effect' which Niklas Luhmann suggested.

- These results do not give any support to, but rather shed doubt on, the prevailing and dominant European policy of 'paid employment as the royal road to societal inclusion'.

The INPART findings about vicious and virtuous circles are partly supported by data from the Danish level-of-living investigation, which shows that there are almost no tendencies to accumulation of 'the good life' and also that accumulation of 'the bad life' is not often seen. It is reported there (Hansen et al, 1980) that only 5% of the whole population (aged 20-69) have 'a good position' in three systems and almost no one in four or five systems (the systems under study were: health, education, social relations, housing, employment, environment and economy). Vicious circles, however, are more evident, data show that 17%, 10% and 5% of the Danes have 'a bad position' in three, four and five systems, respectively. Unemployed people are over-represented in the vicious circles.

As for the question of patterns of compensation (theme 3), the Danish data again provide us with much information. The prevalence and the size of any negative associations among the five systems are taken as expressions of patterns of compensation, and negative gamma coefficients are applied as indicators of negative association between the five systems (Table 6.1). A finding of absent negative gamma coefficients can be taken as an empirical objective observation (cf Chapter Two). In the next section of this chapter, we report on subjective data about 'compensation', that is, individuals' strategies for compensating for unwanted exclusion/marginalisation from one or more systems.

As can be read from Table 6.1, there are very few negative coefficients, and when they do appear they are frequently small. This result indicates that it is very rarely that exclusion from or a marginal position within one system is compensated by inclusion into other systems. At first sight, this result seems somewhat contrary to the observation that unemployed and activated persons often are as much included into the social networks system and the system of leisure-time activities as are the employed. The 'lack of' negative gamma coefficients in Table 6.1 can be taken to show, however, that unemployed and activated persons' marginalisation and exclusion from the system of work is not counterweighted by strong, but only by average, positions in the system of networks and in the system of leisure-time (and is indeed accompanied by weak positions in the system of consumption/income and politics).

Our fourth theme (theme 4) focuses on the issue of whether or not a strong position within one system leads to patterns of exclusion from or marginalisation within other systems as a consequence of limited economic resources or shortage of time. The negative gamma coefficients in Table 6.1 can also be applied as indicators of this relationship since interpretations can be made 'both ways'. They indicate little support for this theme. The INPART study is, however, also able by way of the qualitative data to deliver other evidence.

From the Spanish cooperatives, based on the capitalisation of unemployment benefits scheme (CUB), it is frequently reported that, particularly among those persons with nuclear families, people put so much energy into their work(place) that they thereby exclude or marginalise themselves from other systems and subsystems (friends and neighbours, the cultural system, the leisure-time system, the political system) – though seldom the family which has second or first priority. In the cooperatives nearly all associated workers spend relatively more time on the job than workers in other firms. However, while those without a nuclear family are quite often included in the social network subsystems of friends, neighbours, the cultural and political system, the mothers and fathers of families concentrate their time on inclusion into work, consumption/income and the nuclear family.

Observations from the Danish qualitative studies show that the social activities of full-time employed persons sometimes seem to satisfy their need for social contacts to such an extent that they voluntarily reduce their contacts to the extended family, to neighbours and to friends.

The UK part-time study points out that some of the respondents explained that because they worked (part-time), they felt that they had to spend the remaining time with their children. Therefore, paid employment in this respect added to the obstacles that 'time poverty' can pose to inclusion.

Strategies for inclusion, exclusion and marginalisation

As we observed earlier, the associations between individuals' positions within the different systems are, in general, surprisingly few and low (with several other systems' associations with the system of consumption/income as the only but important exception). This leads to the conclusion that there seems to be little 'automatic' inclusion into, or exclusion from, positions in one system based on positions in other systems. It is furthermore our contention that many people realise that they are not 'automatically' included into a second system by their inclusion into the first (and vice versa so far as exclusion and marginalisation are concerned). Consequently people start thinking and acting strategically.

Some non-representative Dutch observations, however, indicate that such strategic thinking is not always the first step; and that some people believe, at least for some of their first spells of unemployment, that paid work will 'automatically' include them into other systems, for example new networks. The process of strategic thinking, we suggest, will then gradually gather pace from people's acknowledgement of the fact that there is nothing 'automatic' about either inclusion through re-employment or compensation for unwanted exclusion from a system. Sooner or later they have to develop and pursue their own strategies of inclusion and exclusion and they have to make up their minds as to where they want and where they do not want to be included. That is what this part of this chapter is about. More specifically, we shall deal with five different types of individual strategic thinking:

1. strategies for voluntary exclusion;
2. strategies for inclusion into paid employment and activation schemes;
3. strategies for a stronger position within the system of consumption/income (coping with poverty);
4. strategies for compensating unwanted exclusion/marginalisation from one system by inclusion into other systems;
5. strategies for bridging inclusion into two or more systems at the same time.

Chapter Two pointed to the fact that inclusion is not necessarily always something good and that there are numerous situations during people's life trajectories where they do not want to be included into this or that system. Not surprisingly, the case studies are full of examples of people who do not want to be included into the system of politics, the system of religion, the system of sport, different subsystems of fine art and culture, the subsystem of pop-culture, and so on. And most people are, for shorter or longer periods of their life and some even for their whole life, indifferent to, or even have aversions towards, one or more of the specific systems or subsystems. They *voluntarily* exclude themselves and normally do so without problems in relation to other people. Other people may disapprove or deplore their decision but most often politics, sport, religion and cultural activities are considered to belong strictly to the individual's 'private sphere' and seldom imply much involvement of other persons.

The same type of relationship to other people does not apply to the nuclear and extended families which nonetheless are also the subject for strategies of inclusion and exclusion. For example, some Portuguese women said that they decided to get married young (and thereby include themselves – sometimes temporarily – into a newly established family) in order to escape and be excluded from excessive paternalistic authority (in their original nuclear or extended family).

> "I can honestly say that I thought I could just get married to run away from there, and then after I had got married I could go and do my own stuff.... I mean, I was married.... I did feel something for the person I was going to marry, but I didn't want to be married forever, I wanted to get my independence so that no one else could ever again tell me what to do."

Some of the young Danish participants also reported plans for leaving the family where they were raised. However, they did not need to establish another family to leave home, and their voluntary exclusion from the family system would not necessarily be temporary, given the large and growing share of the population who already now live in one-adult households.

However people may have reasons for their preference not to be included other than indifference or aversion towards a system. From one of the Portuguese case studies a story was reported about a man who refused his neighbours' offer to help with building his house since he was afraid he would not be able to repay the favour. Therefore he excluded himself from or, at least, voluntarily restricted his inclusion into the subsystem of community/neighbourhood network. This was mainly due to the relational nature of participating in social life, involving a reciprocity that imposes obligations on those who benefit from others' help. So too the case study on informal work in the UK points to reciprocity as often being a basic assumption in informal exchange – a phenomenon which makes some people choose not to be included into this subsystem of work.

Looking at people's *preferences* for being included in paid work and activation, the overall impression from the INPART data is one of strong commitment to inclusion in paid work. This observation can, at least partly, be explained by the fact mentioned earlier, that some people believe for some initial stage of unemployment that paid work will 'automatically' include them into other systems as well. The strong commitment to paid work goes for the employed, the unemployed and the activated. There seem to be no national, regional, cultural or other exceptions from this general picture, which is also in line with Gallie and Paugam's observations (Gallie and Paugam, 2000). However, while they could report "that the unemployed were more committed to employment than people who were currently in jobs" (2000, p 357), the INPART data show the highest commitment to be among the employed (only the Danish INPART data, however, include both employed and unemployed persons, and the relevant questions are not directly comparable with Gallie and Paugam's observations).

Conversely, to be excluded from the system of paid work is perceived by the overwhelming majority of employed persons as a situation associated with fear of being socially isolated, of being economically deprived or of being unable to pass time.

The Belgian case study, among others, also gives examples of strategic motives for inclusion in an activation project:

> "I participate because I can carry on activity, I can learn a job, I can have some extra money and that helps pay for my children's needs and with the hope of finding a new job."

The points underlined here, as the significant exceptions to the generally few and low associations between individuals' positions in different systems, are the many and high associations between the system of consumption/income on the one hand, and most other systems on the other. It is again worth noting that these associations are examples of deliberate strategies which people adopt to use money as the 'entrance ticket' to the systems of culture, of leisure-time activities, of sports, and so on.

Other people include themselves into education which is then used as a stepping stone to inclusion into work. One Portuguese woman said:

> "And so, when I got married ... because before I got married I had stopped before I'd finished ninth grade ... and now last year I went back.... I wouldn't get it otherwise. Not ... just with ninth grade! If I reply to an advertisement

and there are other people applying with the twelfth grade, or even more, I know I'll never be chosen."

As we showed earlier, by means of the rather large extent to which it is possible to separate the effects of inclusion into paid work from the effects of inclusion into the system of consumption/income (see earlier), a person's inclusion into the system of consumption/income will often be more important for her/his inclusion into other systems than her/his inclusion into the system of paid work. It is therefore relevant to identify the *coping strategies* adopted by activated and unemployed persons to reduce their marginality and gain a stronger position within the system of consumption/income. Unfortunately, the INPART study has very few data on this. In fact only the Dutch, Portuguese and Danish studies provide us with some evidence.

The Dutch study reports about people doing voluntary work who perceive their social assistance benefits as so low that they want to be included into a Social Activation scheme. These schemes are non-compulsory, designed for the most long-term unemployed persons, often with other purposes than inclusion into the labour market and with €1.50 per day to supplement the benefit.

Compared to the Danish data, the Portuguese observations reflect the much lower level of unemployment benefits and other social benefits paid out to activated and unemployed persons. Portuguese coping strategies, as reported in several of the qualitative interviews, also reflect the fact that the process of deruralisation of Portuguese society is far less advanced. There are, first, strategies to increase income and reduce expenses: in rural areas, farming and rearing of animals for home consumption, or cultivating a small vegetable plot or even a larger garden at the edge of the town, are typical strategies of inclusion. Furthermore, there are possibilities of taking odd jobs, such as personal or domestic service, cleaning, or street selling. The other family members, typically, can take overtime work or take more than one job. Many of these activities take place in the informal market as a normal and essential means of economic survival for many of the families studied. Expenses are most often reduced by a tightening of the belt. An illustration of this is the case of a respondent who had to remove her daughter from school because she could no longer bear the costs of transport, clothing and educational material. The second type of strategy focuses on increasing support by investing in primary solidarity networks. Despite scant resources, these Portuguese families show a huge willingness to help the most needy. Their family solidarity is manifested in the form of mutual aid, in caring for the elderly, for children, for disabled kinfolk, in sharing goods, such as land, homes, clothes and food.

Danish coping strategies are very different from the Portuguese and reflect a predominantly service society without pre-modern modes of production, in which the great majority of activated and unemployed persons live in one-person households (Gallie and Paugam, 2000, p 262). Two types of coping strategies prevail. First, material aspirations are observed to be lower among the activated and unemployed than among the rest of the population. Secondly, the activated and unemployed show some acquiescence in their situation. The latter is sometimes combined with hopes for a future in which the degree of inclusion into the system of consumption/income will be stronger.

In the first part of this chapter, objective data indicated a low degree of compensation for unwanted exclusion/marginalisation. This result is not invalidated by the fact that some of the INPART study's subjective data point to strategies of compensation on the part of excluded or marginalised individuals. Having been hit by unemployment once, or never having had access to paid employment, unemployed and activated persons may still develop strategies to *compensate* their exclusion/marginalisation from paid employment by *including themselves* into other systems. Unfortunately the INPART data do not provide systematic or comprehensive information on this matter. The few data available confirm that such strategies come into play, but how frequent they are remains uncertain.

The most general observations come from the Dutch social activation scheme which some participants join as a strategy for inclusion into the system of unpaid work as a kind of compensation for their exclusion from paid work.

Another example concerns a young Danish woman whose education was cut off by illness. At present she is activated in a project where the participants are informed about and gain an insight into various types of employment and education/training schemes. In her leisure-time, she plays the violin and so has a position in the cultural system. At the same time, however, she sometimes feels a bit lonely and consequently has decided to play in an orchestra in the hope of enlarging her network. She has also recently found a boyfriend among the other activated people. In other words, she utilises her inclusion into the cultural system and the subsystem of activation to strengthen her position in the social network system.

A third example is that of a former firefighter and top-level ice hockey player who long ago suffered a mental and physical breakdown that lasted for years. At present, he is activated a few hours a week in a voluntary cafe in a deprived part of Copenhagen. To enlarge his network which was totally destroyed with his breakdown, and since his physical capacity is still very limited, he has started as a voluntary rollerskate instructor for working-class children in another deprived area of the city.

A fourth example is an activated Belgian person (quoted earlier) who can be seen both as an illustration of strategic inclusion into activation for the purpose of finding a job, and as a strategy to strengthen the individual's position within the subsystem of family relations by getting some extra money for his/her children.

Finally, we shall point to the *strategies* people adopt *for bridging their inclusion into two or more systems* at the same time. One of the most widespread examples is women's engagement in part-time employment as a strategy to combine inclusion into paid employment with inclusion into the family. One of the UK case studies says that one of the reasons why women chose part-time work in retail and catering was the flexible hours available in these jobs. The ability to structure their working day around childcare responsibilities is a major benefit of their paid employment. This bridge, however, is at the same time a consequence of the relatively low wages and the limited social protection often attached to part-time employment, one that reduces these women's inclusion into the system of consumption/income, the system of culture and the system of leisure-time activities.

Summary

In the first part of this chapter, three different patterns were applied in order to shed light on four different themes. The first theme, 'the royal road to inclusion' (that is, the contention that inclusion into paid work is the only or most important way to inclusion into other systems) found only little support from our data. What turned out to be of much more importance for inclusion into other systems is inclusion into the system of income/consumption. This system appeared to be the only one with several and strong associations to other systems.

The second theme concerned the prevalence of *vicious and virtuous circles*. Here, no evidence was found of the former; and virtuous circles were observed only in Portugal, where they were based on the prevalence of the extended family and where inclusion into this subsystem was often observed to be an important basis for inclusion into other systems (leisure-time activities, the cultural system and the system of paid informal or formal work). All in all, however, we found very little support for both the 'full St Matthew principle' and for the Luhmannian 'half St Matthew principle'. It is rather well documented, then, that a 'bad position' within one system is rarely followed by a series of other bad positions, and vice versa so far as 'good positions' are concerned.

In general, our study has revealed that activated and unemployed people have weaker positions than the employed in the system of consumption/income and in the system of politics, whereas the same cannot be observed in the system of social networks, in the system of leisure-time activities and in the cultural system. There are tendencies for unemployed and activated persons to be positioned into the less expensive parts of the cultural system and the leisure-time system, but that apart, they are all in all as frequently and as strongly included as employed persons.

The third theme concerned 'compensations', that is, the conjecture that unwanted exclusion from one system is compensated by inclusion into other systems. Here our data show that compensations are very rarely found. Unemployed and activated persons seem often not to have strong positions in other systems – only moderately good positions in the systems of social networks and of leisure-time activities (and significantly weak positions in the system of consumption/income and the political system).

The fourth theme concerned the influence of a strong (and resource demanding) inclusion into one system on the same person's inclusion into other systems. The clearest example in the INPART study is from the Spanish cooperatives, where workers often have to put so much energy and time into their workplace that they partly exclude or marginalise themselves from all other systems except the family system. However, full-time employed Danish and part-time employed UK women also report both a lack of interest and limited time to enter into other systems than the nuclear family system.

The lack of 'automatic' compensation for exclusion from, or a marginalised position within, one system was the background for our focus in the second part of the chapter on individuals' strategies for inclusion/exclusion. The INPART study illustrates a variety of strategies that are applied by individuals in various countries, as outlined on p 150:

- strategies for voluntary exclusion;
- strategies for inclusion into paid employment and activation schemes;
- strategies for a stronger position within the system of consumption/income (coping with poverty);
- strategies for compensating unwanted exclusion/marginalisation from one system by inclusion into other systems;
- strategies for bridging inclusion into two or more systems at the same time.

Notes

[1] 'Better off' here means to be more included, although it is acknowledged that there are persons who prefer to be marginalised or excluded.

[2] The strength of position in the system of work is measured by stability of employment, employment prospects and expected possibilities of finding another job if needed (for the employed); employment record and expected possibilities of finding another job (for the activated); employment record (for the unemployed). The strength of position in the system of income/consumption is, for all three groups, measured by disposable income and satisfaction with present level of living.

References

Gallie, D. (1999) 'Unemployment and social exclusion in the European Union', *European Societies*, vol 1, no 2, pp 139-69.

Gallie, D. (2000) 'Unemployment, work and welfare', Paper presented to the seminar 'Towards a learning society: Innovation and competence building with social cohesion for Europe', Quinta da Marinha, Guincho, Lisbon, 28–30 May.

Gallie, D. and Paugam, S. (2000) 'The social regulation of unemployment', in D. Gallie and S. Paugam (eds) *Welfare regimes and the experience of unemployment in Europe*, Oxford/New York, NY: Oxford University Press.

Hansen, E.J. et al (1980) *Fordeling af levekårene II*, Socialforskningsinstituttets Publikation No 82, Copenhagen: Teknisk Forlag.

Hansen, H. (2001) *Arbejde, aktivering og arbejdsløshed – integration i det hele liv*, Copenhagen: Samfundslitteratur.

Jahoda, M., Lazarsfeld, P. and Zeisel, H. (1975) *Die Arbeitslosen von Marienthal. Ein soziographischer Versuch über die Wirkungen Langandauernder Arbeitslosigkeit*, Frankfurt: Campus.

Johannessen, A. (1998) 'Social tilhørlighet – inntekt viktigere enn lønnet arbeid', *Nordisk Socialt Arbeide*, no 4, pp 231-37.

Møller, I. (2000) *Understanding integration and differentiation – inclusion, marginalisation and exclusion*, Coimbra: Oficina do Centro de Estudos Sociais, University of Coimbra.

National Reports (1999) *Inclusion through participation*, Work Package 3: The case studies, Annex to comparative report, Report in the context of the INPART research project, Contract no SOE2-CT97-3043.

Paugam, S. (1996) 'Poverty and social disqualification: a comparative analysis of cumulative and social disadvantage in Europe', *Journal of European Social Policy*, no 6, pp 287-303.

Statistisk sentralbyrå (1996) *Levekårsundersøgelsen 1995*, Oslo: Statistisk sentralbyrå.

SEVEN

Entrepreneurial activation: the Spanish Capitalisation of Unemployment Benefits programme

Aitor Gómez González

Introduction

In Southern Europe, the male breadwinner model constitutes the core of citizenship in terms of income provision, and this model is still being reproduced by the state. State intervention is mostly passive, and this changes only when family support fails, and not before (Mingione, 2001). Consequently, people rely heavily on family and social network support when they do not manage labour market inclusion. Therefore, family and social networks are the main decommodification elements. Of course, employment entitlements exist in the form of unemployment benefits, but they offer only temporary relief and are accessible after a period of labour market participation only. The passive role of the state is also one of the causes of a high incidence of irregular work, family business and self-employment activities, which are alternative ways to obtain an income.

The prevalence of the male breadwinner model and the importance of the family as a welfare provider have a clear effect on the situation of women. Nowadays young people stay at their parents' home for a longer period than in the past (Andreotti et al, 2001). Public childcare facilities are very limited compared to Northern Europe, and taking care of elderly people is still the work of women in the private sphere of the family. These facts make it difficult for women to participate in the labour market since they invest so much of their time in family responsibilities, going some way to explain why women participate less in the formal labour market, either full-time or part-time. At the same time, this fact also explains why women take part-time jobs and irregular work in larger numbers than men (Mingione, 2001; see also Atkinson, 1986).

In Spain, it is this welfare-state regime context into which active labour market policies are introduced. Different kinds of active measures which are described in the Spanish National Action Plan (NAP) are introduced to reach the objectives of the four pillars on which the NAPs are based (see Chapter

Five). The major part of active measures is located in the first pillar – employability – but there are various measures located in the other pillars as well. Some of the measures that are being introduced aim to bridge the gender gap (which is related to the problems described earlier), and there are also individualised active measures addressed to incorporating the most excluded people into the labour market.

Generally, active measures in Spain relate for the most part either to training schemes or to a combination of training and labour insertion schemes. Spanish policies are hardly directed at the creation of new jobs; insofar as they are, this is normally connected with the implementation of active measures. Jobs which are created in this context are temporary. When the measure comes to an end, the participants' new job finishes as well and the person needs to find another job.

This chapter focuses on a specific activation scheme: the Capitalisation of Unemployment Benefits scheme (CUB). The case of CUB differs from the general characteristics of Spanish activation schemes that I have just described because it involves, potentially at least, the creation of permanent new jobs. The core of CUB can be summarised as follows. Through CUB, workers obtain the total amount of money of their unemployment benefit – the main passive policy in Spain[1] – they are entitled to at one time. Therefore, CUB is the result of a transformation process of a 'passive' policy (unemployment benefit) into an 'active' measure. The measure's objective is to include participants into a social economy business that they create, as will be explained later in this chapter. They are obliged to invest their capitalised benefits in a new social company or in a previously existing one[2]. Little more state support is involved in CUB other than the opportunity for the capitalisation of unemployment benefit entitlements. In terms of activation approaches (see Chapter Three of this volume), CUB has some of the characteristics of the autonomy optimists' approach. For example, its emphasis on people's own initiative – even though, of course, the capitalisation option is quite different from an unconditional basic income.

From the perspective of social policies, the opportunity to capitalise one's unemployment benefits is considered to be an emancipation mechanism: the money people receive should stimulate them to start their own business. For the participants themselves, the real emancipation mechanism is the new business created, partly because they need to change their workers' mentality into that of 'co-owner'. In that sense they are changing their attitude to work. In turn, this change provokes other changes in different systems, for instance family and social networks.

Potentially, CUB is an important mechanism for promoting labour market inclusion of people who have lost their jobs and are at risk of exclusion from the labour market and from other systems. When the scheme was introduced, its target group consisted mainly of male breadwinners who lost their jobs in the industrial sector. The measure offered these workers an opportunity to continue their professional activity, to maintain an income and to begin a new activity in another sector of the economy.

The worker who uses CUB buys shares in a new company, thereby transforming his situation from worker into that of owner; that is, having capitalised his benefits he is one of the owners of the company. This job can be permanent: whether or not he is able to keep the job does not depend on the activation measure, but on the success of the new business.

CUB is an inclusive measure that encourages an entrepreneurial mentality that differs from other entrepreneurial contexts, in the sense that it creates a mechanism for collective participation of workers as co-owners in the different decision-making organs.

Contextualisation and evolution of CUB from 1985 to 2000

Contextualisation

In 1984, the Unemployment Protection Law established the possibility for a worker to receive the total amount of money he is entitled to in the context of the contributory unemployment benefit. Of course, this amount depends on the period of time the worker was contributing (Trigo, 1996). The conditions under which people can apply for CUB were specified by royal decree[3].

The main objective of CUB is to create new employment and to maintain jobs in threatened companies. The scheme facilitates the incorporation of the unemployed – or people at risk of becoming unemployed – in self-employment activities, in cooperatives or in Anonymous Labour Societies (ALS) – alternative CUB options that are discussed later in this chapter. The money that workers obtain by capitalising their unemployment benefit has to be invested in one of the following three ways:

- The creation of a new social economy business (cooperatives and ALS);
- Investment in an already existing social economy company with the objective of becoming an associated worker of that company;
- The establishment of the worker as self-employee[4] (an option abolished in 1992).

Workers who choose the first and second options are investing their unemployment benefits into a business which differs from a private company. In the case of cooperatives, it is important to highlight their long history and tradition, as well as their economic, social and legal framework. They date back to 1844, when the workers of Rochdale created the first consumer cooperative[5] and established a set of principles that laid the foundations of the first legislation on cooperatives (Vidal, 1987). The workers of Rochdale developed values of equality, equity, democracy and solidarity through principles such as equal voting rights; the creation of a non-sharing cooperative patrimony (profits should be invested in the cooperative only, workers cannot use it for themselves); and having a majority of workers with decision-making power (Chavez and Monzón, 2000).

The absence of legislation on cooperatives that had adjusted to the situation of the Spanish labour market at the beginning of the 1970s did not prevent workers who had lost their jobs in the industrial sector from establishing new cooperatives. This was one of the workers' possibilities during the crisis of the 1970s. Another option was irregular work: a large number of workers decided to start working in the submerged economy or in self-employment, because it was very difficult to re-enter the labour market and find jobs under similar conditions as they had (Vidal, 1987). Concentrating here on the first possibility, the creation of cooperatives during this period of economic crisis should be interpreted as part of workers' survival strategies within the exigencies of the labour market. Therefore, their main reason for establishing cooperatives was not a reaffirmation of basic values of equality and responsibility within this kind of business (even though this kind of spirit was at times present). Rather, their first motive was to maintain jobs and, subsequently, to create more occupations (Vidal, 1987).

The cooperative principles approved in the last Cooperative Act in Spain are very much related to the principles approved during the Congress of the International Cooperative Alliance (ICA) in 1995[6]. Besides, the development of a more flexible and private labour market has influenced the wording of some points of the new act on cooperatives. It makes an attempt to combine increased privatisation in the regular labour market with the special social character of cooperative companies, thereby stimulating a more flexible type of cooperative[7].

As an alternative to cooperatives, people can invest CUB money in the ALS, mentioned earlier, and, since 1997, in a Limited Labour Society (LLS). From the mid-1960s onwards, a new type of company business came into existence in Spain, which differs from both the cooperative and private companies. These companies were the predecessors of the ALS, a terminology that was introduced at the end of the 1970s. Initially, the ALS concept began to consolidate without a legal framework to regulate them. The first legal framework was introduced in 1986 (Vidal and Vilaplana, 1999).

The ALS differs from a private company basically in that its workers must own at least 51% of the company's shares. In these companies workers work on indefinite and full-time contracts[8]. As in the case of the cooperatives, a distinction can be made between associated workers, non-associated workers and associated non-workers. An associated worker has invested money in a social economy company by buying shares, but also works in the company. A non-associated worker works in a social economy company temporarily and has no shares in it. An associated non-worker is a person who has shares in a social economy company but does not work in it. A single worker cannot own more than 25% of the company's shares. Public companies can participate as associated companies with a maximum 49% share of the capital[9]. In an ALS, a maximum of 15% of all employed workers can be non-associated workers with indefinite contracts. This percentage is 10% in the case of cooperatives.

In a similar way to the cooperatives, ALS must invest a percentage of their profits in a non-sharing Special Reserve Fund. This means that there is no possibility to share profits among workers: profits have to be reinvested in the cooperative. The ALS have no Education and Social Promotion Fund, and training workers in a specific entrepreneurial mentality is not one of their objectives[10]. As in the case of the cooperatives, the ALS have some special benefits and some fiscal exemptions.

The minimum amount of money needed to create an ALS is €60,103. This fact explains why a large number of companies are based on the other legal option of business, the LLS, that was approved by law in 1997[11]. The minimum amount of money to establish an LLS was set at only €3,005, and the number of associated workers at only three. These facts made LLS the best formula for encouraging the participation of workers in social companies.

Evolution

As a legal framework, CUB is not very complicated, and in terms of economic resources involved it is quite small. These resources do not exceed the unemployment benefit contributions of the workers; in other words, the government does not invest extra resources. In fact, the Spanish and regional governments only invest in the bureaucratic system of registration. No investment is made, for example, in resources to improve workers' possibilities to use the measure. However, the results of the scheme in terms of labour insertion and indirectly in terms of inclusion are considerable.

The main institution that used to be in charge of the measure was the National Employment Institute (INEM). Nowadays, the main responsibility to approve company plans lies in some cases with central government and in others with local governments.

Table 7.1 clearly shows that, between 1985 and 1992, a total number of 499,769 unemployed people used the measure. If we compare, as an example, the total amount of participants in 1989 (82,097) with the total number of unemployed people that same year (2,560,750) we obtain a percentage of 3.2%. In other words, the importance of the measure should not be looked for in its quantitative impact. Rather, the importance is located in the kind of mentality and type of work that this measure encourages. Therefore, one can say that it has a high incidence of inclusion.

It is important to highlight that from 1985 to 1992, around 87% of CUB investments took place in self-employment activities. During this period, investing CUB capital in a new business was the common way in which workers made use of the scheme. CUB investments in cooperatives amounted to 5%, and in ALSs to 8% (Trigo, 1996). This situation changed from 1992 onwards. It was in 1992 that the promulgation of the R.D. Act 1/1992 (3 April) on Urgent

Table 7.1: Unemployed people who capitalised unemployment benefits by type of employment in Spain (1985-2000)

Year	Total	Self-employment	Associated workers in cooperatives	Associated workers in ALS and LLS
1985	16,840	12,446	1,389	3,013
1986	59,240	48,108	3,933	7,199
1987	64,192	53,052	2,998	8,142
1988	74,827	65,147	2,948	6,732
1989	82,097	74,256	2,773	5,050
1990	76,451	70,698	2,287	3,466
1991	81,513	75,444	2,485	3,584
1992	44,609	37,337	3,956	3,316
1993	10,798	613	5,298	4,887
1994	10,935	135	5,632	5,168
1995	8,174	86	4,785	3,303
1996	7,541	93	4,568	2,880
1997	7,144	38	3,927	3,179
1998	8,931	20	3,348	5,563
1999	9,384	38	3,432	5,914
2000	10,589	92	4,090	6,407

Source: Labour Statistic Bulletin Number 140, January 1997 and Number 163, March 2001

Employment Measures took place. These measures prohibited the investment of the money of the capitalisation scheme in self-employment[12].

Several factors influenced the growth of the use of CUB between 1985 and 1992. Here, I wish to mention the process of industrial restructuring, the destruction of industrial jobs and the introduction of the law on ALS. Obviously, the main factor that provokes the use of the measure is unemployment, which was one of the main problems in Spain during the 1970s and 1980s, especially in the industrial sector, but also in the service sector. Furthermore, the approval of the Act on Anonymous Labour Societies of 1986 normalised the situation of ALS in Spain. Besides this, the rich cooperative history in Spain offered a breeding ground for the creation of new social economy businesses by using the measure[13].

In 1992, Spain was confronted with a serious crisis in its economy. A lot of companies crashed and the unemployment rate rocketed once again, reaching 24.2% in 1994. This factor contributed to the increasing number of capitalisations used to create new social economy businesses from old private companies.

As was pointed out earlier in the chapter, 1997 saw another legal modification that influenced the use of CUB. That year, the creation of LLS was approved. Compared to the ALS, this new type of business offers some advantages. One of the most important advantages has been mentioned already: workers need

€3,005 to create an LLS compared to €60,103 in the case of a new ALS. Consequently, the last few years have seen a large number of new LLS registrations, whereas the number of cooperatives and ALS have remained about the same.

Generally speaking, the target group of the measure has remained the same since CUB was introduced; that is, people who have the right to receive unemployment benefits and, therefore, people with labour market experience. However, there are differences between people who made use of the measure in the past and the people who are using it now. In the past, the persons who capitalised their unemployment benefit had considerable labour market experience and an average age of 35. They invested their money in self-employment mainly. They preferred to create their own business, working normally by themselves (without staff). Besides, there were people who invested the money in new social economy businesses. The greater part of these new companies was created from previously crashed private companies in which the people who capitalised had been working for a number of years. That is, the workers bought the company.

After the implementation of the Act on Labour Societies in 1997, the profile of workers who capitalised unemployment benefits changed considerably. Now the average person using CUB is a young person with experience in the labour market but for a considerably shorter period than the average worker who used the CUB in the 1980s. The businesses are also different: they are located in the service sector mainly, whereas during the 1980s, the larger part of the companies was located in the industrial sector. The companies are relatively small: most companies employ less than five workers.

CUB compared to the 'mainstream' of activation policies in Spain and the EU

Capitalisation of Unemployment Benefits is a measure to support business initiatives and to create jobs. Furthermore, it encourages self-employment and work in social economy companies. It has some characteristics that make it very different from the mainstream of activation schemes in Spain and in the EU. This section puts CUB in the broader activation context and discusses some of these differences in more detail.

In Spain, following the OECD recommendations of the end of the 1980s[14], the main goal in terms of employment policy was to diminish passive policy expenses and to increase expenses targeted at the reincorporation of the unemployed in the labour market and at facilitating first job access (ESADE, 1997; Férez et al, 1997). Since 1998, active labour market policies in Spain, as well as in the rest of the EU, are linked to the National Action Plan (NAP). The NAP distinguishes four pillars, of which the first one, *to improve professional insertion capability or employability*, is directed at replacing passive measures with active ones. Within these active measures, three types of action can be distinguished: training, professional orientation, and employment support (CES,

1999). In addition, this has led to a great diversity of actions in Spain; however, in terms of the actual number of unemployed people included into the labour market their impact is limited. The majority of actions in Spain is related to training and professional orientation and not to the direct creation of new jobs[15]. With respect to the latter, again a great diversity of actions can be found[16], with the common objective of including unemployed people in the labour market, and with the common problem of the absence of continuity. For these measures have been created from a 'curative' point of view, incorporating unemployed people into the secondary labour market temporarily, so that jobs end when measures end (Álvarez Aledo, 1996).

Many of the activation schemes in the EU can be seen as 'curative' measures as well. They are measures aimed at target groups such as long-term or young unemployed people; in short, at people who are excluded from or have a marginal position in the labour market which, potentially, may exclude them from other domains of participation in society (see Chapter Six). Their main goal is to reincorporate unemployed people in the labour market, and when job schemes are involved, these are mostly secondary labour market jobs and not jobs in the regular labour market.

The CUB scheme has another orientation. It is not a 'curative' measure addressed to reincorporate excluded people into jobs that have been created for them. Rather it is targeted at short-term unemployed people with labour market experience. Therefore, it is a preventive rather than a curative active measure, since it gives short-term unemployed people with a recent work history the opportunity to capitalise their unemployment benefits and to invest in a social economy company, rather than to wait for state intervention until they are long-term unemployed.

In terms of job creation, CUB is also quite different from the larger part of active measures in Europe, and also those in Spain. Usually, many of the jobs created through these active measures are closely related to the state. The state creates public jobs directly through some of these active measures or it introduces measures to stimulate employers to create jobs for the most excluded people. In the case of CUB, state intervention is almost non-existent. Some guidance is offered by the National Employment Institute[17] and by local employment offices to those workers who want to create a new business with the money coming from unemployment benefits. However, the entire responsibility to create and to begin the activity in the new company lies with the workers who capitalised their benefits. The state prescribes that capitalised benefits must be invested in a social economy company. However, CUB is not stimulating secondary labour market jobs but instead, helps to create jobs in the regular labour market (see Chapters Two and Five). The Spanish state intervenes to encourage employment in cooperatives in general, but not specifically in the context of CUB. The state supports cooperatives through fiscal exemptions and it tries to stimulate employers by giving them more facilities to contract unemployed people.

Unemployed people who use CUB are re-entering the regular labour market as co-owners with indefinite contracts. This is yet another characteristic that makes CUB different from other active measures. Not only, as was mentioned earlier, because these measures normally create temporary employment outside the regular labour market, but also because usually these measures do not encourage company ownership. To have an indefinite work relation inside these social economy companies gives workers a secure income and enables them to make long-term plans. This work relation is not directly related to increased opportunities for inclusion into other systems, but it gives more security, for instance in terms of family and social networks.

The opportunity to become co-owner of the company is probably the most outstanding difference between CUB and the mainstream of active measures in the EU and in Spain. As we will see later in this chapter, the fact that they are working for themselves is an important ingredient of the job satisfaction for many workers who are co-owners of a social economy company. The stimulation of the creation of this kind of worker-owned company in the context of active measures is unique. Insofar as one thinks of autonomy, responsibility, and participation at work as important elements of in-work inclusion, CUB certainly stimulates the creation of companies in which these elements are institutionalised. Of course, the measure does not guarantee that all participants change their worker mentality into one based on a worker–owner mentality. This depends on the workers, a fact representing a potential source of conflict within social companies.

The capitalisation of unemployment benefits in Barcelona and Vizcaya: experiences of inclusion[18]

In Chapter Two, a distinction is introduced between subjective and objective approaches of inclusion and exclusion. The first one analyses inclusion and exclusion 'from the inside', according to the interpretations of actors. This section will focus on CUB participants' interpretations and is based, therefore, on a subjective approach to inclusion and exclusion.

Barcelona and Vizcaya are the Spanish Autonomous Communities that nationally registered most cases of capitalisations during the entire period that the measure has been functioning. The starting point for using CUB is unemployment. Both provinces were confronted with unemployment during the last decades, though not to as great an extent as other parts of Spain. Differences between these two provinces and others relate on the one hand to the higher socio-economic and labour market participation, and on the other hand to the social economy tradition which is stronger here than in other parts of Spain. Traditionally, both provinces have been the most industrialised areas of Spain with, compared to the rest of Spain, a strong workers' movement. The growth and consolidation of the cooperative movement has always been related to this movement. In these provinces, opportunities to create a new business are higher than in others and there is also a higher entrepreneurial mentality.

Many industries closed in Bilbao (the capital of Vizcaya) and Barcelona during the 1970s and 1980s, and CUB was a formula used by workers to invest money and to maintain the company in which they were previously working. Together with the large cooperative tradition in both provinces, this facilitated the creation of new social economy businesses and the incorporation of workers into these companies. It is only to be expected that workers in these provinces should use the measure more often. They have more opportunities to work in already existing social economy companies than in other parts of Spain. Furthermore, they have more opportunities for creating new ones because of the social economy tradition in both provinces.

The increase of the use of CUB from 1997 to 1999 in Spain is caused by the increase in new LLS. Capitalisations and investments of capital in new ALS or new cooperatives occur much less frequently: in these cases, CUB investments take place in previously existing companies rather than in new ones.

The impact of the Law 4/1997 of 24 March about labour societies was very limited in the case of Vizcaya. Here, the cooperative sector is highly consolidated and has a strong position within competitive labour markets. Furthermore, there is also a strong and consolidated ALS movement. Therefore, it is not very difficult for a person to capitalise his unemployment benefit and invest the money in an already consolidated cooperative or ALS, and to start working as an associated worker of that company.

In Barcelona there are also strong cooperative and ALS movements, with more cooperatives having been established in Barcelona than in Vizcaya. In terms of the numbers of workers involved, the differences between both provinces are not very large, especially if we take the active population in both cases into account. In Vizcaya the number of CUB users, relative to the total number of unemployed people, is higher than in Barcelona. In Vizcaya, 1% of the

Table 7.2: Unemployed people using CUB by type of associated worker in Barcelona and Vizcaya (1993-99)[19]

		BARCELONA			VIZCAYA		SPAIN
Year	Total	Associated workers in cooperatives	Associated workers in ALS/LLS	Total	Associated workers in cooperatives	Associated workers in ALS/LLS	Total
1993	2,333	1,629	714	974	321	653	10,798
1994	2,375	1,873	502	889	233	656	10,935
1995	2,019	1,580	439	572	204	368	8,174
1996	1,727	1,489	238	654	351	303	7,541
1997	1,457	1,126	331	589	250	338	7,144
1998	1,401	819	582	701	266	435	8,931
1999	1,153	586	567	801	464	337	9,384
93-99	12,465	9,102	3,373	5,180	2,089	3,090	62,907

Source: Annual Labour Statistic and Social Affairs Bulletin 1993-99

unemployed people use the measure, whereas this percentage is 0.5% in Barcelona. This shows once again, that the importance of CUB should not be sought in the number of unemployed using the measure.

Barcelona has more LLSs and more LLS workers than Vizcaya. In that sense the impact of the new legislation has been more profound there than in Vizcaya. The characteristics of LLS companies in both provinces are quite similar in terms of size and sector of activity. The larger part is composed of a staff of less than five workers (83.7% of the total number of LLS). In the case of cooperatives and ALSs we find medium-sized and also big companies created through CUB.

What follows is a description of the experiences of CUB users in terms of the inclusionary potentials of the measure. In this context it is important to distinguish between the different kinds of companies (ALS, LLS and cooperatives) because there are, as this chapter has already pointed out, many differences between them which partly concern differences in workers' mentality. Workers who use CUB to invest in an ALS normally have a more pragmatic mentality than workers who use the measure to create cooperatives.

Co-ownership, responsibility and autonomy

In both provinces we find a large diversity and a great heterogeneity of life and labour histories among the people who use the measure to start working as associated workers. Compared to workers in 'regular' companies, these workers have more opportunities to participate in the affairs of their respective businesses and more responsibilities and autonomy. In the end, this may result in a higher feeling of inclusion and satisfaction at work, which may have a positive incidence in other life domains (see Chapter Six). However, some workers, for example among those who worked in a private company which crashed and was subsequently transformed into an ALS using CUB, prefer to work as 'regular' workers in the same way as they used to do in the past. In these cases, feelings of satisfaction are the same as in the past or less than in the past if they are confronted with an increase of responsibilities.

Reasons for using CUB are very diverse, but all cases have two things in common: an unemployment situation of the user and the investment of CUB in a social economy company. The worker who uses the measure has shares in the business – he is co-owner. Therefore, objectively, CUB users are changing their worker situation. As a result of their co-ownership, their level of responsibility increases, as does their level of involvement, because they need to initiate and develop the business themselves.

> "[Y]ou have to be responsible for your tasks.... I am doing everything, on Saturdays and Sundays. Because I'm working for myself. Even though I don't get any income. I'm working for me, to get the company going."

Workers who decided to create a new business or transform a previously private company into a social economy company and need to manage it by themselves, have a higher entrepreneurial and activation spirit than workers who capitalised their benefits to be incorporated in already existing companies. Without this kind of entrepreneurial mentality it would not be possible to create a new business. This mentality is encouraged by using CUB, and for this reason the measure has an important activation effect in stimulating this entrepreneurial spirit among workers.

> "It is true that we have created the Anonymous Labour Society, we have an entrepreneurial spirit, if we wouldn't have had it we wouldn't have got involved."

These workers who have shares in the social economy business and are very involved consider it to be important that the other workers of the company value their high level of responsibility for the business. This mechanism of positive recognition of the work that all workers develop in a company is an important condition of improving the self-esteem of all of them and, in that way, to create a positive work atmosphere.

> "But I'm this kind of person who believes that responsibility has to be accompanied by something.... At least there must be recognition. We work at an infernal rhythm and that fact has to be recognised by people who do not have the same responsibilities."

The increase of responsibilities also provokes an increase of two other important inclusive factors, participation and autonomy within the company. Autonomy is directly related to the work that workers develop within the business and also to the capability for taking decisions. In terms of efficiency, it is basic to have a high degree of autonomy to decide quickly and correctly. For this reason it is very important for workers in these businesses to find ways of taking consensual decisions, and at the same time to do this efficiently.

Objectively the structure of cooperatives and labour societies allows workers to take decisions and also gives more freedom of action. However, both types of social economy company function differently in this respect. In fact, it seems that these processes seem to work more smoothly in cooperatives, which are functioning according to real cooperative principles and encourage participation of all workers. Especially in Social Initiative Cooperatives[20], in which all important decisions are taken in assemblies.

> "We have assemblies in which the non-associated workers have the right to vote."

In contrast, there are many ALS that were created from a previous private company where workers were highly involved at the beginning of the transformation process but where their involvement diminished once the company began to increase its profits and the labour situation was normalised.

Workers know that they have shares in their company and a secure job, and feel that they do not need to be more involved in the company to obtain the same income as other associated workers who are participating actively in the same business. This is one of the main causes of tensions among associated workers of social economy companies.

> "From the 49 associated workers I can tell you that 44 have not changed, they continue in the same way as in the past.... From this point you need to sacrifice the four or five workers who have tried to change and to adapt to the new project and to resolve new situations."

In such cases the majority of workers do not want to have decision-making power; they are not attracted by extra responsibilities and autonomy. They prefer how things had been in the past, when they were working as workers of private companies. The new situation in which they need to change their worker mentality and to increase their involvement and participation in the company is not good for them.

Taking into account these problematic situations, it is important to highlight the relation between the increase of autonomy and the increase of responsibility. Workers who have many responsibilities have a higher autonomy and freedom to work and to decide. These elements and other workers' recognition of their duties increase feelings of inclusion and the efficiency of their respective social economy companies.

> "[Y]ou are doing your work and you are enjoying it. You have a margin of autonomy that is good and you have a margin of trust that allows you to manage the company and this factor may be the cause of motivation among workers."

Each associated worker that was interviewed was satisfied with his or her job. Normally this feeling of satisfaction is higher among persons who have been involved in a social economy company from its start, taking responsibilities and participating actively in the company, than among workers who become incorporated into an already existing social economy company. For those workers who prefer not to assume more responsibilities and autonomy and are not really involved in the company, satisfaction levels are roughly the same as when they were still working in a private company.

This feeling of satisfaction has a positive effect on workers' experiences of inclusion in their companies, that is, in the system of work. It also has a positive influence on their family and social networks.

Inclusion in work and inclusion in other systems

Workers normally increase their participation in their own companies, but not in other systems. These include, for instance, social, political and cultural domains, underlining the lack of automatic spin-off effects from inclusion in work on inclusion into other (sub)systems of society (see Chapter Six). Workers do not feel the need to participate in other activities outside work. For example, among the interviewees the number of workers who are participating in social movements is very small. Those who do participate in social movements normally work in companies with a real cooperative philosophy, and are working to obtain a social impact, as in the case of one respondent who is working in a cooperative and is also participating in social movements, in this instance a neighbourhood association. This involvement positively affects her feeling of inclusion in the neighbourhood.

> "When you are involved in organisations you know the tangles of different neighbourhoods or areas in more depth, the companies, houses and all those things in which you are involved."

Active political participation is almost non-existent among the interviewed workers. Only in a few cases, the person turned out to participate in political parties or to attend political meetings. In that sense CUB and the type of work that it encourages is not related with participation in the political system. More workers are involved in trade unions than in political parties, because unions allow them to participate more directly. However, workers who were involved in trade unions at the end of the 1970s and at the beginning of the 1980s now have negative perceptions of these bureaucratised organisations.

The CUB has a positive impact in terms of income or economic participation. Inclusion in this domain is encouraged by the new situation of the CUB user, because he or she is co-owner of a business, and in this way has a secure job and income. Normally, workers reported that initially, when they created a new social economy company, their incomes diminished.

> "All of us have changed our salaries, in order to make the company solvent and we have lowered our quality of life, this is clear."

However, after some time – usually two years, approximately – they manage to earn a similar salary to what they were earning in the past. Nevertheless, workers who experienced a decrease of their incomes are satisfied with their situation, because other factors, such as autonomy, freedom and the possibility to participate in decision-making organisms of the company, compensate for this 'deterioration' of their situation in terms of income.

The majority of the interviewees now have a more consolidated position in their companies. In many cases their income is more or less the same as in the past. However the feeling to have a secure job and income allows workers to increase their levels of consumption, for example by buying new flats and cars or by experiencing opportunities to invest money in other matters.

"Now I have bought a flat. That fact has given me a certain independence to do all that I want without giving explanations to anybody.... I don't need to give explanations and I don't need to ask my parents for money.... These facts increase my security and independence."

Economic participation is related directly to standard of living, but not always to quality of life. Different opinions on this issue were found among workers who are involved in social initiative cooperatives, revealing that quality of life depends on many factors (such as free time), and not just income.

"You can have an income of one million pesetas per month, but if you have no time to enjoy it.... I prefer to have a lower income but more freedom.... I need to enjoy all I have."

Family and social networks, the social domain, are basic elements of inclusion for all the interviewees. Sometimes associated workers who are highly involved in their company reported difficulties in combining these different spheres. Workers who create a new business invest a lot of time in establishing it. They feel responsible for their work and they want their company to survive in a competitive market.

"Whenever you spend a lot of working hours, always, unquestionably, it is in detriment of your social life. That is very clear. It could affect the family ambit. If the person who lives with you doesn't support you, you are in a very difficult situation, very difficult. Of course, there are a lot of things and a lot of problems, divorces and a lot of things that appear in that way."

Normally workers separate their social from their labour life. However, it is very difficult to do this when you are a co-owner of a company and know that its success depends on you. In that sense, workers who feel responsible and have long working days consider family support to be very important. The combination of work and family is vital to maintain equilibrium.

"If you don't have family support in a project with these characteristics.... It is basic to have family support. Because when you are faced with a big project you need to fight for that and if you need also to fight for the family.... They are two different fights and totally opposite. Then, you lose one of them, if you need to control family and the project ... something must be lost, you lose one fight."

To what degree the family is a strong inclusive element is dependent on the situation of the worker. The young workers who have not yet formed a family, attach more importance to their social networks and jobs as conditions for experiencing feelings of inclusion. They use CUB to consolidate their position in the labour market and to have more possibilities to become independent from their family of origin. When a person has formed a family, however, the situation is different. For male workers who need to take care of their families because they earn the family's only income, CUB is a measure that allows them to maintain a job and an income under more or less similar conditions as in the past.

The role of the state

All work done by associated workers is a product of their involvement and their entrepreneurial mentality. As we saw earlier, the role of the state is limited to some supportive measures addressed to social economy companies. However, the state hardly intervenes in CUB as such. It is only involved in some guidance tasks during the initial phase, through the National Employment Institute and local employment organisms. After that, support from the state ceases.

The person who decides to make use of CUB runs all the risks of the process of establishing a new social economy company. He invests all his unemployment benefit entitlements in the company. However, often more economic resources are needed and banks are not very supportive of this kind of new business. A second problem appears when workers who never managed a company before now attempt to manage their own company. They need time to get accustomed and gain the necessary skills, but such time is hard to find in a competitive market. Finally, workers have no unemployment benefit entitlements should a company crash less than two years after starting up. They invested their previous benefits in the company and have not yet been able to build up new entitlements.

> "The state does not intervene. We manage by ourselves and we carry on with the project. The only positive thing has been the capitalisation."

To be an associated worker in a social company may be an attractive and unique solution for many workers who have been working in the industrial sector for many years and have elementary education. Some social initiative companies employ people who otherwise could only access paid jobs through support measures from the state, such as temporary jobs which are located predominantly in the public sector. In other words, from the point of view of the state it is preferable that these people capitalise their unemployment benefits to work by themselves, because this way the state does not have to invest resources to reincorporate them into the labour market.

> "[T]he treasury of the state receives a lot of money from our companies (social economy companies). They give less than they receive. We are playing a strong compensatory role, because now they don't need to compensate unemployment. They must give more facilities."

In summary, all workers consider CUB a very positive measure, because it provides them the minimum resources to start a new business or to invest in an already existing one. In addition, the scheme is also valued highly because it enables the person making use of it to transform his worker status into the status of co-owner. In that sense, capitalisation is not only a measure preventing prolonged unemployment. It is also a measure that facilitates the incorporation of unemployed people into new or existing companies in a new status.

Concluding remarks

In Southern Europe, where countries are characterised by a lack of strong state intervention, paid work and the family are fundamental systems preventing situations of exclusion. Now, with a more flexible labour market in which the number of non-stable jobs is increasing and non-qualified workers occupy the lowest levels in private companies, the family strengthens its inclusive role. Labour is becoming increasingly precarious, and the concept of lifelong employment is disappearing in favour of temporary contracts in a flexible market. In this context, the family and other social networks become increasingly important as inclusive factors.

Between 1985 and 2000, CUB reincorporated 573,265 unemployed people into the regular labour market. Money was invested in various ways: self-employment activities, new cooperatives, ALS and LLS, or already existing social economy businesses. In contrast to many activation measures, CUB facilitates the creation of jobs in the regular labour market, in companies of which the person who invests the money becomes one of the owners. This leads to significant changes in workers' working and social lives. Although there is a large variety of personal situations among CUB participants, in general the great majority of interviewed workers are satisfied with their jobs in social economy companies, and each values the CUB scheme.

The CUB scheme, in accordance with Southern European traditions, is characterised by the absence of a central role of the state. It is also a measure that encourages a very different type of work and work mentality compared to the 'normal' working context in private enterprises. Workers who use CUB are creating an indefinite job in a social economy company in which more examples of solidarity can be found than in private companies. Male workers with low qualification levels who lost their jobs, or women with similar qualification levels and with limited labour experience in the regular labour market have the opportunity to capitalise and to become co-owners of a social economy company with a secure job and income. These women, for instance, have the opportunity to capitalise, because they have been working previously in the same social economy company in which they invest the money of CUB. However, it is also a positive measure for qualified people with a higher entrepreneurial mentality who, although they have other possibilities in regular paid jobs, prefer to create their own business.

Objectively, CUB produces transformation processes that increase workers' opportunities to participate in decision making in the companies. An increase of autonomy is also made possible, as are responsibilities and a feeling of satisfaction with the job. In that sense this measure is unique, because it is encouraging a kind of workers' mentality that reinforces an entrepreneurial mentality. At the same time, autonomy in work, involvement in decision making inside the company and sharing of responsibilities among workers are encouraged with the objective of increasing the efficiency and productivity of the company.

Workers who became co-owners have more stability in terms of their contractual situation, and reinforce inclusion in economic and labour participation. In this respect, there are differences between cooperative workers and ALS workers. Among the former we find more cases of an increase of responsibilities, autonomy and participation at work, with a more accentuated sense of solidarity. In the latter case, there are many instances of social companies created from previous private industrial companies. In these instances, the majority of workers do not change their mentality. They prefer a worker role similar to that which they were used to in the past, and do not want extra responsibility and autonomy.

Associated workers who do not really want to change their workers' mentality are working with other associated workers who have changed. This may create tension and, eventually, trouble within the company. Both types of workers have used CUB to maintain their previous job; in that sense, the measure is very positive for both. Although the measure is not an incentive for the first group to change and to improve their working conditions, it is the beginning of a process of change for the latter.

When explaining how a Greek bakery had changed in the last 25 years according to the new requirements of a more flexible labour market, Richard Sennett (1998) highlighted the opinion of a foreman. According to this foreman, most of the problems related to bad salaries, and short-term and precarious contracts could be solved if workers owned the bakery. This is exactly what CUB makes possible. It is an example of a local measure (at a national level) within a global and competitive market. Taking into account the future scenarios of work that Beck (2000) analyses in the context of the second modernity, we can observe how CUB supports the consolidation of a more responsible, participative and solidarity-based mentality among workers, which may prevent negative effects of the individualisation of work.

For these reasons, I think that it is necessary to encourage active measures such as the CUB. Many current active measures have no significant impact in terms of job creation and those that do, fail to do so by inclusion in the regular labour market. At the same time I would advocate increasing support and protection by the state, though not in a paternalistic way, of initiatives in the context of CUB.

It is necessary to invest more resources in non-paternalistic, active labour market policies that encourage the inclusion of their participants in work and social networks. Although training measures, combined with short periods of work, can be necessary, they are not sufficient by themselves. These kinds of active measures are curative, their conception of unemployed workers is negative in the sense that they are based on their deficits and not on their capabilities.

We need to introduce more active measures that are based on the capabilities of workers to begin new businesses and to increase their responsibilities and participation at work. We need active measures that create active workers.

Notes

[1] The main passive unemployment policy in Spain is the unemployment benefit that has two levels: contributory payments and assistance payments. Unemployed people use the first as payment with the CUB.

[2] Under 'Social economy' we found, until the 1980s, associations, mutual benefit societies and cooperatives. In the Spanish context, the labour societies (Anonymous Labour Societies and Limited Labour Societies) were included under this denomination by law in the 1980s. This chapter deals with the development of social economy companies created through the capitalisation of unemployment benefits, but it refers to cooperatives, ALSs and LLSs only, and not to associations and mutual benefit societies.

[3] Official State Bulletin (OSB) no 157, 2 July 1985. Publication of R.D. 19 June 1985, no 1044/85 (Social and Labour Affairs Department), through which the CUB scheme was regulated.

[4] OSB no 157, 2 July 1985: articles 1 and 2.

[5] In Spain the first cooperative – 'La Fabril' – was registered in 1842, and was located in Barcelona. Its main goal was to create and maintain jobs in a period of crisis (Reventos Carner, 1960).

[6] This congress formulated the so-called 'seven principles': voluntary and open membership; democratic member control; member economic participation; autonomy and independence; education, training and information; cooperation among cooperatives; concern for the community (www.ilo.org/public/english/employment/ent/coop/origin.htm).

[7] OSB no 170, 17 July, 1999: chapter 1, "General dispositions".

[8] Act 15/1986, 25 April (OSB no 103, 30 April): article 1.

[9] Act 15/1986, 25 April (OSB no 103, 30 April): articles 5 and 6.

[10] Act 15/1986, 25 April (OSB no 103, 30 April): article 17.

[11] R.D. Act 1564/1989, 22 December (OSB no 310, 27 December): article 4.

[12] OSB no 84, 7 April 1992. The self-employment cases that appear after 1992 are related to special cases of capitalisation.

[13] The next section elaborates on the social and economic context of cooperatives and ALSs in Spain.

[14] In 1988 the OECD proposed the concept of active labour market policies. It classified public expenses in the labour market according to seven broad categories. The active ones were: employment services; training; special measures to encourage labour insertion of young people; subsidies to encourage employment through direct creation of jobs in the public and private sectors and specific measures to employ disabled people.

[15] Important training measures are the Professional Training Programme (which is divided into three subsystems, Continuous Training; Vocational Training and Professional Formal Training), and the Work Schools and Profession Houses (for more information see MTAS, 1995; CES, 1996; CES, 1999). Within professional orientation it is important to highlight the role of the Public Employment Services which are in a process of decentralisation in Spain (for more information, see ESADE, 1997).

[16] Focusing on active measures addressed to encourage employment through non-training measures, the following can be distinguished: social economy companies; to encourage autonomous employment; labour incorporation through special contracts of groups at risk of falling into processes of social exclusion; local initiatives for employment; employment plans (for more information, see MTAS, 1995; CES, 1996; Vidal, 1996a, 1996b; ESADE, 1997; CES, 1999).

[17] The National Employment Institute is the organisation in charge of the passive policies in Spain and the institution managing the CUB at a national level. In some autonomous communities, the local governments have competencies regarding the CUB (for instance, Catalonia).

[18] For INPART, 100 CUB participants were interviewed using in-depth interviews (60 in Barcelona and 40 in Bilbao, the capital of Vizcaya, one of the three provinces of Euskadi, the Basque country). Part of this information is presented in this section.

[19] The table presents data from 1993 to 1999, since the possibility to invest CUB money in self-employment activities was abolished in 1992.

[20] Social Initiative Cooperatives are a type of cooperative strongly embedded in the community. Many workers in these cooperatives are involved in social movements. Normally, these cooperatives used to be associations that worked closely together with the neighbourhood in which they were located. When the decision was made to transform into a social economy company, their close connection with their neighbourhood was maintained. Now, some of these cooperatives are discussing with the Euskal Cooperative Federation ways to create a legal basis for this type of cooperative.

References

Álvarez Aledo, C. (1996) 'Políticas activas de creación de empleo y colectivos desaventajados', *Economistas*, vol 14, no 70, pp 23-32.

Andreotti, A., García, S., Gómez, A., Hespanha, P., Kazepov, Y. and Mingione, E. (2001) 'The Southern European model', *Journal of European Area Studies*, vol 9, no 1, pp 43-63.

Atkinson, J. (1986) *Employment flexibility in internal and external labour markets*, Brighton: Institute of Manpower Studies.

Beck, U. (2000) *Un nuevo mundo feliz: La precariedad del trabajo en la era de la globalización*, Barcelona: Paidós.

CES (Consejo Económico y Social) (1996) *Economía, trabajo y sociedad: Memoria sobre la situación socioeconómica y laboral: España 1995*, Madrid: CES, Departamento de Publicaciones.

CES (1999) *Memoria sobre la situación socioeconómica y laboral: España 1998*, Madrid: CES, Departamento de Publicaciones.

Chavez, R. and Monzón, J.L. (2000) 'Las cooperativas en las modernas economías de mercado: perspectiva española', *Economistas*, no 83, pp 113-24.

Del Arco Álvarez, J.L. (1977) *Cooperativismo una filosofia una técnica*, Zaragoza: Centro Nacional de Educación Cooperativa.

ESADE (Escola Superior d'Administracío i direcció d'empreses) (1997) *L'Estat del Benestar i el Mercat de Treball*, Barcelona: Generalitat de Catalunya, Departament de Presidència.

Escuela de Estudios Cooperativos (1988) *Las sociedades cooperativas en la nueva legislación española*, Madrid: CDN (Ciencias de la Dirección).

Férez, M., Güell, M., Obesco, C., Recio, E. and De Sebastián, L. (1997) *El trabajo en el futuro*, Bilbao: Deusto Coop.

Generalitat de Catalunya (1987) *Llei de Cooperatives de Catalunya*, Barcelona: Generalitat de Catalunya, Departament de Treball, Direcció General de Cooperatives.

Gómez-Calcerrada Gascón, J.L. (1987) *La cooperativa de trabajo*, Barcelona: Ediciones CEAC, SA.

Jiménez, R. (1987) *La legislación cooperativa en España en Generalitat de Catalunya 1987, Legislació sobre cooperatives als Estats membres de la CEE*, Barcelona: Generalitat, Departament de Treball.

Mingione, E. (2001) 'Labour market segmentation and informal work', in H.D. Gibson (ed) *Economic transformation, democratisation and integration into the European Union. Southern Europe in comparative perspective*, New York, NY: Palgrave.

Ministerio de Trabajo y Asuntos Sociales (1995) *La política de empleo en España*, Madrid: Centro de Publicaciones Ministerio de Trabajo y Seguridad Social.

Monzón Campos, J.L. and Morales Gutiérrez, A.C. (1996) 'Las empresas de Trabajo Asociado', in J. Barea and J.L. Monzón Campos (eds) *Informe sobre la situación de las cooperativas y las Sociedades Laborales en España*, Madrid: CIRIEC, pp 77-121.

Monzón Campos, J.L. (1989) *Las cooperativas de trabajo asociado en la literatura económica y los hechos*, Madrid: Centro de publicaciones del MTAS.

Ortiz Lallana, M.C. (1989) *La prestación laboral de los socios en las Cooperativas de Trabajo Asociado*, Barcelona: Bosch, Casa Editorial SA.

Reventos Carner, J. (1960) *El movimiento cooperativo en España*, Barcelona: Ariel.

Rosembuj, T. (1983) *Ley de Cooperativas. Catalunya-Euskadi*, Barcelona: Ediciones CEAC SA.

Sennet, R. (1998) *La corrosión del carácter: Las consecuencias personales del trabajo en el nuevo capitalismo*, Barcelona: Anagrama.

Textos Civitas (1999) *Legislación sobre cooperativas y Sociedades Laborales*, Madrid: Civitas.

Trigo, J. (1996) *Bienestar social y mecanismos de mercado*, Madrid: Unión Editorial SA.

Vidal, I. (1987) *Crisis económica y transformaciones en el mercado de trabajo*, Barcelona: Diputación de Barcelona.

Vidal, I. (1996a) 'Historia y presente de las empresas SAL en Catalunya 1979-1993', in J. Rojo i Carbellido (ed) *Autogestión y sindicalismo, una crónica de la transición*, Barcelona: FESALC, pp 141-54.

Vidal, I. (1996b) *Inserción social por el trabajo: Una visión internacional*, Barcelona: Centro de Iniciativa de la Economía Social.

Vidal, I. (1998) 'The workers' cooperatives: an answer to unemployment', Paper presented during an INPART meeting at the University of Barcelona, 25 April.

Vidal, I. and Vilaplana, A. (1999) *Perspectivas empresariales de las Sociedades Laborales en la Unión Europea*, Barcelona: FESALC.

Vidal, I. (ed) (2001) *El tercer sector i l'economia social a Barcelona*, Barcelona: Consell Econòmic i Social de Barcelona.

EIGHT

Orthodoxy and reflexivity in international comparative analysis

Ben Valkenburg and Jens Lind

Introduction

Life is easy for social scientists engaged in international comparative research. Yet, at the same time, it is also hard. Within the social sciences, this kind of research is regarded as the ultimate in terms of scientific quality, especially when the results are international publications. The interest in international comparative research among policy makers has been growing over the years, due to, among others, processes of globalisation. Where globalisation goes hand-in-hand with political integration, as is the case in Europe, policy makers do not only want information about other countries. This information should also help them to develop, evaluate and implement policy measures. In this situation substantial resources are made available for international, comparative research.

The empirical research on this international level is predominantly based on a scientific model that can be referred to, in Giddens' (1979) phrase, as the 'orthodox consensus'. At the centre of the orthodox consensus is the empirical-analytical research model that emphasises theory testing, large-scale research, primarily based on quantifiable data and aimed at finding general explanations of social behaviour in terms of causality. The orthodox consensus is based on methodological principles (objectivity, generalisation, decontextualisation, and so on) that are not only well-adapted to international comparative research, but also invite and encourage researchers to do this kind of research. In most cases, the policy maker too has an image of social research that is in line with the orthodox consensus. In this sense, life for the international, comparative researcher is easy.

At the same time, though, his or her life is hard or, at least, should be hard. Within the social sciences, the methodological principles which lie at the root of the orthodox consensus have been fundamentally criticised. As a result of this criticism, more emphasis is being put on trying to understand the way people think and act as social and reflexive actors in a specific social context. Central notions in this so-called 'reflexive social science' are the competent actor, a relation between common sense and scientific knowledge based on reciprocal adequacy, and the contextuality of knowledge. The contradiction between empirical research dominated by the orthodox consensus on the one hand, and the direction in which the methodological discussion is taking us on the other, is getting more acute. This contradiction, often in an implicit way, is also reflected in the experience of the policy maker. Social research based on the orthodox consensus often yields results that lack practical relevance and, for that reason, they end up in the bottom drawer.

Against this background, this chapter focuses on the following subjects. First we argue that reflexive social science is more adequate than the orthodox consensus. In current practice, social scientists share much of the criticism on the orthodox consensus on a theoretical level, without considering the implications, and acting upon the consequences on the level of empirical research. We want to avoid doing so, and the second and third subjects we discuss are the practical implications of reflexivity for empirical research and for social policy, respectively. Our discussion is based on the practical experience gained in INPART, in which we have tried to deal with these consequences. We do not intend here, however, to go into the details of the methodology applied by the project, nor do we intend to give an account of the methods used (although we will at times direct the reader to other chapters in this book). Our intention with this chapter is to present some reflections on methods and methodology which we developed during and after INPART.

In view of the complex situation characterising the current state of social science, we cannot be expected (nor, for that matter, can other researchers) to have definitive answers to all the complicated questions raised by a reflexive approach to international comparative research. What may be expected, though, is explicit reflection on our attempts to find these answers. That is what we will try to do here. Fourth, and hopefully as a result of the first three aims, we want to argue that a reflexive approach to international, comparative research is not only desirable, but attainable as well.

In order to achieve this, we begin with a short discussion of the main methodological principles of the orthodox consensus and the empirical-analytical research model that is based upon them. We also argue that this approach apparently gives adherents few problems in doing international research. We then explore and elaborate on the main issues in the so-called 'reflexive approach' and consider the main consequences of this approach for both social science and social policy. Against this background we discuss the implications for comparative research, the general experiences of INPART and a few central issues for further debate.

The orthodox consensus: the prediction of a distorted picture

Much has been written about the orthodox consensus. It is not our aim here to present an elaborate analysis of it. Rather, we concentrate on a critical discussion of the main methodological principles.

From the orthodox point of view, objective and scientifically adequate knowledge is knowledge in which the subjectivity of the researcher – and of the people (s)he is researching – is kept out of the research situation as much as possible. To do this, the researcher should be able to enforce a dualism between himself as a private person with values and political ideas on the one hand, and, on the other, her/his role as a scientist who refrains from these values and political ideas in her/his scientific research. In this second role, the social scientist has to find ways of dealing with the no longer disputed fact that all observations are theory-impregnated and that value-free knowledge is (therefore) an impossibility. To find a solution for this difficulty, a compromise is found in a separation between a 'context of discovery', in which (value-laden) observations are made which form the basis for theory formation, and a 'context of justification', in which the hypotheses are tested, and consequently falsified or corroborated. The constant remaining threat of 'pollution' in this testing phase is to be combated by the strict rules and methods for data assembly, analysis and theory testing the researcher has to follow.

This points to another assumption inherent in the orthodox consensus; that is, that there is a fundamental distinction to be made between scientific knowledge and common sense. Consequently, strictly separated roles are defined for both parties in the research process. The researcher is supposed to have the systematic theoretical knowledge and the methods to collect relevant data to produce scientific knowledge. The researched party is kept in a passive role. Objectivity on the part of the researched party is thought to be secured by limiting their role to data-delivery, such as answering survey questions, the relevant theoretical background and meaning of which is only known to the researcher.

As regards the type and status of the knowledge produced, the social scientist, just like the natural scientist, is searching for universal causality, or at least relationships between specifically defined circumstances and outcomes that are not limited to the specific context under investigation. The goal of the researcher is to predict social behaviour in other contexts and in future times. Though it is not possible to predict that whenever condition *a* occurs, it will *necessarily* lead to outcome *b*, at least it is true to say that such an outcome is *highly probable*.

Against this background, generalisation implies that the data and theoretical conclusions are produced, as much as possible, independently of the specific context in which the research project has been conducted. The way to do this is to take representative samples in a way that excludes the subjective 'distortions' of the respondents, to follow strict statistical rules for extrapolation, and to test theoretical hypotheses in different contexts.

These methodological principles find expression in the empirical-analytical research model, which is characterised by the following steps:

• The social scientist formulates hypotheses (causal relationships between independent and dependent variables [causes and outcomes]) based on previously developed theories;

- These hypotheses are empirically tested, following strict rules;
- This testing leads to confirmation, confutation or further elaboration of the original hypotheses, and of the original theories.

The most important basis for testing hypotheses is provided by quantifiable data. In the process of gathering and analysing data they are supposed to form the best means, and offer the best possibilities, for excluding the subjectivity of the researcher and the respondents. Furthermore, quantifiable data fit in with the large-scale data gathering that is considered a precondition for generalisation.

One overall criticism, which goes back a long way, is that social science cannot and should not try to copy the natural sciences, since social reality fundamentally differs from natural reality. One of the reasons is that people, contrary to natural objects, give meaning to their social reality as a basis for their actions. This means that they will always react in an uncontrollable, subjective way, to the researcher and the research situation. A social science that denies interpretations, meaning and subjectivity as constituting elements of social behaviour, and focuses solely on the causes or determining factors in the actions of individuals, inescapably risks concluding for determinism. While there certainly may be causes influencing people's behaviour (for example, biological, neurological), these never tell the full story of the factors that play a role in social action.

Another criticism is that a social science operating under these assumptions, promises something it cannot deliver: the explanation and prediction of social behaviour. In other words, social science does not produce knowledge that can be used as a tool for intervention. The only prediction that is confirmed time and again is that social science reduces the complexity of social reality to serve its own goals, taking insufficient account of the goals of policy makers and other involved parties.

To say that each and every international comparative research project is based extensively on the methodological principles and the empirical-analytical model mentioned above would be an overstatement. What can be said, however, is that in the overall picture the orthodox consensus is still as dominant as it ever has been. Most international comparative research conforms to the methodological principles outlined earlier, and contributes to their realisation by offering a high level of aggregation on which research data can be gathered and compared. It is for that reason that, within the orthodox consensus, it is seen as both a feasible and desirable form of research, the results of which – in terms of international publications – are considered to be the most important criterion for assessing the scientific quality of the researcher. By limiting the numbers of variables and working only with one-way (causal) relationships, the empirical-analytical research model offers the possibility to compensate for the growing complexity that is concomitant to an international research perspective. If the adherents of the orthodox consensus see any problems at all, these are of a technical nature and typically concern the availability and comparability of data.

Meanwhile, the problems entailed by this model are growing ever more distinct. With regard to the social sciences, one could say that the theoretical and methodological discussion is eroding its very principles. Eventually, the discussion must inevitably lead to the conclusion that the orthodox consensus comes up with a distorted, simplified picture of the complex social reality that is being studied.

The reflexive turn

Against this background, the discussion on a new, or at least alternative, model for social science has made significant progress and has gained considerable importance, mainly due to two factors.

The first concerns the rise, growth, and institutionalisation of methodological discussions in the social sciences themselves during the 1960s and 1970s. Previously, the interpretative approach was labelled to a specific discipline – cultural anthropology – and in that sense marginalised in relation to the mainstream of 'modern' social science. After the 1970s, however, the discussions shifted towards the disciplines forming the core of social science as such. What could (and should, for that matter) be disputed was the content of argumentation. What could no longer be denied, though, was that the discussion concerned basic methodological issues relevant for *all* social sciences.

The second factor concerns the ongoing theoretical discussion on modernisation. In this discussion one of the arguments is that, compared to the 'old' ideals of the Enlightenment, the meaning and role of knowledge has changed fundamentally. In the natural sciences, the production of knowledge can perhaps still be seen as the work of specialists. After all, which lay person really understands the ins and outs of gentechnology or quantum physics? Social scientific knowledge on the other hand has become an integral part of practically everyone's everyday social life. Compared to the natural sciences, the social sciences seem to be the weaker member of the scientific family. After all, have they ever discovered anything that revolutionised social life? In fact, however, the extent to which the social sciences are part of the modernisation of social life is actually rather comparable to that of the natural sciences, albeit in a different way. With regard to this phenomenon, Giddens (1984) has pointed to concepts like capital, investment and markets, which were developed in the 18th and 19th centuries to analyse ongoing social changes. Meanwhile, they have become integral to, and form constituting elements of, modern economic life. Economic activities would be inconceivable if members of society did not have access to and make use of these concepts. Though a lay person may not be able to formally define them, every person that has a savings account acts in accordance with the principles underlying these definitions. The concepts are not just 'handy descriptions' that help the actor to understand what (s)he is doing. They also constitute these actions as such, though this often happens in a routine manner and therefore does not involve a process consciously brought about by the actors. At the same time, the concepts are continuously being evaluated and developed during this process. Therefore, social scientific knowledge "spirals in and out of the universe of social life, reconstructing both itself and that universe as an integral part of that process" (Giddens, 1990, pp 15-16).

This means that the object of social science itself has learnt to think along social scientific lines. The expert only has a relative advantage over the well-informed lay person. This is especially true in the current situation, where the social space for action (that is, our view of the social world around us, as a basis for reflection on our individual identity and actions) can be expanded to the whole world with one click of the mouse of our personal computers.

In this process, the meaning of knowledge has changed fundamentally. Knowledge can no longer be regarded as a cumulating source of certainties. Knowledge is being permanently used, discussed and developed in everyday practice. That is to say, it involves a reciprocal process taking place in the context of everyday interaction. If the contexts are different, this reciprocal process may also be different. General statements can only be expressed in modest terms, and certainly not in terms of general decontextualised laws of social behaviour and predictions.

This changing meaning of knowledge is at the same time an important factor in, and the outcome of, processes of individualisation. Based on a permanent flow of new knowledge, and in different contexts, actors develop their individual identity and actions. Individual identity has become a reflexive project. In this process, knowledge is not primarily linked with cumulation, universality and certainty, but with contextuality, reciprocity and uncertainty. Perhaps we have begun to realise only recently that this process of reflexive modernisation has far-reaching and radical implications, not only as regards its consequences for the flexibility of individual action and social structures, but also with regard to the meaning and role of knowledge (Beck, 1986; Giddens, 1990, 1991; Beck et al, 1994).

Coenen (1993) summarises the implications of reflexivity for social science in two points. The first point is connected with the work of Bourdieu. For the latter, reflexivity means that the social scientist should clarify the influence the researcher exerts on her/his object of research. To do this, (s)he is required to explicitly articulate her/his own background, presuppositions and values. Moreover, (s)he has to take into account:

> ... the *intellectualist bias* which entices us to construe the world as a *spectacle*, as a set of significations to be interpreted rather than as concrete problems to be solved practically.... Whenever we fail to subject to systematic critique the 'presuppositions inscribed in the fact of thinking the world, of retiring from the world and from action in the world in order to think that action' (Bourdieu, 1990, p 382), we risk collapsing practical logic into theoretical logic. Given that these presuppositions are built into concepts, instruments of analyses ... and in practical operations of research ... reflexivity calls less for intellectual introspection than for the permanent sociological analysis and control of

sociological practice. (Wacquant, in Bourdieu and Wacquant, 1992, pp 39-40)

With his second point Coenen is referring to Giddens, who emphasises the reflexivity of the actor:

> I have already pointed out that in most traditional schools of social thought reflexivity is treated as merely a nuisance, the consequences of which can either be ignored, or are to be minimised as far as possible. This is true both in respect of methodology, where 'introspection' is swingeingly condemned as contrary to science, and in respect of the conceptual representation of human conduct itself. But nothing is more central to, and distinctive of, human life than the reflexive monitoring of behaviour, which is expected by all 'competent' members of society of others. (Giddens, 1976, p 114)

The reflexive monitoring of action means that actors use their knowledge of themselves and their social context to translate their motivations and intentions into actions, and at the same time to monitor this process. In this sense people are competent actors; that is, able to steer and give direction to their own lives. The monitoring of their action, however, largely takes place unconsciously and in a routine way. In their daily behaviour, people make use of matter-of-fact knowledge and common-sense insights that are usually taken for granted, so one is hardly conscious of having this knowledge. More than often, people find it difficult to put this kind of pre-reflective knowledge into words. Asked and trained to do so, they are able to give reasons for their actions. By doing so, practical knowledge can be turned into discursive knowledge. All this does not mean that people cannot be wrong about the reasons for their actions, though, or lack insight into the way their actions link with other people's actions to form structural patterns that turn out to be quite hard to change.

Implications for social science: towards a reflexive approach

The discussion on reflexivity has far-reaching implications for the social sciences, not only on the level of methodology, but also on the level of theory and research practice. In this section we elaborate on these implications, using the study of processes of inclusion and exclusion in general, and INPART in particular, as an example of the implications. We realise that these implications cannot be directly translated into, and taken over in the practice of, social scientific research. We think it important, though, to be as explicit and radical as possible on the central issues in the discussion about the methodology of international, comparative research. For only that way, we can elaborate further on how to work out these principles into manageable, practical devices.

The first implication of a reflexive approach of social science is that we should strive to get rid of, and find alternatives for, the many conceptual dualisms that up till now have characterised social science. Some of the most fundamental dualisms are probably those concerning the objectivism–subjectivism distinction and the actor–structure distinction. According to Bourdieu, these dualisms primarily represent a theoretical distortion of the complex reality they refer to. As in social science in general, these dualisms explicitly crop up in the study of inclusion and exclusion. One of the most important ones is reflected in the tendency to either 'blame the victim' (actor) or 'blame the system' (structure) for any fault. Is it people's own fault that they do not have a job, or is their unemployment due to excluding mechanisms operating within the labour market (this theme is also taken up in Chapter Two)? On an individual level the question often raised is: is unemployment caused by 'objective' factors (such as age, ethnicity, sex, level of education, and so on) or by 'subjective' factors (such as motivation, self-esteem, self-image)? Another variant is: is it the professional who is doing a bad job, or is it rather the unemployed person who is unwilling? When the frequent failure of policy delivery is concerned, the question put forward is: is government policy failing or does the problem just lie with the delivery of the policy?

These kind of dualisms are not only characteristic for the social scientific study of inclusion and exclusion, where they are translated and laid down in distinguishable variables (that is, when traditional research is implied). Strengthened by 'scientific arguments', they play an important role in everyday practice and policy as well. In the Netherlands, for example, there is a rather large amount of empirical research that concludes that the number of low-qualified jobs has not decreased but rather increased. In certain sectors of the labour market, many low-qualified positions are vacant. In this situation, thinking in terms of dualisms leads to the conclusion that the cause of unemployment is to be attributed to the unemployed themselves. The logic of thinking implies that if it is not objective factors that determine unemployment (low level of education is not a problem for these vacancies), it must 'therefore' be subjective characteristics (lack of motivation) that cause people to be out of work. At the end of this line of argument, the unemployed are faced with stigmatisation and a government policy that confronts them with sanctions to get them into paid work.

In view of failing efforts to conquer unemployment, it must be clear by now that the reality of this phenomenon cannot be adequately captured with these kinds of dualisms. When a person is unemployed, this is the result of a complex of interactions (between the unemployed person, employers, the professionals that are supposed to provide support, the policy makers, and so on), interactions that can only be fully understood in the specific context where they are conducted. A social scientist who wants to study this complex process often feels that, unless this complexity is dissected, (s)he cannot investigate the process. Justified by the orthodox consensus, the answer given by many researchers to this problem is to reduce complexity. The result is a distorted picture of reality. The task of a reflexive social scientist, however, is to take the life world of the unemployed, and other actors relevant for the study, for the real one, and not what (s)he himself makes of it behind her/his desk. (S)he is to accept the complexity of this reality, has to try to deal with it theoretically and – the proof of the pudding being in the eating – must incorporate the consequences in the way (s)he does her/his research. This at least means that (s)he has to reckon with the various parties involved in the research field and work out how their (re)actions interrelate. The researcher should also keep an eye open for the way existing social patterns are reproduced by the usual, daily action patterns of the actors in the field under study, and how these action patterns may have been reified in institutionalised forms. This is a first, necessary though not sufficient, step towards gaining insight and trying to improve the current situation.

A second implication of a reflexive approach in social science is the need for a reconsideration of the importance and impact of 'subjectivity' within research situations. To elaborate on the example above: constitutive for the job-seeking actions of an unemployed person is not her/his level of education, but her/his interpretation of its relevance in her/his individual, specific situation, including her/his estimations of the potential employers' interpretations of her/his capabilities. Comparable remarks can be made with regard to the employer. Of course, the formal level of education of a jobseeker is an important issue for the employer. Its specific meaning for the decision (s)he makes, however, depends on a lot of other things: the motivation and image of the jobseeker, existing stigmas, the company culture, the background of the employer her/himself, and so on. In the orthodox consensus, this kind of subjectivity of the researched (in this case unemployed persons and potential employers) is more or less excluded from the research process, or is at least reduced to a limited number of more or less objective variables, as it is seen as a distorting factor for the development of a real scientific understanding of the process under study.

In this case, criticising this approach is not just an academic matter either. To give an example: within the context of active policies, education is seen and treated as an independent variable that to a large extent determines whether people find paid employment or not. In practice, it is not that simple, however. Education can help if – and only if – it is relevant for the specific context and interpretations of an unemployed person and her/his potential employers. Clarity on this point cannot be generated unless the subjective perspective of both parties is taken into account. If this is left out or limited, the relevance of education remains a coincidental factor, as it is now. In the current situation, input on the level of education is a matter of trial and error. For the unemployed, the end result often is a(nother) negative experience.

As a first move in the direction of a more reflexive approach, the view of subjectivity as a 'polluting' factor should be abandoned. Instead, the researcher should use double hermeneutics as a basic methodological principle. That is to say, researchers are always interpreting social reality and simultaneously interpreting the interpretations of the actors that constitute that reality. As we saw earlier, people give specific meanings to the things happening around them, just as they have their own specific norms and values, and take a particular view of the power relations they are involved in. Sometimes they are hardly conscious of these taken-for-granted meanings, norms and power relations which form part of their practical knowledge and which they help reproduce in their daily actions. Within a reflexive approach, it is important that the social scientist tries to get a picture of the meanings, norms and power aspects related to the situation under study. Moreover, since researchers are always interpreting these interpretations as well, they should make sure to double-check their own interpretations with the people involved (a point discussed later in this chapter).

A third implication of a reflexive approach in social science is that no fundamental distinction can be made between social scientific knowledge and common sense. This, of course, does not mean that social scientific knowledge has nothing to offer. It can contribute considerably to consistency, to the articulation of concepts, theories and relationships, to the broadening of empirical scope and to a systematic discussion. In the end, though, all this does not imply that a strict, fundamental line can be drawn between common sense and social scientific knowledge. Common sense also uses theories and concepts, permanently relates these to everyday practice and develops both in a reciprocal way.

Reflexive social scientists who want to understand the actions of the people within a specific field of study, have to take as a starting point that, especially in the beginning of a research project, the people under investigation know more about their actions than the social scientists do. This knowledge is related to 'facts', but also to theories about and complexities within people's social context. For example, the decision of an unemployed person to pick up education is not only based on the factual information this person has about a specific course, but also on the theoretical notions (s)he employs regarding the relations between education and paid work in relation to her/his practical experiences.

Here, we also see the importance of taking into account what meanings are given, which norms are used and which power relations exist in the eyes of the people under study, to at least be able to understand the situation in which the research project is being executed.

A fourth implication of a reflexive approach in social science is that we should realise that the generation of knowledge is always context-bound. This contextuality of knowledge and knowledge production does not mean that the social scientist's scope is by definition limited to the specific context under study. Of course, her/his aim is also to study broader developments, relations and structures. For a reflexive social scientist too, generalisation is an important aspect of research. It does mean, however, that the starting point is the way actors reflexively shape their actions in their specific social context. The people under study are considered to be competent actors with valuable insights and capacities, and as such are approached, in principle, as fellow researchers.

A fifth and final implication is that social scientific research should be based on the methodological principle of reciprocal adequacy. This principle implies that knowledge generated during a research process can only be considered scientifically adequate when both researchers and those researched acknowledge the explicitly articulated research findings.

Negatively speaking, the methodological principle of reciprocal adequacy prohibits the researcher from withdrawing from the social field under study and from presenting a reduced, distorted picture of reality. Positively speaking, the principle constitutes an expression of the fact that scientific knowledge and common sense are seen as complementary, not only on a theoretical level but also on the level of practical research activities. They are complementary in that the knowledge of the research subjects can be supplemented with the knowledge or other special skills of the researcher, and the other way around. Consequently, in a reflexive approach, researcher and researched are seen to fulfil different, but equally important roles within the research process. The researched are considered to be competent actors with valuable insights and capacities and, as such, are approached as fellow researchers. Finally, the principle of reciprocal adequacy is a precondition for a relation of trust between the researcher and the researched. In the orthodox consensus this relation of trust is seen as a threat to objectivity and the adequacy of scientific knowledge. In a reflexive approach it is seen as a condition: an adequate understanding of what people do in their everyday practice is possible only when they are willing to inform the researcher on the reflexive backgrounds of their actions. Their willingness to do this requires that they know what the research is about, have control of the information they supply and can influence the research process. An unemployed person will only tell what it really means to be unemployed if (s)he trusts the researcher in these respects. If (s)he does not trust her/him, (s)he will be talking with her/his mouth shut.

In short, the emphasis in a reflexive approach is on trying to understand the way people think and act, as social and reflexive actors in a specific social context. Central notions in a reflexive social science are: the competent actor, the interrelation of common sense and scientific knowledge, reciprocal adequacy (as a precondition for scientific knowledge and for a relation of trust between the researcher and the people under study), and the contextuality of knowledge. For the sake of argument we have laid down this approach of social science in a radical way. Even if we take it in a less radical way, though, we are still far removed from the orthodox consensus.

The need for a turnaround in social policy

Social policy – active policies included – also has its 'orthodox consensus' in which it is the policy maker that defines problems, analyses the causes, and develops strategies and instruments. It is not until the end of this process that the individual client comes into the picture. At this stage the way of looking at problems and solutions has been defined, everything is ready and often institutionalised in rules, resources and organisations, and should be delivered to the client. This predominant traditional way of making and delivering social policy can be characterised as an institutional, supply-oriented approach (Coenen-Hanegraaf, 1998).

This approach is often implicitly based on a concept of knowledge that is strongly linked to the concept of knowledge characteristic of the orthodox consensus in social science in at least two respects.

First, traditional social policy aims at general policy measures. Forms of education or subsidised labour that are seen as adequate for all low-qualified unemployed, forms of financial advantages for all employers that employ long-term unemployed, and so on. These policy measures are based on and aimed at the features that people (in this case both the unemployed and the employers) have in common. These common features are seen as the most important causes for their problems and as the most important variables that should be tackled by social policy. In other words, traditional social policy implies a concept of knowledge that emphasises generalisation in more or less the same way as the orthodox consensus in social science does.

Second, traditional social policy is based on the assumption that adequate policy can be developed without the involvement of the individual client in this process. To put it another way, often the idea of the policy maker is that involvement of the client in defining problems, analysing causes and finding strategies will lead to an over-subjective and particularistic policy, and the erosion of the general goals and frameworks that the policy maker her/himself is supposed to serve. This exclusion of the individual client, of her/his subjectivity and contextuality, in the production of knowledge that social policy is based upon, also has strong parallels with the orthodox consensus in social science.

What goes for the orthodox consensus in social sciences, goes for traditional social policy as well. The traditional approach is based on an old view of knowledge, whereas in the meantime, and under current social conditions, knowledge has acquired a meaning that radically differs from the earlier situation. Individualisation and reflexivity mean that people orient themselves on a broad stream of constantly renewed knowledge. Tradition and 'grand narratives' still fulfil an important role; they form an important source for the development of an individual identity. However, this no longer is a role in the form of collective interpretative frameworks, which are 'taken over by others' and which prescribe what people ought to do and what they ought not to do. They are continuously examined for their specific meaning for individual identity. In this process, the citizen is no longer prepared to set aside her/his own competences in favour of, for instance, a policy maker who, from an institutional, supply-oriented approach, is in a position to define the problems of that citizen, to determine which causes play a role in these problems, to establish what could be appropriate solutions, and which instruments are needed to solve the problems.

A social policy that is based on an institutional, supply-oriented approach is outdated, since it does not do justice to the process of individualisation and reflexivity (see also Chapter Nine). Consequently, it cannot be expected to contribute to emancipation, equality, identity constitution and solidarity with due regard for this process. For those groups that can manage without the social policies of the welfare state and welfare society, this will not be of great importance. They can manage, and will make it on their own. For them, the emphasis in the process of individualisation is mainly on 'being able to'; they find they have more possibilities to choose for themselves and they have sufficient knowledge to be able to make those choices. For groups in a situation of relative deprivation, it is a different story. Their identity has become a reflexive project too; a project they have to develop on the basis of their competence. They too are constantly confronted with choices. However they see and/or get far fewer chances to find a proper connection between their project, competences and choices on the one hand and the complex society they are part of on the other. In many cases an institutional, supply-oriented approach will not push them forwards, but backwards. It does not link up with their everyday context and reflexivity and, at the same time, emphasises their incompetence.

If social policy is to be successful, the links between social policy and the motivations, perspectives and competences of the individual have to be taken into consideration. To develop a more modern approach, the individual himself should be actively involved in defining problems, analysing causes, developing strategies and using instruments. Social policy, just like social science, should be characterised by reciprocal adequacy between the policy maker and the clients.

Back to international comparative research

Whereas the criteria of international comparative research based on the orthodox consensus force us to concentrate on gathering general data, a reflexive approach primarily implies contextual research. In the former, quantitative data are the main basis for scientific knowledge; qualitative data are seen as helpful. In contextual research, it is the other way around. Additionally, we saw that the reflexive turn in social policy supposes an understanding of the needs, motives, aspirations and (practical and theoretical) knowledge of the actors concerned. It was this perspective that triggered INPART.

In the theoretical, conceptual and methodological strategy of INPART, we have tried to find answers to the many questions raised by this reflexive approach of international, comparative research. From the start, it was clear that in the project, which dealt with processes of inclusion and exclusion, complexity and contextuality were at stake at different levels.

First, there is the national level. If we want to do research on, say, subsidised labour in the Netherlands, we will have to deal with issues such as the composition and background of the target group, the routines, cultures and traditions of the organisations that are delivering the policies, relevant segments of the labour market, and so on, and the interrelations between all of these factors. And then we have to realise that for a research project on inclusion and exclusion, the issue of subsidised labour is only one of the subjects to be examined.

Secondly, we have to consider the differences and similarities between the national levels under study. These differences and similarities do not only concern the content and meaning of national conditions, factors and developments, but also the cohesion and interrelation between them. Family structures, for instance, can play an important role. What these family structures stand for and the role they play in processes of inclusion and exclusion, however, is different for the national contexts under study. For example, if we want to do research on subsidised labour in Belgium and the Netherlands, we are to a certain extent dealing with comparable issues. But at the same time we are dealing with specific national issues, like differences in government policy, cultures, institutional frameworks, and so on, which are probably even more important. And while it seems logical to examine and compare the differences and similarities within closely related countries like Belgium and the Netherlands, it is even more evident that there are large differences between Northern and Southern Europe, or, for that matter, between countries in different parts of the world.

Thirdly, it will be clear by now that at the international level, the complexity of converging or rather diverging conditions, factors and developments that are relevant for the research project, will be substantial.

In the research strategy of INPART, the central instrument has been the case study (see Chapter Five). The research was (partly) focused on specific active policy measures of national governments, and case studies gave optimal possibilities to do justice to the complexity and contextuality of policies. These national case studies drew on the everyday experiences and interpretations of the people under study, and therefore on the principle of double hermeneutics. These case studies were contextualised by extensive analyses of the national contexts they were part of.

With the contextualised case studies forming the basis for the project, comparability was approached by elaborating on what is specific in the contextualised case under investigation, and then, from there on, to look for general features. Therefore a principle of generalisation is practised that is different from the principle underlying the orthodox consensus.

Of course the question whether or not INPART's theoretical, conceptual and methodological strategy has been executed in an adequate way and in every possible respect, is open to debate. Like all other researchers, we are human, make mistakes, do not always have enough time and energy to do what we want to do, and so on. Furthermore, and this is not just an opportunistic defence against possible criticism, the current rules and regulations for research projects on a European level are not in all respects adequate to allow for a reflexive approach.

Nevertheless, we think that the general direction of INPART is defensible and has proven to be a fruitful one in terms of the empirical results. Furthermore, the project gives food for thought on how to further develop a reflexive approach in international comparative research on at least three central issues that, in this respect, need further discussion.

First, we need further theoretical elaboration on the issue of *contextualisation*. If we take seriously the idea that we cannot understand anything without understanding the social context, we would conclude that we could not make any comparisons, since we cannot single out any elements from its social context. This radical implication depends, however, on our starting point or perspective. In other words: what do we mean by a social context? Is it a family, a part of a town, a municipality, a nation, or the entire world? If we take the entire world as a starting point and, for instance, analyse the poor and rich countries as deviations from some sort of broad average, or consider individual nations as subdivisions of the entire world society, we can compare deviations and variations. If we take a local municipality as the relevant social context, however, we cannot compare it with other contexts without violating our principles.

A less radical description of the problem – but basically one which deals with the same controversy – is the difference between what Ebbinghaus (1998, p 302) terms "cross-national comparison" and "international relations theory". The former tends to "study the commonalities and differences between European nation states" while the latter "deals with political regulation within a multi-level policy" (Ebbinghaus, 1998, p 302).

In recent years, most comparative research on social policy has departed from 'welfare-state models'. Individual nation states are categorised into some four or five broad models that are constructed from similarities and differences. The models presented by Esping-Andersen have been especially influential in this comparative discourse, and this methodology makes comparisons between a high number of nation states less complicated to survey. Yet the basic issue remains: are the models variations within the same basic model, or are they completely independent and separate from each other? Are they variations within a common social context or not? One can actually argue that they are and that they are not. It all depends on one's point of view and argumentation.

Therefore, from our criterion that comparisons must not be made without including the social context, we cannot reject this methodology of comparing 'models'. If we assume that they are deviations of basically the same 'society' we can compare them without violating our principles. Comparisons need a basic assumption that the subcontexts we are comparing are part of a common order or society. A very pragmatic formulation of this could be that, in order to compare European nation states, we must assume that they have some basic features in common (such as democratically elected government, a basic level of guaranteed institutions, and so on). Otherwise comparisons are taken out of their context.

When we study special social phenomena like active and inclusion policies we cannot just assume, however, that they are part of the same European context. Although the EU (especially during the second half of the 1990s) has developed comprehensive and wide-ranging policies as part of a European Employment Strategy and procedures of open coordination via the National Action Plans (NAPs; see Chapters Five and Nine), these policies are set mainly in a national context (although there are examples of imitation effects, where one nation state makes reforms which are inspired by neighbour nation states). Active social policies are national matters, and the related institutions are set up and operate mainly in a national and even local context. This means that policies, institutions and actors have to be analysed in their national contexts. As Jensen (2000, p 31) puts it: "A social phenomenon that at first glance looks similar in different countries may have entirely different meanings and effects at different times in history and in different historical spaces". How can we overcome this fact if we want to compare such phenomena without losing the social (national) context?

One solution is to find out how the institutions are related to each other and how the individuals and the institutions are referring to each other in the nation states that are to be compared. Jensen recommends the construction of "hidden, structural analogies" (2000, p 35) between core institutions in the countries compared. This means that social phenomena must be studied in their specific nation state context, and then compared with the same phenomena in other countries, taking into account that they must be interpreted in their own institutional setting and configuration of institutions. The comparison must be based upon a national case study which includes the understanding of the meaning and effect of the specific configuration of institutions in the individual nation state.

The second issue that needs further discussion is the *principle of generalisation* and, more specifically, its consequences for choosing case studies. Without going into too much detail here, we were not able to solve all the problems of our methodology's application in our project. Some case studies were made without thorough consideration of the fact that they were to be compared with one another. To put it very crudely, some of the national case studies were insufficiently subject to the principles of the comparative approach we have outlined in this chapter. When the case studies were completed and we were about to sum up our findings from a comparative perspective, the task turned out to be very complicated. It was obvious that the analysis demanded further and thorough discussions. With hindsight, the major issue in this respect was the choice of case studies. In a reflexive approach the choice of case studies is a complex process. The starting point is to develop a shared notion of generalisation from a reflexive approach. This may sound obvious, but it is not. In a situation where international comparative research is still strongly dominated by the orthodox consensus this requires an intensive discussion. The next step is to answer the question: which case studies will offer sufficient opportunities to elaborate on what is specific to them and then, thereafter, to look for general features? This general question should be translated into more specific criteria for the choice of case studies. The eventual choice of case studies requires research and should therefore be part of the research project as such. In the project, we have approached this choice more pragmatically: content is closely connected to conditions. The rules and regulations for EU-funded research projects give little room for such an investment. They require that the choice of case studies is made beforehand, in the process of making an application.

The third issue is *reciprocal adequacy*. Given the complexity of the issue we will not elaborate too extensively on it here. The national case studies offer possibilities for discussion between researchers and the researched on the results of the research project. These possibilities at a national level should be connected to a discussion on a comparative, European level. This raises practical questions. If the 'researched' are seen as 'all the people under investigation in the national case studies' it is not easy to imagine how such a discussion should or could be organised. Discussion on a comparative, European level will, almost by definition, have to be organised through some form of representation of those researched. A more fundamental problem is that such a discussion presupposes that the comparative, European level on which this discussion is organised is a 'living reality' for them. They must have some interest in it, have some sort of a picture of it, and must be motivated to be actively involved in it. Both in this practical and in a more fundamental respect, there is still a lot of work to be done.

As we stated in the introduction to this chapter, we did not intend to elaborate on the details of the way in which INPART dealt with this reflexive method, nor the reasons why the project did not meet all the ideal criteria of this method. We have mentioned some of its most obvious weak points and could add more. We could also explain some of the specific reasons why INPART – despite its initial (naïve) aspirations – did not end up as the ideal example of reflexive comparative method. This was not, of course, our intention. Our intention was to use the experiences of INPART to contribute to the general discussion on international comparative research. Whether or not we succeeded is a matter for the reader to decide.

References

Beck, U. (1986) *Risikogesellschaft. Auf dem Weg in eine andere Moderne*, Frankfurt am Main: Suhrkamp.

Beck, U., Giddens, A. and Lash, S. (1994) *Reflexive modernisation*, Cambridge: Polity Press.

Bourdieu, P. (1990) 'The scholastic point of view', *Cultural Anthropology*, vol 5, no 4, pp 380-91.

Bourdieu, P. and Wacquant, L.D. (1992) *An invitation to reflexive sociology*, Chicago, IL: University of Chicago Press.

Coenen, H. (1993) 'Het gelukkig gesternte van handelingsonderzoek', in H. Coenen, L. Keune and B. Boog (eds) *De actualiteit van handelingsonderzoek*, Tilburg: Tilburg University Press.

Coenen, H. and Leisink, P. (1993) *Work and citizenship in the new Europe*, Aldershot: Edward Elgar.

Coenen-Hanegraaf, M., Ploeg, M, Valkenburg, B. and Coenen, H. (1998) *Begeleid Werken: Theorie en methodiek van een individuele, vraaggerichte benadering*, Utrecht: Van Arkel.

Ebbinghaus, B. (1998) 'Europe through the looking-glass: comparative and multi-level perspectives', *Acta Sociologica*, vol 41, no 4, pp 301-13.

Giddens, A. (1976) *New rules of sociological method*, New York, NY: Basic Books.

Giddens, A. (1979) *Central problems in social theory. Action, structure and contradiction in social analysis*, Berkeley/Los Angeles, CA: University of California Press.

Giddens, A. (1990) *The consequences of modernity*, Cambridge: Polity Press.

Giddens, A. (1991) *Modernity and self-identity*, Cambridge: Polity Press.

Jensen, P.H. (2000) 'Kontekstuelle og tværnationale komparative analyser', *Dansk Sociologi*, vol 11, no 3, pp 29-48.

Lipsky, M. (1980) *Street-level bureaucracy: Dilemmas of the individual in public services*, New York, NY: Russell Sage Foundation.

Smith, S. and Lipsky, M. (1993) *Nonprofits for hire: The welfare state and the age of contracting*, Cambridge, MA: Harvard University Press.

NINE

Activation policies as reflexive social policies

Rik van Berkel and Maurice Roche

Introduction

This chapter reflects upon the results of INPART from the perspective of social policy. What could be the implications of these results for current and future activation policies? We present recommendations for activation policies based on the findings presented in the earlier chapters of this book. In order to understand the origins of these recommendations, it is important once again to make explicit some characteristics of our research (also see Chapter Five).

The research project, INPART, was not a systematic evaluation of activation programmes, but rather a study into the inclusionary and exclusionary potentials of different types of work. The case studies on which we reported in Chapters Five to Seven were not limited to activation programmes, even though quite a few focused on these programmes. We also focused on regular work – the 'participation' or 'inclusion standard' – and on unpaid and informal work that, up until now, have hardly played any serious role in policies that aim to promote inclusion. The experiences of the respondents did tell us a great deal about the contribution of types of work to inclusion, and about aspects of the policy context that may increase this inclusionary potential. In this chapter, these lessons are translated into recommendations for social policies.

In the case studies we were interested in mapping people's experiences and situations in terms of inclusion and exclusion, both within and across the types of work under investigation. In terms of representativeness, we were interested in the variety and diversity of experiences and situations rather than in their precise frequency or incidence. A range of quantitative and qualitative research methods has been used to gather the empirical data.

In assessing the inclusionary potential of types of work and activation programmes, we did not use the usual, institutionally defined criteria for evaluation. That is, we did not focus on input–output ratios, savings on expenditures on income protection schemes, regular labour-market outflow of participants, and so on. Instead, we were interested in participants' perspectives and priorities that can be, but certainly not always, similar to those of the institutions involved in activation. In fact, the tension between institutional aims and objectives on the one hand, and target groups' or policy clients' aims and objectives on the other was an important motivation for instigating INPART, and will be a core issue in our recommendations.

Activation policies or, more generally, policies aimed at inclusion need to be understood by all actors involved (clients and their advocates on the one hand, and state administrators and social policy professionals on the other) in relation to the development of the EU. In the contemporary period, the EU is beginning to contextualise these policies in terms of locating them within a broader transnational framework of citizenship, institutions and policies. To adequately understand the nature of contemporary activation and inclusion policies, and the challenge they imply, we first need to explore this deeper and broader socio-political context further in its own terms. Then, in the discussions which follow, we return to the policy recommendations. First, some general comments will be made regarding inclusion and exclusion in modern society and the challenges this poses for activation policies, in terms of both aims and means of these policies, and of the activation approaches underlying them. We begin by elaborating the concept of 'reflexive activation policies', which has already been introduced in Chapter Eight. We then present some recommendations on how the inclusionary potentials of activation programmes and schemes might be strengthened. Finally, we deal with the issue of 'institutional activation'. Reflexive policies call for a process of reciprocal activation of clients and institutions, rather than for a process in which institutions are seen as the 'activators' and clients as the 'activated'.

The changing context of European social and activation policies: the EU

The national-level citizenship regimes of the member states of the EU, together with their national-level social rights and social policy regimes, now exist (for better or worse) and are reproducing or reforming themselves within the context of a dynamic and historically unprecedented multinational and transnational multilevel governance system (Leibfried and Pierson, 1995; Marks et al, 1995). It is reasonable to suppose, then, that this context will have important implications for these regimes and for their experiences and systems of social citizenship. While these implications cannot be addressed definitively at the present time, it is possible to explore some relevant aspects in a provisional way (also see Roche and van Berkel, 1997). In this section we consider some of the main relevant dynamics of the EU's integration process, before considering some key factors in this integration project, which are having, and will increasingly have, impacts on national social citizenship.

The EU: integration dynamics

The approach to social and economic policy within the EU, given the leading role of the Franco–German axis within it, has tended to be influenced particularly by the corporatist social model, for example in the attempted institutionalisation of a 'social dialogue' approach to policy making. However, as the single market project developed in the 1990s, this policy dynamic could be argued to have come into conflict with market-building and market-based imperatives of the kind arguably more familiar in the historical and political experience of liberal market model societies like the US and the UK. Ironically, this fundamental policy dilemma has arisen during a period in which the UK has appeared to commit itself, under successive Conservative and New Labour governments, to playing a marginal role within the EU. In addition, the EU is still absorbing the impact of the relatively recent addition to its ranks of Sweden and Finland in 1995, a process which has brought the traditions of social democratic model societies and their concerns for promoting the full complex of civil, political and social rights of citizenship to bear more directly and critically on EU institutions and policy making.

What does the development of the transnational EU project mean for the national-level citizenship regimes of member states in general, and their social citizenship regimes in particular? It is not easy to answer this question, not only because we are currently participating in a rapidly changing, hotly debated and ill-defined transitional stage in the development of the EU (see Leibfried and Pierson, 1995; Beck et al, 1997; Geyer, 1999). On the one hand, and in the short to medium term, there is the possibility that there may be few implications. This is for a number of reasons. Firstly there is the diversity in national social models around Europe noted earlier, and the fact that, to a certain extent, these differences within the EU systems can be protected because of the subsidiarity principle and the current persistence of national control and veto power over taxation and welfare policies. These principles were reaffirmed in the Treaty of Nice of 2000. Secondly, and more generally, the pace of the integration process may continue to be periodically slowed down because of the objections of particular member states, notably the UK. Arguably a 'multispeed' EU is likely to emerge in the medium term, and countries like the UK may or may not decide to locate themselves in the core group of member states which is willing to push the integration agenda most strongly. On the other hand, in the medium to long term, and with or without the UK, it is evident that there is a political and social logic connected with the economic logic of the construction of the single market, the single currency and the Economic and Monetary Union (EMU) project in general. This is likely to generate policy 'spillovers' into the spheres of social and citizenship policy, comparable with 'spillover' processes in many policy areas which have long characterised the process of development in the EU. In addition, the enlargement process and the EMU integrative process in general, if they are successful, are each likely to lead to increases in intra-EU labour mobility and also related concerns about 'social dumping' (Alber and

Standing, 2000). These issues are likely to increase the pressure to develop more standardised and portable EU-level citizenship and social rights systems, and this in turn may require a reorganisation and relative standardisation of elements of national social policies and welfare systems.

Key factors in the integration process: EU citizenship

The status of 'EU citizen' was created in the Maastricht Treaty of 1992. It was intended to supplement national citizenship, and indeed is (controversially) only available to people who are already citizens of member states. Currently it is defined very narrowly and technically in Article 8 of the treaty. However, it is arguable that this represents the tip of the iceberg of the effective rights of individuals and corporate actors which exist by virtue of EU laws as interpreted by the European Court of Justice. In fact this court has taken an activist role in developing these rights over a long period of time.

For many years, and certainly since the Maastricht Treaty, in which the status was first officially constructed, the European Commission (EC) has used the concept of European citizenship and citizens' rights (Roche and van Berkel, 1997; O'Leary and Tiilikainen, 1998). In particular the EC has long seen it as a strategically important part of its policy discourse concerned with identifying and acting against forms of social exclusion at EU level (Roche, 1992; CEC, 1993a, 1993b, 1995a, 1995b). The EC's continuing reliance on the discourse of citizenship was evident, for instance, in its views on the need for EC constitutional reform in 1996 in the run-up to the Amsterdam Treaty (Roche, 1997). The EC's agenda setting for Amsterdam included the presentation of a wide-ranging conception of European citizenship which we can analyse in terms of civil-political and socio-economic dimensions of EU citizenship, constitution and public sphere. The EC sees citizenship as the answer to exclusion and argues strongly for the critical need for the member states to make major constitutional reform and political development to develop EU citizenship both for its own sake and as a means of countering increasingly structural problems of exclusion in European society.

The Amsterdam Treaty was ratified and given force of law by all of the member states in 1999. This enabled the EU's Social Charter, from which the UK had previously opted out, to become fully part of the EU's legal system. This charter embodies substantial rights for employees (in part-time and temporary employment as well as full-time employment) which have been rolled out over a number of years through a programme of legally enforceable Directives to the member states. These rights include the right to a decent wage, maximum working hours, join a trade union and to strike, equal treatment for male and female employees, and to social security. However, it is worth mentioning that these rights are restricted to citizens who happen to be in employment, and therefore they do not apply to all citizens.

Economic and Monetary Union (EMU)

With all due allowance for subsidiarity and differential national reform processes, the implications of the EMU single market and single currency projects, as they are worked through in the medium term, are likely to increase convergence between member states' mainstream work and welfare systems. The first stage of the single currency project, launched in 1999, involves, among other things, the centralised control of the exchange rates of the national currencies of the 11 member states in the 'eurozone' by the European Central Bank together with a significant constraint on their levels of public expenditure – at least that part of it which might be generated through governmental borrowing and increases in the national debt. This stage of the EMU system, together with the monitored economic convergence that it involves, clearly implies a 'pooling' of economic sovereignty by eurozone members. That is, it already seems to imply significant constraints on participating state's traditional capacities for independent and nationally distinctive versions of macro-economic policy (Crouch, 2000).

The working out of the economic policy logic of EMU in the medium term involves drawing out both of the implications of a single currency for independent national tax and benefit systems and also, in relation to this, the implications of the single market project for independent and nationally distinctive work and welfare systems. The crucial point for the future of the latter issue is not just the current and ongoing unification and 'Europeanisation' of capital and commodity markets but, in particular – and, because of the evident durability of barriers of language and tradition, necessarily in a longer-term perspective – the progressive unification and Europeanisation of member states' labour markets and Europe-wide labour mobility and migration during the early decades of the 21st century.

The single currency project's implications for tax and benefit systems (Huws, 1997) and the current policy goal of constructing a single labour market within the EU, are both binding treaty-based commitments. Both separately and together they necessarily carry profound implications for the capacity of member states to retain control, as they currently do, of employment and welfare policies. The agreements which member states have entered into in their attempt to converge their employment and welfare policies remain technically voluntaristic and not legally binding. However, even in the post-Maastricht and pre-Amsterdam period of the mid-1990s, these agreements were capable of being analysed as distinctive systems of multilevel governance involving a significant pooling of sovereignty by a group of what have become merely 'semi-sovereign' welfare states (Leibfried and Pierson, 1995).

Employment policy: the European Employment Strategy

The final key factor we will discuss here is most directly and clearly linked to activation policies: the EU employment policy, also known as the European

Employment Strategy. The development of the EU's employment policy is likely to be the crucial axis for new developments in EU social and economic rights, and social citizenship. In the post-Amsterdam period of the late 1990s we could first see the beginning of a process of 'open coordination': a coordinated EU employment policy and regulatory system which member states are obliged to take into account, and which is likely to consolidate in the short to medium term. Agreed in Luxembourg in 1997 and first implemented in 1998, annual Employment Guidelines require member states to submit annual employment action plans and attempts to promote 'best practice' policy sharing and a coordinated approach between the member states. The system has recently been further institutionalised by the creation of an intergovernmental EU Employment Committee charged with the annual monitoring – reported in a Joint Employment Report – of member states' National Action Plans (NAPs). They are also responsible for the coordination of NAPs in relation to the EU's overall Employment Action Plan policy from 2000 onwards. With all due recognition for the current voluntary nature of the process and the diversity it allows, it remains the case that these policies now have to be presented and accounted for to the European Council and are open to scrutiny and debate in the European Parliament and in other EU institutions, such as the Economic and Social Committee (ECOSOC). At the very least it can be reasonably assumed that, from now on, policies which are incompatible with the overall intergovernmentally agreed thrust of employment policy for Europe are unlikely to be created or promoted in member states. At the Lisbon Summit in 2000, a similar method of open coordination on social inclusion was agreed upon. The first 'joint report' on social inclusion presents this new initiative in the social policy field as complementing the objectives of the European Employment Strategy (CEC, 2001). This social inclusion initiative opens up a broader approach to exclusion than the 'unemployment equals exclusion' and 'employment equals inclusion' theses so characteristic for employment policies. Nevertheless, the joint report on social inclusion seems to adhere to the 'royal road to inclusion' view on employment when it states:

> In this respect it puts due emphasis on the key role of participation in employment, especially by groups that are underrepresented or disadvantaged in it, in line with the objectives of the European Employment Strategy. (CEC, 2001, p 5)

Returning now to the European Employment Strategy, the guidelines for the NAPs employment are centred around four pillars representing the key themes in EU employment policy:

• Improving employability;
• Developing entrepreneurship and job creation;
• Encouraging adaptability of businesses and their employees;
• Strengthening equal opportunities policies for women and men.

From an activation perspective, the first pillar is the most crucial one (see the appendix to this chapter). By means of these guidelines, one of the major decisions of the Lisbon Summit in 2000 should be realised:

> The Lisbon Summit agreed on a new comprehensive strategy towards employment, economic reform and social cohesion as part of the knowledge-based society and made a commitment to regaining the conditions of full employment. (CEC, 2000, p 3)

The employment strategy pursues a "preventative" approach to unemployment and emphasises the new and long-term state obligation to support citizens' lifelong "employability" as well as, generally, a society of "full" or "secure employability" through education and training opportunities and active rather than passive approaches to the distribution of welfare benefits and services (Bosco and Chassard, 1999). These policy approaches, particularly the preventative and employability approaches, have undoubtedly been registered in the recent employment policy discourses and practices of EU member states as they begin to undertake reforms in their mainstream work and welfare systems (SEDEC, 2000).

This development of EU-level employment policy runs parallel to the existing agreements in the social rights field. These include, firstly, agreements (from Maastricht) to monitor social policy convergence, and (from Amsterdam) to exercise an increased competence for EU institutions in the sphere of social inclusion policy actions. They also include new commitments to human rights and to the European Social Charter's social rights agreed in the Amsterdam Treaty. These commitments are now embodied in the movement for the EU Charter of Fundamental Rights which was given Declaration status in the Treaty of Nice of 2000 (EP, 2000). Taken together, these developments begin to amount to the construction of a framework for socio-economic policy making and for the addressing of citizens' socio-economic rights at EU level. They may be said to amount to the beginning of what can be referred to as a process of civil and social union. While this undoubtedly currently lags behind the EMU and political union processes, it is logically required by it and it may ultimately be more substantially developed to complement it.

The EU dimension in employment policy is relatively recent, its connections with changes in national employment policies are not always clearly articulated within national policy debates, and it presents an intrinsically complex picture. So there are limits to which its impacts can be fully grasped as a whole and adequately evaluated at the present time. Nevertheless it is reasonable to assume that they are likely to be significant in the medium term, and that national policies which are compatible with the overall agreed range of EU policy strategies will increasingly be considered and experimented with by member states. This process may provide a context for more rapid policy learning (policy cloning and social technology transfers) between member states, particularly in respect of effective policies. This in turn presages the possibility of a qualitatively greater degree of commonality across the EU in employment policy, compatible with the long-term development of a more integrated labour market. Currently, this is already happening in terms of the spread of the policies we have discussed in this book, namely active approaches to social policy and the development of activation programmes around European countries; even though, as we also saw, diversity is still significant. In relation to this it is also happening in terms of the spread of elements of a cross-national common policy discourse in this field in which national policies are conceptualised and framed using the common strategic concepts of activation, employability and related EU-level policy concepts.

Overall then, the spillover effects of the EMU, the European Employment Strategy and, recently, the NAPs social inclusion process are likely to stimulate the development of a cross-EU level of social and economic policy. In principle at least, this ought to stimulate related social and economic rights of the citizens of Europe. However, if existing transnational social rights, for instance in relation to work and employment, are to be developed further, they should not be built up in isolation and disconnection from civil and political rights. This kind of decontextualisation is a temptation and a weakness in political and policy discourses, particularly those which have often issued from the EC in the 1980s and 1990s, which operate one-dimensionally with concepts like 'the European Social Model', 'Social Europe' and so on. It is suggested that the promotion of such goals for European social citizenship needs to be undertaken in parallel and in conjunction with projects to democratise the EU and to politically and socially regulate the single market.

Reflexive activation: general issues

This and the following sections will direct attention to activation policies and the lessons for the future of these policies that may be learnt from our research results. As we saw earlier in this chapter, EU-level policy is of increasing importance in coordinating and stimulating social policy developments, particularly where the 'transformation' of social policies into more active policies is concerned. Therefore, our reflections on activation policies will be of relevance to both national and transnational policy making.

In terms of the typology of activation approaches developed in Chapter Three, the starting point of our recommendations can be outlined as follows. We think that 'active policies' can, under certain conditions and for some groups of socially disadvantaged people, contribute to the inclusionary potential of a variety of types of work and participation. In our view, active policies should be positive and enabling, facilitating the access to resources that are essential if people are to meet their needs, rather than enforcing or prescribing certain types of participation while discouraging or punishing others. In other words, the activation approach on which our policy recommendations will be based tends towards that of the activation optimists rather than the paternalism optimists. At the same time, inclusion into society and its (sub)systems requires both income support and participation support. That is, we recognise the claim of the autonomy optimists that income is an important precondition for broader inclusion and may for some be sufficient to realise full participation. This is in line with the conclusion of Chapter Six that inclusion in the system of income/consumption has the strongest association with inclusion in other systems.

Active and passive policies are conceived here as instruments to reallocate resources or, put differently, to provide capital (in the broad sense of the word as developed by Bourdieu) in the form of income, participation support and recognition (Bourdieu, 1999; SEDEC, 2000). Obviously, modernisation processes have changed the context in which social policies operate and intervene (Valkenburg and Coenen, 2002). Contrary to some 'modernisation optimists', we do not share the view that modern society has been able to overcome social inequality. Therefore, in order to combat processes and mitigate outcomes of social inequality, the redistributive and reallocative functions of social policies are still of major importance. Nevertheless, individualisation and detraditionalisation, which are considered to be important characteristics of the 'second modernity' (Beck, 2000) or of 'post-Fordist modernity' (for example, Gorz, 1999), and which produce new social risks and opportunities, have a significant impact on the conditions under which social policies operate. Consequently, they should influence their objectives, means and modus operandi.

This issue is elaborated in an inspiring publication by Leisering and Leibfried, *Time and poverty in Western welfare states* (1999), which concerns itself with social policies in modern societies. They elaborate four new policy orientations which, in their view, are necessary in adjusting social policies to the challenges of modernity, and are also relevant for our discussion. We can summarise these challenges as follows.

Firstly, processes of individualisation and differentiation which have contributed to the heterogeneity among target groups of social policies imply the need for a reconceptualisation of these policies as life course policies (see also Giddens, 1994; Leisering and Walker, 1998). Undifferentiated and static social policies are inadequate for dealing with diversity and 'subjective and biographical' time, referring to people's experiences with 'objective' inclusion and the meanings they attach to these experiences.

Secondly, social policies should treat clients as competent actors whose capabilities and skills should be enabled by these policies. This implies, on the one hand, recognising and using in a positive way the action potential of poor people, rather than conceiving of them as passive (or as frauds and scroungers). On the other, enabling approaches are directed at escaping from rather than compensating for poverty (also see Chapter Three).

Thirdly, social policies should advocate an integrated approach. Although Leisering and Leibfried mainly refer to the distinction in many welfare states between systems of social insurance and residual social assistance, we can interpret this in a broader sense as a plea in favour of a decompartmentalisation of social interventions. The multidimensional character of problems of exclusion calls for integration and coordination, rather than for fragmentation and compartmentalisation.

Fourthly, the authors advocate a transformation of social policy into *reflexive* social policy. By this they refer to a process of continuously monitoring the effects of social policies and reporting on them. Again, we will use this concept in a broader sense here. It not only refers to monitoring the intended and unintended effects and outcomes of policies, but also to a reflexive attitude with respect to their suppositions and conditions of operation including the competence and knowledge of the people at which policies are targeted (Chapter Eight), and state–citizen relationships in policy making and delivery.

Based on these policy orientations, we can present some general reflections on activation policies.

Heterogeneity and policy differentiation

As we have elaborated in this book, both in a theoretical (Chapter Two) and an empirical way (Chapters Five to Seven), problems of exclusion can be very diverse. They can relate to a variety of (sub)systems, can involve a lack of a wide range of resources, and can occur in various combinations of types of exclusion, even though the associations between various types of exclusion are anything but simple (Chapter Six). Temporal dimensions of exclusion can be very different as well, both in 'objective' terms – duration of exclusion – and in 'subjective' or 'biographical' terms – experiences of (severity of) exclusion and 'involuntary' versus 'voluntary' exclusion (see Chapter Six). Finally, prospects of inclusion can vary, once again both in objective terms: usually defined as labour-market distance or employability; and in subjective terms: in terms of the types of inclusion excluded people want to establish. Furthermore, contrary to common sense and to the suppositions underlying many activation policies, the distinction between 'the included' and 'the excluded' does not run parallel to that between the employed and the unemployed; at least, when the concepts of inclusion and exclusion are not reduced to employment and unemployment respectively. Therefore, policies aiming at combating exclusion should be targeted ideally not only at (groups of) people who are excluded from the labour market, but also at (parts of) the so-called included. But even when we limit ourselves to traditional target groups of activation, heterogeneity is substantial. Consequently, the problems inclusion policies set themselves to resolve, can be quite different for different groups of excluded people or, in more conventional terms, for different groups of the unemployed and the poor. It could even be argued that unemployment or poverty are not always the major – and certainly not the only – problems excluded people are confronted with. This implies that the starting point of active social policy interventions can differ considerably. Furthermore, objective characteristics of activation clients such as age, gender and nationality – the kind of information social workers usually collect about their clients if only because these data need to be stored in files – are, in individual cases, at most partial. They are also not very good indicators of the nature and severity of exclusion problems. Therefore, activation processes should start with an investigation or assessment of the kind of problems that should be solved through activation.

By now, assessment and gateway procedures are standard components of many activation programmes. However, these are not necessarily directed at mapping exclusion problems. More regularly, they focus on determining the employability and labour-market distance of individual clients, which is deemed necessary in order to decide on the nature of activation measures to be employed. Potentially, this may amount to ignoring the point of view of clients, who may have other concerns than their 'employability', and to reducing clients' situation to one of unemployment. Ultimately, these practices may lead to situations – and we saw examples of them in our case studies – that activation has solved the problems of the institutions involved in activation (realising placements, cutting on benefit expenditures) but not those of activated clients.

We can also interpret this in a different way. Heterogeneity not only refers to the problems activation has to solve, but also to the solutions it should offer and the objectives it should try to realise. Just as many activation schemes are one-sided in presupposing that unemployment is the most important exclusion problem, they are one-sided in recognising one objective only: economic 'independence' (from benefits and public income support) through labour-market participation. Recognising heterogeneity implies a differentiation of potential exclusion problems *and* of potential inclusion roads. Of course, activation policies, especially in countries with a longer tradition in activation, have been differentiating their activation programmes substantially. However, the types of participation involved in these different programmes (ranging from regular work via subsidised work, training and education to unpaid activities) are often classified according to a clear participation hierarchy rather than as different types of participation of equal value. Regular paid work is undisputed and unrivalled at the top of this hierarchy, whereas unpaid activities, if seen as an inclusion option at all, constitute a kind of participation safety net for the most disadvantaged (read: non-employable).

The objective of activation: employment or inclusion?

Most activation policies are employment rather than inclusion policies. They are, as Standing (1999) calls it, labourist. That is, labour market participation or, maybe even more importantly, social security independence, is the most important goal of these policies, and not inclusion in its broader sense. In this respect, it is quite unclear why the concepts of inclusion and exclusion have been introduced at all into policy debates on participation. Given the definition of these concepts in current activation policies, they are used as synonyms of employment and unemployment rather than reflecting a broader approach to challenges to welfare states. From this point of view, the European Employment Strategy – and the NAPs breathe the same spirit – is exactly what it claims to be: a set of measures to combat unemployment (and welfare-state dependency), not a strategy to promote inclusion in a broader sense. Against this background it will be interesting to see how the method of open coordination on social inclusion which started during the Portuguese EU presidency in 2000, will develop and will relate to the employment strategy.

What is at stake here, of course, is what Leisering and Leibfried (1999) termed "political time": the debate on the recognition of certain 'lifestyles' or, to be more specific, of certain types of participation. Which types of participation are recognised as useful, both for the individuals involved in them and for society at large, and can therefore be considered as legitimate activities of people dependent on income transfers? Current debates on the obligations in terms of labour-market participation of single parents (most of them women) are just one example of this (see, for example, Levitas, 1998; Saraceno, 2002). Increasingly, single parents on social assistance are losing the right to take care of their (young) children and are subjected to labour-market activation (see also, Lødemel and Trickey, 2001). Paternalism is often unambiguously present: labour-market participation is considered to be of far more emancipatory importance to women than taking care of their children. In his discussion on workfare, Standing summarises these points as follows:

> Workfare is a labourist and paternalistic response to the crisis of insecurity. There is room for disquiet. Workfare stigmatises the poor by associating certain activities with prior failure and by eroding the right to income security even further than recent labour market developments have done. It is coercive social policy. It is also morally a soft option. When the paternalistic family was seen as the social norm, women were expected to stay out of the labour force, so that labour conditionality was not regarded as reasonable. Now the norm is that women should be in wage jobs, so the paternalism dictates that women, even with young children and without a regular partner, should be obliged to take jobs. (Standing, 1999, p 334)

Of course, the issue here is not to take employment rights and support in realising labour-market participation away from single parents or (groups of) the unemployed in general. The issue is whether other inclusion options are recognised and whether people are granted voice and choice in deciding which inclusion options they prefer. As much as it is useless to talk about inclusion and exclusion as dichotomous concepts, it is also useless to exaggerate the inclusionary potentials of regular labour-market participation (which is exactly what those who support the 'royal road to inclusion' view of employment are doing), and to downplay the inclusionary potentials of other types of participation. In our view, the main issue is not whether certain types of work potentially contribute more to inclusion than others. This approach is inherently paternalistic in its consequences since it assumes that this question can be answered irrespective of the needs of the people involved. Rather, the main issue is what resources are offered by certain types of work, and how these do or do not match the inclusion needs of potential participants.

The main challenge of activation: matching resources and people's needs

We have so far formulated two conclusions with respect to activation policies. We have highlighted the heterogeneity among target groups of these policies. People are included and excluded in different ways and in various degrees, and have different needs with respect to inclusion (and 'voluntary' exclusion). On the other hand, types of participation or work are very diverse in terms of the resources they offer. Employment in itself is diverse, and diversity is even increased when other types of work are taken into consideration. Combining these two conclusions means that activation policies should consider it as their main challenge to match people's needs with the resources of types of work and participation, keeping in mind that these resources are partly shaped by social policies. This is how we interpret Leisering and Leibfried's as well as others' pleas to transform activation policies into enabling or empowering policies. This approach is quite different from many current activation programmes, which either presume that people's needs are clear from the outset and do not need further assessment ('they want to work'), or that needs should be paternalistically enforced upon them ('they should [want to] work').

In terms of citizenship rights and obligations, this approach to activation does not imply that activation is only about rights and not about obligations. Rather, what rights and obligations mean in concrete situations and circumstances is subject to negotiation at the policy delivery level. Rights and obligations are not defined without any involvement of clients, but are agreed upon intersubjectively, which means that they are liable to reciprocal adequacy. In fact, this amounts to a democratisation of the activation process. This is one of the core characteristics of what Jordan called 'new politics of welfare',

> ... in which responsibilities are negotiated rather than imposed, and the division of labour – in households, as in the public sphere – results from democratic dialogue and compromise, rather than a struggle for power and domination. (Jordan, 1998, pp 181-2)

In this sense, responsibilities might be seen as 'positive obligations', a concept used by Rosanvallon (2000) in outlining a third way of "mutual involvement of the individual and society" (p 88) that is emerging between traditional social rights and paternalistic social aid. Evidently, conceiving of clients as 'competent actors' in their activation processes and of responsibilities as negotiable in a democratic process implies that (s)he is also equipped with the resources (in terms of information, power, direction opportunities) to enter this negotiation process. Various EU countries are already experimenting with instruments that can increase clients' involvement and autonomy in activation, for example, by introducing individual activation budgets.

Participation and income

Chapter Six concluded by stating that inclusion in the system of income/consumption is often important for inclusion in other systems. Evidently, our societies are not fully monetarised, and forms of non-monetarised mutuality, exchange and trade still exist. Nevertheless, the latter are under constant pressure, partly as a consequence of the labourist orientation of social policies, as became clear in our British case study into informal work and in the Spanish and Portuguese case studies where respondents referred to the changing role of the family. These developments are likely to strengthen the importance and necessity of income as a crucial resource for participation, for example, in the domains of consumption, social networks, culture and leisure ('income before participation'). At the same time, activation policies often increase the conditionality of income by making it into a reward for participation ('participation before income'). As we saw in Chapter Three, income is often transformed in an activation context into the main instrument to enforce participation obligations upon social security claimants.

One might state that the introduction of activation policies is based on the correct assumption that problems of exclusion cannot be reduced to lack of income only. Exclusion often means more than financial hardship, and realising participation often requires more than income, even though income is likely to facilitate participation in other systems. However, the reverse holds as well: exclusion problems cannot be reduced to lack of participation. Therefore, in assessing people's needs and determining the resources necessary to combat exclusion, there is no a priori reason to subordinate income to participation. In a 'labourist' policy context, the importance of income as a dimension of inclusion is seen as strengthening rather than weakening the employment orientation of activation policies. In work-based societies like ours, for most people the road towards income improvement runs through the labour market. Apart from the debate on the desirability of an increasing monetarisation of social relations, the working poor debate has emphasised that labour-market participation does not guarantee income improvement and security. The flexibility and differentiation processes that are taking place on the labour market have weakened the relationship between labour-market participation and income security and improvement. Activation programmes themselves have contributed to these processes: subsidised and additional employment programmes for the unemployed have created a labour-market segment of low-paid jobs that often hardly offer any income improvement to (former) social security claimants. Furthermore, these programmes do not always encourage regular labour-market participation. In fact, they can sometimes actively impede it, which constitutes another barrier for potential income improvement. This weakens the case for a 'royal road to inclusion' view of employment, and calls for specific attention to inclusion into the system of income/consumption, rather than seeing the latter as an automatic effect of inclusion in employment.

From a labourist perspective, one can approach this problem by developing a strategy aimed at strengthening the degree to which employment guarantees inclusion in the system of income/consumption, for example by improving prospects for income improvement or by providing more job-related income security. From a less labour-market centred perspective, access to income improvement, economic independence or purchasing power can be created beyond the labour market as well. For example, so-called Time Currency or LETS systems reward involvement in unpaid and reciprocal activities by converting the contribution people make into a form of currency that can be used to acquire goods and services that one needs or desires (for example, see Offe and Heinze, 1990; Williams, 1998). A more 'monetary' and radical approach has already been mentioned as the core of the autonomy optimists' activation approach (see Chapter Three), that is the introduction of a Basic Income or Citizens' Income (Coenen and Leisink, 1993; Jordan, 1998; Gorz, 1999). These schemes are advocated in many different forms. Some adherents are in favour of a fully unconditional basic or citizens' income, which should be sufficient to meet people's basic needs. Others propagate more conditional versions (for example, the Active Citizen Credit scheme) which entitles people to an income not as an unconditional citizens' right but as a reward for participation and contributing to society, whatever form that contribution takes. A more modest non-labourist solution to increase people's inclusion into the domains of income and consumption is to reward participants in unpaid activities with some kind of financial bonus or incentive as is currently happening in some of the Dutch municipal social activation schemes (see Chapter Five).

This is not the place to elaborate these income improvement options in more detail. These examples suffice to show that theoretically, alternatives exist for the increasingly insecure labourist road to income improvement which can increase the inclusionary potential of types of work outside the labour market substantially.

Recognising and facilitating inclusion strategies beyond the labour market

Conceiving the target groups of activation as competent actors and broadening the concepts of inclusion, work and participation create opportunities for activation programmes to recognise inclusion strategies that go beyond labour-market participation, and to facilitate and support these. This plea to make the politics of welfare 'go with the grain' of individual and collective strategies instead of enforcing obligations is a recurrent theme in Bill Jordan's work on welfare and his critical assessment of what he labels the "new orthodoxy of welfare" of third way politicians (Jordan, 1998, 2000). It is also reflected in Standing's work when he concludes his analysis of workfare policies as follows:

> In the more flexible society emerging in industrialised economies and elsewhere, *diversity* of behaviour should be facilitated, rather than curtailed by mechanisms designed to pressurise the poor to conform to some State-determined norm. (Standing, 1999, p 334)

Table 9.1: The 'orthodox consensus' of activation versus reflexive activation

Activation issues	Orthodox consensus	Reflexive activation
Activation approach	Paternalism optimists' activation approach.	Combining elements from the autonomy optimists' and the activation optimists' activation approaches.
Heterogeneity of clients	Relevant in as far as heterogeneity influences employability and selection processes with respect to placements.	Relevant for the definition of the problems to be solved by activation and for determining the objectives of the activation process.
Heterogeneity of work/ participation	Mainly relevant as far as employment is concerned; employability determines where in the participation hierarchy individual placements take place.	Relevant for the variety of resources that different types of paid and unpaid work/participation give access to.
Main challenge	Matching employability of clients with the corresponding position on the participation hierarchy.	Matching individual needs with resources offered by types of work and participation.
Characteristics of activation process	Paternalistic or enforcing: rights and obligations are predefined and hardly subject to negotiation.	Rights and obligations are negotiable and subject to a process of 'mutual adequacy'.
Linking participation and income	Income improvement through labour-market participation.	Alternative ways of income improvement, unconditional (income as a basic citizens' right) or conditional (income as a reward for participation and contributing to society).
Informal, non-labourist inclusion strategies	Neglected or counteracted (penalised or criminalised).	Recognition and facilitation.

In the dominant approach to activation, non-labour-market centred inclusion strategies are either neglected or counteracted, the latter because they are considered fraudulent, since they are seen as diminishing people's labour market availability or because they are seen as incompatible with policies aimed at reducing social security expenditures. This creates a paradoxical situation in which activation makes people passive or makes them *look* passive because they will feel encouraged to hide their informal or unpaid activities from activation professionals. From a labourist point of view, this way of dealing with informal strategies is logical and sensible. From an activation approach founded on a broader concept of inclusion, however, it is quite counterproductive.

In many countries of the EU there is an increasing awareness that bottom-up, community based initiatives are important instruments in tackling exclusion. An example of these initiatives were (some of) the Belgian Third System Organisations and the Dutch Social Activation scheme that were studied in our research (Chapter Five). Nevertheless, in the context of a labourist activation approach these initiatives run the risk of only being valued in as far as they promote employment creation and labour-market participation. Starting from a broader perspective on inclusion and participation, bottom-up initiatives rooted in people's own attempts to realise types of inclusion should be encouraged as well, due to their ability to enable people to help themselves, inside or outside the labour market.

Summary

In Table 9.1 we have summarised the main differences in the ways the 'orthodox consensus' of activation and reflexive activation deal with central activation issues. In terms of the activation approaches developed in Chapter Three, the 'orthodox consensus' of activation is closely akin to the activation approach of the paternalism optimists, whereas reflexive activation incorporates elements of the activation optimists' and autonomy optimists' approaches.

Strengthening the inclusionary potential of activation schemes

In the previous section broader issues regarding activation and activation approaches have been discussed. There, we characterised the main challenge of what we called 'reflexive activation' as empowering people by providing them with resources to meet their needs, in an intervention context that recognises the autonomy and competence of the target groups of activation. In this section we focus on a more concrete level, namely the schemes and programmes or 'types of participation' developed and employed in the context of activation. Against the background of the former section, we formulate some conditions that may strengthen the inclusionary potential of activation programmes, irrespective of the type of work or participation involved, and reduce their exclusion risks. Of course, from an outsiders' point of view, participation in activation programmes by definition implies some form of inclusion. However, here we are interested in participants' experiences of inclusion, in terms of the match between their needs and resources offered by types of work, as elaborated before. The same goes for exclusion: when we talk about reducing exclusion risks, we mean reducing experiences and instances of involuntary exclusion. Once again it should be emphasised that what we have been labelling throughout this book as the inclusionary and exclusionary potentials of types of work are shaped and can be modified to an important degree by social and, we would like to stress, in-company personnel or human resource management policies. Apart from that, active social policies can play a vital role in matching the needs of people involved in an activation process with the resources offered by types of work.

In their comparative study of workfare programmes, Lødemel and Trickey (2001) distinguish Human Resource Development from Labour Market Attachment programmes. Whereas the former focus on the development of human resources and opportunities, the latter merely aim at ending welfare dependency by employment. From our case studies it becomes clear that the former is the preferred approach. The 'labour market attachment' approach may seem attractive because it gets people off benefits in the short term; but it has less to offer in terms of longer-term and sustainable inclusion, at least, when we recognise that inclusion and exclusion cannot be defined adequately without taking people's own experiences and needs seriously. Furthermore, it may create exclusion risks in terms of a lack of resources to be able to participate in the systems people would like to participate in, in a way they see fit. On the one hand, the 'labour market attachment' approach may not be very adequate in helping people to cope with multidimensional exclusion problems, therefore excluding the most disadvantaged from participation and producing drop-out risks. On the other, it may produce participation traps for participants, for example, when the activation offer does not match people's needs or when no new participation perspectives come up. Therefore, activation programmes should provide ideally, tailor-made mixes of participation, learning and support, not only to realise successful placements, but also to anticipate new needs and ambitions. Such needs and ambitions, as our case studies show, are very likely to crop up during activation and participation. Of course, this raises the issue where the responsibilities of activation programmes end and those of human resource management policies of the companies where placements take place, begin. It also focuses attention to the question whether participants in activation programmes that are placed in 'regular' companies have similar rights to in-company employability measures as other workers. Some of our case studies revealed that placing activation clients in the context of specific activation programmes in regular companies may offer inclusion opportunities but may also involve serious marginalisation risks. We encountered the latter, for example, in cases where participants in activation programmes are confronted with status differences, and are entitled to different employment rights and benefits as their 'regular' colleagues (see Chapter Five).

Risks of involuntary exclusion can arise when activation participants are confronted with a lack of prospects, which can be the case in both temporary and permanent activation schemes. Temporary schemes do not always succeed in bringing about more permanent or sustainable inclusion. After the scheme has finished, participants run the risk of finding themselves in a situation of unemployment again. For them, the best current activation can offer is semi-permanent participation in temporary schemes that are designed to get them into regular paid work but do not manage to do so. In the case of permanent schemes a more lasting form of participation is realised which, however, involves high risks of marginalisation. This may be due to a lack of income improvement opportunities and to institutionalised stigmatisation at policy or shop floor level, or due to the absence of possibilities to find more 'regular', challenging or interesting employment. Solutions to these and similar risks can be sought in two directions:

- Improvements in the secondary labour-market schemes themselves, which are particularly important for those for whom participation in these schemes will have a more permanent character;
- Improvements in opportunities to exit the scheme and to find types of work that match people's needs. Evidently, this will often imply regular employment, but this does not always have to be the case, since regular employment will not always be the best solution when optimising inclusion is concerned.

Whatever direction these new steps in the activation process will take, they imply the need for some kind of follow-up support once placements in a scheme have been realised, in terms of social policy or personnel management interventions and measures with respect to, for example, guidance, training and education.

We have repeatedly criticised top-down approaches in current activation policies. One of the effects of top-down approaches is that people whose needs, possibilities and capacities do not match with the activation offers being made, run the risk to drop out of schemes or not to be able to enter them at all. This problem will become increasingly manifest, we think, given the emphasis current EU social policies put on developing so-called full coverage approaches to activation. This means that targets are set to activate all members of certain target groups – the young unemployed, the new unemployed, the long-term unemployed – within a specific period of time (see the appendix at the end of this chapter, guideline no 1). A quite cynical but not unlikely strategy to realise this objective – which in itself is ambitious, given the resources needed – would be to reduce activation to individual intake interviews. During these interviews, an assessment is made to determine which clients fit the requirements of existing programmes and become 'included', whereas those who do not fit these requirements are excluded. In order for the full coverage approach to really provide inclusion opportunities for all members of the target groups, activation offers have to be flexible, which is a logical consequence of the recognition of the heterogeneity of activation clients. A tailor-made approach to activation requires that new programmes can be developed, existing programmes can be combined, and separate programmes can be modified and adjusted to the needs and possibilities of individual clients. For example, secondary labour-market schemes that demand full-time involvement or are restricted to low-skilled and low-productivity jobs will not be able to meet the needs of various categories of unemployed. These include people with health problems that are not able to work full-time and would like to work in part-time or casual employment; people who have been unemployed for a long time and would like to be able to gradually increase the number of working hours; people who have caring responsibilities for children or sick relatives who prioritise these responsibilities over labour-market participation; highly qualified people who are unemployed for other reasons than a lack of formal qualifications; people looking for career and development prospects in the context of secondary labour-market programmes. All of this may sound obvious, but excluding from participation those who do not fit the requirements of the available activation schemes is still common practice in many activation contexts.

Institutional activation

Introducing activation policies in general, and transforming the 'orthodox consensus' approach to activation into a more reflexive approach in particular, requires a major process of institutional activation. This side of the introduction of activation policies cannot be emphasised enough, especially since the activation debate is usually highly biased towards the behaviour and attitudes of clients. Public debate is dominated by endless examples of 'unwilling clients' that are used to legitimise tough approaches towards clients. Much less attention is paid to examples of willing clients who run up against 'unwilling institutions' and see their individual activation attempts fail because of a lack of adequate support. Therefore, this section will elaborate on some issues of institutional activation.

The case we are making here for a reflexive approach to activation and the institutional activation that implies, calls for resources for activation, not only in terms of money but also in terms of service providers' time (for example, caseloads) and skills. This may be seen as conflicting with governments' attempt to decrease social expenditure and taxes, but at the same time it corresponds with the objective to invest in human capital and social cohesion. Without going into great detail, it should be pointed out that high-quality activation services may involve higher costs but also produce gains, for instance, in terms of the effectiveness of activation and in terms of a more 'inclusive' society, the outcomes of which should not only be measured in terms of economic but also in terms of social returns. The *Joint Report* on social inclusion also emphasises the importance of the quality of policy delivery in realising more inclusive and integrated services.

> This involves designing and delivering policies as close to people as possible; ensuring that services are delivered in an integrated and holistic way; ensuring transparent and accountable decision making; making services more user friendly, responsive and efficient; promoting partnership between different actors; emphasising equality, rights and non discrimination; fostering the participation of those affected by poverty and social exclusion; emphasising the autonomy and empowerment of the users of services; and emphasising a process of continuous improvement and the sustainability of services. (CEC, 2001, pp 7-8)

We will return to several of these issues later in this chapter.

The first issue with respect to institutional activation we would like to mention concerns inter-institutional cooperation and coordination that effective and efficient activation requires. The reasons for the increasing importance of cooperation and coordination are twofold. First, the multidimensional character of problems of exclusion calls for an interdisciplinary approach in assessing and tackling these problems. Therefore, a non-reductionist approach to exclusion requires that a variety of skills and professions can be mobilised in the activation process. Secondly, regulatory changes in the institutional context itself also make institutional cooperation and coordination more urgent (also see Chapter Three). For example, the privatisation[1] of the activation component of social policies taking place in several countries increases the number and changes the nature of institutions and actors involved in administering and delivering activation: public institutions, private reintegration companies, non-governmental organisations (NGOs), the voluntary sector, social partners, and so on.

The second issue concerns the transformation of top-down approaches of policy making and delivery into bottom-up approaches. Currently, policy makers define the problems that activation policies – or social policies more generally – have to solve and the direction in which solutions to these problems should be found. This top-down and paternalistic 'structuration' (Giddens, 1984) of social policy interventions is deeply ingrained at all levels of policy making, from the political decision-making process via the routine or 'habitus' in the daily practices of social workers to the expectations and 'consumer attitudes' of social policy users. Transforming these practices into bottom-up, tailor-made and client-centred approaches of activation is a radical process, the consequences of which can hardly be overestimated. It will not only affect the level of policy delivery (the 'primary process'), starting with reconsidering the position of clients in the activation process and restructuring client–consultant interactions. It will also influence intra-institutional work and management processes, as well as the process of policy making itself (see Bosselaar et al, 2002).

Thirdly, some comments should be made regarding the issue of compulsory activation. It is quite clear that the introduction of the activation approach has been accompanied by a strengthening of obligations of clients, as well as by increasing control and surveillance of their behaviour and attitudes. In the public and political debate this redefinition of rights and obligations is morally justified by pointing out the reciprocal character of welfare-state support and by the emancipatory impact of (labour-market) participation. A more hidden motive for this redefinition is institutional activation itself: by explicitly imposing obligations upon clients, social policy institutions are implicitly being forced to take their role as activators more seriously. For it is not uncommon procedure for these institutions, in trying to deal with a shortage of resources and a high workload, to focus activation efforts on clients with activation obligations while discouraging 'willing' clients free from participation obligations.

From a more pragmatic point of view one might ask why imposing obligations upon clients is necessary at all. When social policy institutions would be allowed to focus attention on providing high quality, client-centred activation for 'willing' clients who 'voluntarily' ask for activation in some way or another, they would probably have impressive caseloads for years to come.

Besides, as far as we know there is little evidence that compulsory activation is more effective in realising successful and sustainable inclusion than voluntary activation. Of course, this partly depends on one's preferred definition of success, an issue discussed later in this chapter. Apart from that, voluntary activation would challenge activation institutions to deliver high quality activation services to their clients or, in other words, to optimise the match between clients' needs and activation offers. The client-centred policy perspective we have been developing here also weakens the case for compulsion. Most people want to be included to a certain degree in social networks, in the systems of income and consumption, and in work or activities of some sort; and most of them want to contribute to society in some way. From this point of view, the motive underlying compulsion in current activation seems to be to enforce specific, predefined obligations, that is, types of inclusion, upon people who do not see these as meeting their needs. In the 'orthodox consensus' of activation the concept of 'unwilling clients' refers to clients who refuse to accept activation offers. However, the phenomenon of declining activation offers can also be interpreted as reflecting a lack of recognition for, or unwillingness to recognise, other types of inclusion and other ways of taking one's responsibilities, and therefore as a mismatch between people's needs and activation offers.

The introduction of activation programmes is often accompanied by processes of decentralisation which increase the discretion of regional or local authorities and policy agencies in the design or delivery of policies (Chapter Three). Degrees of decentralisation can differ considerably across countries and across target groups within countries (see Lødemel and Trickey, 2001). For example, social assistance schemes in many countries are more decentralised than social insurance schemes, and this may affect the degree of delivery-level discretion in activation schemes directed at the non-insured and the insured respectively. Nevertheless, the issue of decentralisation in activation is an important one. Critics of decentralisation have pointed out that its main purpose is to decentralise national governments' inability to deal with exclusion effectively, and to put the burden of insufficient resources for activation on regional and local authorities. Furthermore, they are afraid that it will make activation clients subject to inequality of justice and arbitrariness, since they will have different rights and obligations in different local contexts. In addition, they fear that local authorities will have less favourable and tolerant attitudes towards minority groups such as refugees, the homeless, gypsies, and so on. These potential consequences of decentralisation are all but imaginary. At the same time, we think that forms of local discretion are necessary to be able to adjust activation to local circumstances and to individual needs. The issue is not whether activation should be either centralised or decentralised. The issue is how reflexive, client-centred activation policies can be embedded in a regulatory context that facilitates tailor-made policy delivery and an adequate match of clients' needs with activation offers. This implies that ways out of the decentralisation–centralisation dilemma should not be sought in an 'either/or' direction, but an 'and/and' direction.

The final institutional issue raised here concerns the importance of monitoring. For reflexive policies, insight into their intended and unintended effects is of major importance, which makes monitoring an essential part of them. However, monitoring activation policies in itself is insufficient. Just as important is the issue of what exactly is being monitored, which also relates to the question what constitutes a success of activation. Where monitoring is already a regular practice, success is usually defined in an institutional way: that is, success is measured in terms of the number and nature of placements realised, or in terms of the number of activated people no longer dependent on income support. Furthermore, monitoring is frequently limited to short-term effects of activation. In the context of the activation approach that has been developed in this chapter, monitoring should have the following characteristics. First of all, attention should be paid to the degree to which target groups consider activation a success. As we saw in earlier chapters, there can be a considerable difference in what constitutes a success from an institutional as compared to a client point of view. When successful activation is defined in terms of the quality of the match between clients' needs and activation offers, clients' experiences cannot be discarded in monitoring the effects of activation. Secondly, as much attention in monitoring should be paid to those who have been placed in schemes as to those who drop out or never manage to enter the schemes. Furthermore, comparisons between these groups should not be limited to the usual 'objective' characteristics in comparative social scientific research. It is equally important, if not more so, to focus these comparisons on differences in people's needs, possibilities, dimensions of exclusion, social and psychological situation, and so on. Finally, monitoring should involve a longitudinal element. Our case studies as well as other studies have shown that even though activation may result in short-term successes – also in the experiences of participants – there is significant risk that they do not contribute to long-term, sustainable inclusion. Temporary programmes can keep people in a revolving door process of permanent activation or can be followed by another period of unemployment; permanent programmes can turn into participation traps. The question whether activation programmes contribute to sustainable inclusion or not can only be answered when activation experiences are monitored over an extended period of time.

Appendix: European guidelines for member states' employment policies 2001 (selected items)

The Employment Guidelines for 2001 start with a section discussing some 'horizontal objectives' which are the result of the Lisbon summit and the Feira meeting during the Portuguese EU presidency in 2000. In the introductory section it is stated that:

> [T]he European Council embraced full employment as an overarching objective of the EU's employment and social policy.... It also requires a continued implementation of an effective and well balanced and mutually supportive policy mix, based on macroeconomic policy, structural reforms promoting adaptable and flexible labour markets, innovation and competitiveness, and an active welfare state promoting human resources development, participation, inclusion and solidarity. (CEC, 2000, p 8)

In order to achieve the full employment objective, among other things it is stated that the following should be realised:

> Enhancing job opportunities and providing adequate incentives for all those willing to take up gainful employment with the aim of moving towards full employment. To this end, Member States should set national targets for raising the rate of employment, in order to contribute to the overall European objectives of reaching by 2010 an overall employment rate of 70 per cent and an employment rate of more than 60 per cent for women. In pursuing these targets, the aim of increasing the quality of jobs should also be taken into consideration. (CEC, 2000, p 8)

Furthermore, the development of a "comprehensive and coherent strategy for Lifelong Learning" as well as "a comprehensive partnership with the Social Partners" (pp 8-9) are considered of major importance in this context.

As far as the four pillars structuring the guidelines are concerned, the first pillar on improving employability contains the most explicit reference to activation policies. For example:

> In order to influence the trend in youth and long-term unemployment, the Member States will intensify their efforts to develop preventive and employability-oriented strategies, building on the early identification of individual needs; within a period to be determined by each Member State which may not exceed two years and which may be longer in Member States with particularly high unemployment, Member States will ensure that: [follows Guideline 1] Every unemployed person is offered a new start before reaching six months of unemployment in the case of young people, and twelve months of unemployment in the case of adults in the form of training, retraining, work practice, a job, or other employability measure, and, if necessary, with

accompanying individual vocational guidance and counselling with a view to effective integration into the labour market. (CEC, 2000, p 10)

Guideline 2 is also aimed at strengthening activation:

Each Member State will
- review and, where appropriate, reform its benefit and tax system to remove poverty traps, and provide incentives for unemployed or inactive people to seek and take up work.
- endeavour to increase significantly the proportion of persons benefiting from active measures to improve their employability with a view to effective integration into the labour market, and will increase, in the light of its starting situation, its per capita expenditure on active measures, taking into account cost effectiveness and the overall budgetary balance. (p 10)

Guideline 6 underlines the importance attached to skill upgrading of the unemployed, by stating:

Member States will promote measures for unemployed people to acquire upgrade skills including IT and communication skills, thereby facilitating their access to the labour market and reducing skill gaps. To this end, each Member State will fix a target for active measures involving training offered to the unemployed, thereby aiming at gradually achieving the average of the three most advanced Member States, and at least 20 per cent. (p 12)

The last guideline under this pillar reads as follows:

Each Member State will
- Develop pathways consisting of effective preventive and active policy measures to promote the integration into the labour market of groups and individuals at risk or with a disadvantage, in order to avoid marginalisation, the emergence of 'working poor' and a drift into exclusion.
- Identify and combat discrimination on grounds of sex, racial or ethnic origin, religion or belief, disability, age or sexual orientation in access to the labour market and education and training.
- Implement appropriate measures to meet the needs of the disabled, ethnic minorities and migrant workers as regards their integration into the labour market and set national targets for this purpose, in accordance with the national situation. (p 13)

Under the fourth pillar, strengthening equal opportunities policies for women and men, women's participation in activation policies is addressed explicitly. The following target is set: "To ensure that active labour market policies are made available for women in proportion to their share of unemployment" (CEC, 2000, p 18).

Note

[1] It should be emphasised here that 'privatisation' can take different forms in different welfare states. For example, Mingione et al (2002) show the importance of civil society (third sector organisations, the Church, NGOs) in the provision of local welfare in Southern Europe. In the context of the Dutch welfare state, to mention another example, privatisation takes a different form. There, it means that public welfare institutions responsible for the administration of social security or social assistance hire private reintegration companies to provide activation services.

References

Alber, J. and Standing, G. (2000) 'Social dumping, catch-up or convergence? Europe in a comparative global context', *Journal of European social policy*, vol 10, no 2, pp 99-119.

Beck, U. (2000) *The brave new world of work*, Cambridge: Polity Press.

Beck, W., Maessen, L. and Walker, A. (eds) (1997) *Social quality in Europe*, The Hague: Kluwer Law International.

Bosco, A. and Chassard, Y. (1999) 'A shift in the paradigm. Surveying the EU discourse on welfare and work', in European Foundation for the Improvement of Living and Working Conditions, *Linking welfare and work*, Dublin: European Foundation for the Improvement of Living and Working Conditions.

Bosselaar, H., van der Wolk, J., Zwart, K. and Spies, H. (eds) (2002) *Vraagsturing. De cliënt aan het roer in de sociale zekerheid en zorg*, Utrecht: Jan van Arkel.

Bourdieu, P. (ed) (1999) *The weight of the world. Social suffering in contemporary society*, Cambridge: Polity Press.

CEC (Commission of the European Communities) (1993a) *Growth, competitiveness, employment*, The Delors White Paper, Luxembourg: CEC.

CEC (1993b) *European social policy: Options for the Union*, The Green Paper, Luxembourg: CEC.

CEC (1995a) *Social protection in Europe*, Brussels: Directorate General Employment, Industrial Relations and Social Affairs.

CEC (1995b) *European social policy: The medium term action plan*, Luxembourg: CEC.

CEC (2000) *Proposal for a council decision on guidelines for member states' employment policies for the year 2001*, Brussels: CEC.

CEC (2001) *Draft joint report on social inclusion*, Brussels: CEC.

Coenen, H. and Leisink, P. (eds) (1993) *Work and citizenship in the new Europe*, Aldershot: Edward Elgar.

Crouch, C. (2000) *After the Euro: Shaping institutions for governance in the wake of European monetary union*, Oxford: Oxford University Press.

EP (European Parliament) (2000) *The European charter of fundamental rights*, Draft Paper, Brussels: EP.

Geyer, R. (1999) *Exploring European social policy*, Cambridge: Polity Press.

Giddens, A. (1994) *Beyond left and right. The future of radical politics*, Cambridge: Polity Press.

Gorz, A. (1999) *Reclaiming work. Beyond the wage-based society*, Cambridge: Polity Press.

Huws, U. (1997) *Flexibility and security: Towards a new European balance*, Citizens Income Trust Discussion Paper No 3, London: Citizens Income Trust.

Jordan, B. (1998) *The new politics of welfare. Social justice in a global context*, London: Sage Publications.

Jordan, B. (2000) *Social work and the third way. Tough love in social policy*, London: Sage Publications.

Leibfried, S. and Pierson, C. (eds) (1995) *European social policy*, Washington, DC: Brookings Institute.

Leisering, L. and Walker, R. (1998) *The dynamics of modern society: Poverty, policy and welfare*, Bristol: The Policy Press.

Leisering, L. and Leibfried, S. (1999) *Time and poverty in Western welfare states. United Germany in perspective*, Cambridge: Cambridge University Press.

Levitas, R. (1998) *The inclusive society? Social exclusion and New Labour*, Basingstoke: Macmillan.

Lødemel, I. and Trickey, H. (eds) (2001) *'An offer you can't refuse': Workfare in international perspective*, Bristol: The Policy Press.

Marks, G., Scharpf, F., Schmitter, P. and Streeck, W. (1996) *Governance in the EU*, London: Sage Publications.

Mingione, E., Oberti, M. and Pereirinha, J. (2002) 'Cities as local systems', in C. Saraceno (ed) *Social assistance dynamics in Europe: National and local poverty regimes*, Bristol: The Policy Press, pp 35-79.

Offe, C. and Heinze, R. (1990) *Organisierte Eigenarbeit. Das Modell Kooperationsring*, Frankfurt am Main: Campus.

O'Leary, S. and Tiilikainen, I. (1998) *Citizenship and nationality status in the new Europe*, London: IPPR/Sweet and Maxwell.

Roche, M. (1992) *Rethinking citizenship: Welfare, ideology and change in modern society*, Cambridge: Polity Press.

Roche, M. (1997) 'Citizenship and exclusion: reconstructing the European Union', in M. Roche and R. van Berkel (eds) *European citizenship and social exclusion*, Aldershot: Avebury, pp 3-23.

Roche, M. and van Berkel, R. (eds) (1997) *European citizenship and social exclusion*, Aldershot: Avebury.

Rosanvallon, P. (2000) *The new social question. Rethinking the welfare state*, Princeton, NJ: Princeton University Press.

Saraceno, C. (ed) (2002) *Social assistance dynamics in Europe: National and local poverty regimes*, Bristol: The Policy Press.

SEDEC (Social Exclusion and the Development of European Citizenship) (2000) *Comparative social inclusion policies and citizenship in Europe*, Final Report, TSER programme, Brussels: DG12/EC.

Standing, G. (1999) *Global labour flexibility. Seeking distributive justice*, Basingstoke: Macmillan.

Valkenburg, B. and Coenen, H. (2002) 'Een aantal overwegingen over de maatschappelijke betekenis van een individuele, vraaggerichte benadering', in H. Bosselaar, J. van der Wolk, K. Zwart and H. Spies (eds) *Vraagsturing. De cliënt aan het roer in de sociale zekerheid en zorg*, Utrecht: Jan van Arkel, pp 26-51.

Williams, C.C. (1998) *Helping people to help themselves: An appraisal of the potential of Local Exchange and Trading Systems (LETS)*, PERC Policy Working Paper No 15, Sheffield: PERC/University of Sheffield.

Williams, C.C. and Windebank, J. (1998) *Informal employment in the advanced economies: Implications for work and welfare*, London: Routledge.

Index

Also available from The Policy Press

Unemployment, welfare policies and citizenship

Edited by **Jørgen Goul Andersen, Jochen Clasen, Wim van Oorschot** and **Knut Halvorsen**

"... provides a useful and timely critique of employment and unemployment policies in a wide range of European countries. The editors are to be commended for including countries not normally covered in comparative policy texts."
Bruce Stafford, Centre for Research in Social Policy, Department of Social Sciences, Loughborough University

Using in-depth, comparative and interdisciplinary analysis of employment, welfare and citizenship in Europe, this book provides:

* a comprehensive critique of the idea of globalisation as a challenge to European welfare states;
* an updated overview of employment and unemployment in Europe;
* detailed country chapters with new and previously inaccessible information about employment and unemployment policies written by national experts.

Paperback £23.99 (US$43.20) • ISBN 1 86134 437 6
Hardback £55.00 (US$99.00) • ISBN 1 86134 438 4
234 x 156mm • 240 pages TBC • November 2002

'An offer you can't refuse'
Workfare in international perspective

Edited by **Ivar Lødemel** and **Heather Trickey**

"A first and a must on work and welfare in comparative perspective."
Stephan Leibfried, Centre for Social Policy Research, University of Bremen

'An offer you can't refuse' compares in-depth, international work-for-welfare (workfare) policies objectively for the first time. It considers well-publicised schemes from the United States alongside more overlooked examples of workfare in Britain, Denmark, France, Germany, The Netherlands and Norway.

Paperback £17.99 (US$32.50) • ISBN 1 86134 195 4
Hardback £45.00 (US$81.00) • ISBN 1 86134 196 2
216 x 148mm • 384 pages • January 2001

Changing labour markets, welfare policies and citizenship

Edited by **Jørgen Goul Andersen** and **Per H. Jensen**

"A state of the art account of the most pressing social policy issue in European countries."
Lutz Leisering, Faculty of Sociology, University of Bielefeld, Germany

Changing labour markets, welfare policies and citizenship addresses the question of how full citizenship may be preserved and developed in the face of enduring labour market pressures.

Paperback £18.99 (US$34.50) • ISBN 1 86134 272 1
Hardback £45.00 (US$81.00) • ISBN 1 86134 273 X
216 x 148mm • 320 pages • January 2002

Social assistance dynamics in Europe

National and local poverty regimes

Edited by **Chiara Saraceno**

"... an original contribution to the understanding of comparative social assistance."
Stewart Miller, School of Social Policy, Sociology and Social Research, University of Kent at Canterbury

Describing social assistance 'careers' in different national and urban contexts, this innovative book documents the strong interplay between personal biographies and policy patterns - a particularly useful perspective which complements the more structural, top-down approach of much international work in social policy.

Paperback £17.99 (US$32.50) • ISBN 1 86134 314 0
Hardback £45.00 (US$81.00) • ISBN 1 86134 315 9
216 x 148mm • 320 pages • January 2002

Lone parents, employment and social policy

Cross-national comparisons

Edited by **Jane Millar** and **Karen Rowlingson**

"... stands as a model not only for the substantive analysis of policies that affect lone parents, but as an example of the way in which the best international social policy research should be conducted."
Nick Manning, School of Sociology and Social Policy, University of Nottingham

This book offers an up-to-date analysis of policies and provisions for lone parents in the UK, US, Australia, France, the Netherlands and Norway.

Paperback £16.99 (US$31.00) • ISBN 1 86134 320 5
Hardback £45.00 (US$81.00) • ISBN 1 86134 321 3
216 x 148mm • 320 pages • November 2001

For further information about these and other titles published by The Policy Press, please visit our website at: www.policypress.org.uk or telephone +44 (0)117 954 6800

To order, please contact:
Marston Book Services
PO Box 269
Abingdon
Oxon OX14 4YN
UK
Tel: +44 (0)1235 465500
Fax: +44 (0)1235 465556
E-mail: direct.orders@marston.co.uk

The POLITY
P̃P
P R E S S